# DRIVEN HEARTS

## FINDING ANSWERS

# ROD DOUGLAS

**BLUEPRINT PRESS**
INTERNATIONALE

ISBN
978-1-959365-07-5 (Paperback)
978-1-959365-08-2 (eBook)
978-1-959365-06-8 (Hardcover)

# TABLE OF CONTENTS

## CHAPTER ONE

# SOMETHING BETTER

Young, headstrong, adventuresome—all good qualities to be found in a man of 18 years of age. That's me, Nikos, or Nic as most of my friends call me. It's 29 A.D. and I enjoy the benefits of coming from a family of ample means and considerable influence in Grecian affairs. Unfortunately there is another quality that I left out of the afore mentioned and that is I felt imprisoned . I was nearing the completion of my schooling in my hometown of Athens and felt a rising tide of curiosity building within me. Word seemed to reach the streets of Athens on an almost daily basis about the teaching and following of men from Israel named John and Jesus. They were gaining much notice, both from those who sought more from them and those who seemed fearful of them. I can recall one particular afternoon when news came that the man they called John had been imprisoned. Many people sought his death, hoping it would be the end of this new teaching and that his followers would become discouraged and disband. However, those people were mistaken. John's imprisonment only helped to stir something deep in the hearts of those who had listened to his teaching. They began to follow the other man, Jesus, and their movement became even stronger. Stories were told of great miracles, healings, and even the dead being restored to life. These tales, or if you possessed a mind like mine, preferred to consider them trustworthy news—these tales stirred within me an insatiable desire to examine the facts for myself. The very thing that stirred the hearts of those people in that land was stirring within me. My imagination would run wild as I tried to sleep at night. The stories I heard during the day became visual realities as I lay in my comfortable bed and let them unfold before me again and again.

Each time they would grow into even more spectacular happenings. Sounds would be ever so intense and descriptive, colors so vivid and glorious, actions so real, and even odors would come into my nostrils. Had anyone else been there with me, there would not have been a single piece left for them to build into there imagination. I had grasped every piece and woven it into the fabric of my most inner thoughts.

Every morning as I woke after only a couple hours of sleep, having spent the majority of the night sailing through the marvelous expanses of thoughts; I would find myself weighing the value of my education against the calling of adventure—of knowing for myself the truth and accuracy of the accounts I had heard for the past many months. This became an ever increasing desire, perhaps an obsession. Many of my companions thought me to be delusional or mentally unbalanced. I was a young man with everything I could need. My future looked brilliant to any who knew my family or knew anything at all about Grecian society. I had not one thing to be worried about. Even my future family was arranged and the young woman who had been selected for me would have been the one of my own choice had I been ready to make it. Perhaps I was one who needed to spend time in the asylum. I found myself in a continual state of turmoil trying to rationalize the whole situation. Peace would not come. The scales holding my future in Athens gave way each day to the scales holding the unanswered adventure calling me to the land of miracles and wonders. This struggle within me had continued for over a year and finally the day came when the intensity of the call raised to the level that it could not be rejected.

I decided to announce my decision to my parents. After further thought, I retreated and waited until my father had left for the forum and approached my mother with my plans. I knew I was heading into confrontation that I could not win and so had predetermined that this would be more of a courtesy of informing them that I was about to leave and to provide them with a general whereabouts as to where I was going. I had not planned on allowing for much discussion on the matter. There were a couple of exceptions though. First of all, I thought it would be wise to have adequate funds to make such a trip and secondly, I didn't want this to cause a severing of our relationship that could not be repaired. Let me be honest here. I had a life ahead of me that I didn't want to throw away. I may have been accused of being mentally unbalanced, but I was not completely insane.

As I poured forth my plans to my mother she went through a progression of emotional states. At first, she thought I was only fantasizing. Shock set in when she saw that this was a serious matter. I watched her face change from a woman whose face had never shown the slightest indication of worry or fret to that of a mother whose child had been pried from her arms as she clutched it to her bosom. That evening was one of the most painful times of my life. I tried to keep busy during the day with anything I could find to do. The mournful sobbing of my mother had an unnatural way of penetrating my ears and sinking right into my heart. The harder I tried to evade those tearful sounds the louder they seemed. I don't think I could have caused my mother more pain if I had torn her heart open with a dagger. But alas, this was a necessary step that had to be taken if any relief was to ever come from the pounding in my heart to know what was happening in the hills of Judah. Some day I would make it up to her. She had to know how much I loved her and she knew I would never cause her this kind of pain without sound reason. I had never inflicted such anguish on anyone in all my life. And then it dawned on me. My father would be home in less than an hour.

What was going to happen then? I couldn't stand it any longer. What had to be done must be done, even if it meant leaving without the assurance of being able to come back home and without the money I knew

I would need. So be it! I would just have to find a way as I went. I knew I must now go. My father would be too insistent and he had the ability to put an end to my plans if he desired to do so. Any confrontation with him would only add to my mother's agony. My father and I did not have the close relationship that my mother and I shared. Besides, he would have all he could do to comfort my mother. There was simply no other choice. I gathered a few clothes, some necessary items, and whatever money I could find in my room. I was desperate to leave but I was determined to leave with some integrity. I would not take anything that was not mine. Ah yes, I made sure to pack an ample supply of paper and writing pens safely in the bottom of my bag. After quickly surveying my room to see if I had everything I needed, I gathered my strength and went to say good-bye to my mother. As I hugged her I felt her tears falling on my shoulder. They would become so precious in the days and months ahead as I was to discover the vastness of the love in those tears. I tried my best to comfort her with the fact that I would be back someday. I can only hope that she had at least some degree of understanding as to why this voyage was so important to me. At this point in time, I'm not sure I even understood the full extent of the forces that were calling upon me to go. After a long and love-filled hug and a quick kiss, I departed.

As I walked down the familiar streets, I began to realize that there was an unfamiliarity creeping in. Each step I took seemed to bring in new details to the streets I had walked for years. The neighborhood I thought I knew so well was filled with things I had never noticed before. It was strange but I seemed to notice so much that had been there for years. Even people drew my attention as I passed them. Life was coming to a fullness that I had missed before. I was being filled with the spirit of adventure and I was only blocks from home. Be still my heart!! I had walked only a short distance more when the spirit of adventure began to give way to a spirit of fear. I suddenly realized that I had failed drastically to make adequate preparation for my voyage. I had not even booked passage or planned a route. Oh, this battle within still rages—excitement to fear—confidence to doubt! I must go on—there will be a way—I can't go back now—I have to know... but why and how? It was then I thought of my friend, Marco.

My family was known to have rolled their eyes and stopped to take a deep breath when I would mention my association with Marco. I don't think it was so much that they disliked him, as it was that he was not from the proper lineage. Now that was a part of my family's heritage that I was more than willing to remove from my way of life. Marco and I had grown to trust and respect each other. He had given me a knowledge of life that our schools knew little about. There was such a refreshing honesty and sincerity to our relationship. I often felt sorry for my family when I saw the pitiful facade of empty words and meaningless promises of their friends and associates. Perhaps this was one of the driving forces that was leading into this adventure. There had to be more to life than what my society was teaching. Marco had helped me to know that much already.

I turned down the next street and quickened my step as I headed to the place where I was almost certain to find Marco. He worked evenings cleaning in the market district, usually washing down the tables of fish vendors. Even though the work was unpleasant at best, the job offered something that the both of us found of great value. It was here in this market place that we found men who had been all over the Mediterranean and brought with them news from nearly every port on it. On occasion, I would spend a few hours helping Marco as we listened to the conversations of the sailors, deck hands, and dockworkers. Whenever the talk would slow or even stop Marco would say something to get it going again. He had an uncanny way of doing that. I swear that fellow could get information out of the mouth of one of those dead fish. I had learned to be still and not say much. There was a noticeable resentment toward me since I represented a social class who held these workingmen in low esteem. My presence was tolerated for the most part as long as I stayed quietly in the background. Sometimes I would become so enthralled in the conversations that I would blurt out a comment or question and that would end the topic of discussion for a good long while. At that point you could count on a few ringleaders to start in on how unfair life was and how it was about time to put an end to social injustice. It was like I had personally contributed to the hardship these men were enduring and on a few occasions, I thought they might be going to take their discontent out on me right then and there. I knew that my presence at the market place after hours caused Marco to be uneasy. It wasn't that he didn't want to associate with me but that he knew how these men felt. It made him edgy—like he was caught in the middle. Because of that and because my parents would have forbidden me to go around such rough characters, I limited my visits to the market.

The evening was still young enough that I had little problem finding Marco. He was scrubbing down a long section of tables that had held the days supply of fish. But Marco wasn't applying himself to the job as he usually did. This evening he was sitting there with his scrub brush in hand listening to some sailors. In fact, they had quite a crowd gathered around them. I hurried up and worked my way to a place directly behind Marco. I placed my hand on his shoulder to let him know I was there and his only response was to turn briefly to see who it was. His attention returned to the conversation. It was not but a few seconds later that I learned why he was so intent on hearing what was said. The sailors were reporting that the daughter of a ruler named Jairus had died. He went to ask Jesus to bring her back to life. All the people thought this was insanity but Jesus went into her home and brought her out alive. Everyone gasped in disbelief at first and then, seeing him with their own eyes and talking to them; ran to tell others. Soon the whole countryside was filled with excitement. This event also caused fear to rise up even more in those who opposed this new teaching. There was talk of more killings in order to stop this movement. .

The sailors continued for nearly an hour telling wonderful stories about Jesus feeding thousands of people with only a few loaves of bread and a couple of fish. I was truly amazed and even found myself questioning how this could really happen. Even more amazing however, was the fact that these rough and hardened seamen were so excited about what they were reporting. There simply had to be a power at work that was far greater than any of us could realize. Human nature could not explain the change I saw in the hearts of these men. In fact, I believe this was the first time I had been at the market place and not been the object of their scorn.

It was getting late in the evening and my excitement was building to the point that I could hardly contain it. I had to get Marco off to ourselves and tell him of my plans to leave. Finally I grabbed his arm and pulled him off to the side.

"Marco, you have got to listen to me! After the things I have heard here tonight, it is more urgent than ever that I leave here tonight and find a way to Judea and Galilee. There is something happening to people there that is changing our world. I must find out what it is." I said as I continued to pull him.

Marco stopped and looked stunned. "Nik, you can't go off by yourself. The next passenger ship isn't due to leave for three more days. How are you going to get there?"

I replied, "I wouldn't have the fare for passage anyway. I need to find a ship leaving tonight. I have to leave now even if it means hiding on board or whatever I must do."

"You know how the men here at the market feel about you. What do you think they would do to you out to sea? You wouldn't live to sunrise tomorrow. Don't be foolish!" Marco warned, "Let me finish up here—I will be just a few more minutes. We need to talk this out some. Wait for me just outside the door over there."

"I'll be waiting, but hurry—I need to get going!" was my reply.

As I was waiting, I realized how difficult my voyage was going to be. Marco had a valid point about how the sailors felt toward me. Most of the security I had felt all my life was now abandoned. I was now going to have to stand on my own. Towering doubts entered my mind along with images of being thrown into the churning sea. I drove those thoughts back with a determination to find out more about this Jesus.

A door suddenly swung out and abruptly captured my attention. It was Marco coming out to find me. It was almost like I had to travel a great distance to come back to where he was. The workings in my head were becoming increasingly more vivid—there was a transformation going on within me—I could physically feel it! It was definitely a strange sensation but one that I was beginning to welcome.

"Let's go!" Marco said as he reached out and grabbed my arm. "We are going by my house. We can talk on the way."

"Alright, but I need to get started as soon as I can. My family will be watching all the ships leaving tonight. Besides that, I really feel an urgency to get to Judea. I can't explain it but it's there." I said.

"We need to get some things from my house. I promise it won't take long. We have to get you some different clothes." Marco said. "You try going on a boat dressed like you are now and there ain't a sailor alive that wouldn't pitch you in. You've got to start thinking like they do if you want to make it across the sea with the likes of sailors. I need to get some things myself anyway."

"What do you mean, 'For your self?'" I exclaimed.

"We are going together on this journey." Marco replied.

"You can't!" I retorted, "In the first place that is too much to ask of you and secondly—"

Marco interrupted, "You haven't asked me—I have just told you I'm going." "Well then, secondly, do you know what this will do to our families? Mine will be blaming you and your family for leading me off on this trip and yours will be accusing mine corrupting their hard working son. This would only add more tension to the problem. Who knows what they might do." I reasoned.

"Your family will be blaming me for this whether I'm there or not. I would just as soon not be there to hear all that. As for my family—well I don't know. I might not be missed as much as you think. Anyway, what makes you think you are the only one who must find out about the teachings of this Jesus? I've heard the same stories as you have. Or do you think I'm not educated enough to understand these teachings? Besides all that, you need me and you know it!" Marco added.

I was silent for a few minutes as we continued our quick pace to his house. He had hurt me deeply with his remark about his education. I knew he probably didn't mean it, but in the back of my mind, I wondered if he thought I held myself to be better than him. He was right about one thing. That was the fact that I did need him. He had the ability to get along with the people we would encounter on every step of the way. I realized how much I had yet to learn from him. I also realized that I had been guilty of not recognizing his excitement on hearing the same stories that stirred my heart so. I had been so preoccupied with the desires of my heart that I had forgotten to be considerate of those of my best friend.

"The truth of the matter is that I want you to go with me on this trip. It seems just too much to ask of you though. Marco, I'm sorry for not understanding how these stories have touched you in much the same way as they have me and you know that I don't think myself better than anyone. Please don't try to use that on me anymore. You know how deeply I feel about those things." I finally said after much thought.

"Fine! It's settled then. So here's the plan. " Marco replied as if we had not just shared a deep and personal moment. "After you get rid of those clothes, we need to gather up some food. I brought enough fish from the market. We need some bread and water. See what you can find while I get some stuff from home. Now go! I won't be long. Be back here in ten minutes!" he said with all the assurance of a commander.

I smiled and felt a great relief inwardly as I watched him run to his house. I was grateful to have Marco with me. But I had work to do. I ran up the street to find a shop that might still be open. Finding one, I purchased the bread and some dry beans. Finding a container for the water was more difficult. It had to be something that could stand up to the rough handling of our journey. It had to be compact. Why hadn't I thought of such a necessity when I was still at home? Going on down the street I saw the light from a tavern shining out into the street. There hanging beside the door was a wineskin. Perfect! I grabbed it and yelled, "How much for this?"

A stillness came over the room and every head turned to see who had dared to break their fellowship of cursing and brawling. After what seemed like half the night had passed, a gruff voice said. "Sixty drachmas!"

I knew I was being taken for a fool but I also knew I had to get back to Marco with the supplies we needed. Quickly I dug in my pocket and pulled out 20 drachmas and pitched it on the floor. I turned and ran, feeling that I had paid a fair price, that I had secured an ideal water container, and that I had displayed some of that street savvy I was to need as this adventure progressed. I could hear that gruff voice yelling at me from the tavern door but I knew I had left enough money on that floor to satisfy the man's greed. I had noticed that greedy people were often lazy people. There was a point when greed gave way to effort. I found that my calculation was just about exact since the man's head was the only part of him that found energy to leave the tavern.

His greed had been satisfied and he only had to growl to keep up his reputation among his friends. I knew Marco would be proud of me.

I stopped only long enough to rinse out the wineskin and fill it with fresh water and then returned to find Marco waiting. He handed me some clothes and told me to throw what I had on away. I ran into the shadows and quickly returned wearing some of Marco's old clothes. I wanted to show him how successful I had been in getting the things he had ask for and to tell him how I had dealt with the man at the tavern but he had his mind set on what we must do in the next several minutes.

"Grab your stuff and follow me." he said as he threw a sack over his shoulder and headed down the street towards the docks. "I think I know how we can get across the sea, maybe even as far as Tyre. How well can you cook?"

"I don't know—I haven't really tried much. I'm sure I can manage to keep the two of us from starving." I replied.

"I'm not talking about just cooking for the two of us. I want to know if you can cook for a ship's crew. I've done it a couple of times, but just on short trips. The sailors get a bit more particular on voyages across the Mediterranean. You think you can handle the job?" he asked.

"I'll give it a try!"

"Well, try hard because if you can't fix some decent food they won't think long about feeding you to the sharks. Anyway, here's the plan. I know the captain of a ship that is supposed to set sail tonight. He lost his cook on their last voyage and he just might let us sail with them for a while until he finds another cook. If we play everything right, it won't cost us anything and we can eat for free. Just follow my lead and I will do most of the talking. Oh, and while I'm thinking of it, hide any money you have in your socks. That way if anyone finds it at least you will know it's gone." Marco explained.

"How did the captain lose his last cook?" I asked with a tone in my voice that indicated that I wasn't sure I really wanted to know the answer.

"He got sick from something he ate and died." He answered. "Tradition is that the cook has to eat what he fixes. Helps make for good cooks or fewer of them that ain't so good."

I just walked on with Marco now and didn't say much more of anything for a while. I was wondering if Marco was thinking the same thoughts that were going through my head. He seemed to be calm and knew what he was doing. If he was scared at all, he didn't show it. As for me, my heart was pumping about twice as fast as it normally did. I told myself that it was from the excitement and anticipation of the great adventure were embarking on, but I knew that most of the reason was that I was just plain scared. This was my first time away from home without my family and I had never dreamed of working on a ship. I must have had hundreds of pictures running through my mind as we walked. Soon we reached the docks and stopped near a small ship that was tied up there. A few men were busy running up and down planks carrying crates, kegs, barrels, and sacks that must have weighed over a hundred pounds each. I kept looking for a passenger ship when Marco noticed me doing so.

"What are you looking for?" he asked.

"I was just wondering where the ship we're taking is docked." I replied.

"Well, stop wondering. It's right here in front of you." Marco said with just a hint of a chuckle. I grinned, but only briefly as I could see he was not joking. Of all the pictures that had just previously ran through my mind, none of them even resembled the site that my eyes saw now. Not only was this not a passenger ship, it wasn't even much of a cargo vessel. From the appearance of her bow in the moonlight, she had been repaired more than a few times. My heart was still pumping nearly as fast as before but now it was sinking into my stomach. I stood there speechless and with my mouth open.

Marco didn't have much difficulty reading my thoughts and said, "Don't be so worried. She's been a good ship and made it through a lot of storms. Her captain knows the sea and he's been at her wheel since before I can remember. They are quite a pair. Now come on and let's see if we can get hired on."

He didn't wait for my approval but headed towards one of the boarding planks with confidence in his stride. I followed as best I could. The captain was taking stock of cargo as it came on board. We approached him and waited for him to acknowledge our presence. He kept writing and mumbling to himself as we waited. After a couple of minutes he asked without pausing from his writing or even glancing at us, "Are you two going speak up? Don't have time for no standing round. What is it with you?"

Marco was quick to respond, "You're Capt. Vitas and you're headed for Tyre, right?"

Capt. Vitas, still taking stock and only looking up as another deck hand came by with cargo, replied, "What else you going tell me that I already know?"

Marco ignored his remark and went straight to the point, "We heard you needed some help in the galley. How would you like to get two days hard work done for the price of one?"

Capt. Vitas turned to look at us upon hearing Marco's question. His eyes did a thorough search of our bodies, checking for strength; of our faces, checking for character; and our eyes, for honesty. He completed his survey of us in less than half a minute and then asked. "What's your deal?"

"You get us to Tyre and you only pay us for half the number of days it takes to get there. You get a cook and galley help until we reach Tyre." Marco said.

"How do you know I still need a cook?" Capt. Vitas asked.

"If you didn't, you wouldn't be wasting time talking with us now." Marco answered with a tone that revealed a hint of arrogance.

"You get three-quarters of a day's wage for two day's work and do whatever needs doing when the galley works done. Now get below and help get things stowed away. We set sail in less that an hour." Capt. Vitas commanded.

We did it! We were genuine seamen now. Just think of the stories we would be able to tell someday and think of the places we would see. Imagine the people we would meet. Imagine the—I felt a hand grasp my arm and pull me around. It was Marco trying to bring me back to reality.

"Come on! We got work to do. Let's get below and get started. There is a lot of stuff to be stacked and tied secure before we set sail. Capt. Vitas is a fair man but he wants the work done. Follow me!" Marco ordered.

I followed him down to the hold. As I went I wonder whatever made me think it was such a good idea to have Marco along. He sure was a bossy fellow, but I had to admit, he knew what he was doing.

" Marco, how long do you think it will take us to reach Tyre?" I asked as I surveyed the dark spaces of the hold, hoping his answer would tell me it wouldn't be long.

"Depends." he responded, "Depends on the wind and if we don't run into any storms. Could be just less than a month if goin's good. A couple if it ain't. Beside that, I'm not sure how many ports we will stop in."

Our conservation was ended by the thudding and creaking of a platform that was lowered by ropes through a large hole in the upper deck. No sooner than the platform had cleared the opening and made its way to the toward us, a man yelled down to us to get the load cleared off and made ready for the next one. Marco and I worked feverously to clear the cargo from the platform and finally had it clear.

"O. K. It's ready!" Marco yelled up.

Capt. Vitas appeared above us and told us to secure and stack as much as we could. We had several more loads to be lower into the hold. Apparently they had been working short-handed until we came along. The hold was already getting full and there was hardly room to set anything else. Capt. Vitas came below with two of the deck hands and helped us arrange the cargo. Some of it had to be moved so as to be accessible for the next stop. It was truly amazing to watch the captain manage to arrange the cargo so that a whole new section of the hold was bare and ready for the rest of the shipment.

We worked hard that night. Capt. Vitas didn't get to set sail as early as he had planned. The shipment was larger than he had expected. There was barely enough room left in the hold to walk. The galley was packed full of food and supplies as well as with cargo. Our bunks had to be laid on top of crates. It was nearing mid-night when Capt. Vitas called down for us to come on deck and help raise the sails. Our first job was to help with setting the ship free from the dock. Once it was loose, the deck hands used long slender poles to push the ship away from the dock. The poles had wide blades on the ends that served as oars once the ship was out away from the dock. Ever so slowly the ship made its way out into the bay. The men strained at the those long oars until finally Capt. Vitas gave orders to raise the sails. He showed us how the sails were untied and hoisted up the rigging. He warned us to keep our hands out of the way of the ropes and to watch that we didn't get our feet tangled in them. He had sternness about his character, but that sternness was seasoned with a respect for the wisdom and knowledge that stood behind it. I made a commitment to myself that I was going to learn all I could from him on this voyage.

It was a clear night and there didn't seem to be much of a breeze but when the last sail had been raised it billowed out and stretched itself free of all wrinkles. I soon heard the sound of water being rolled out of the way as the ship sliced through the sea. It was setting much lower in the water now with its full load. Soon we had left the lights of Athens behind us as we traveled out into the darkness of the sea. It was amazing though, how the moon lit up the surface of the water.

"You two get below and catch some sleep. I want breakfast ready by dawn. We'll be heading' for Ephesus, hopefully getting' there in four, maybe five days ." Capt. Vitas commanded.

We went below and climbed into our bunks. The ship was moving ahead smoothly and the water was pretty calm. The only sounds we heard were the groaning and creaking of the ship and noticeable dripping below us.

"Marco, what is that dripping down there?" I ask.

"It's only seepage. Don't worry about it. The deck hand on duty has to keep it bailed out. It will be your turn soon enough." he answered.

We were both tired and our conversation didn't go much further for some time. I began thinking about all the times we had heard the stories that had brought us to this night. The stories had definitely aroused a desire to learn more of the teachings that these stories were centered around. Marco and I were not the only ones who were affected. A growing number of people were becoming less than satisfied with the socially accepted beliefs in the many gods of Grecian culture. A serious challenge to mythology and idolatry was being born in the hearts of many people. And now, Marco and I were on our way to find out more. To think of the magnitude of what we might learn was nearly overwhelming.

Finally I reached a point of being so excited about what was before us that I had to talk to Marco even if he was asleep. "Marco, you still awake?" I whispered, but not too softly.

"Ya. Why?" he answered. "Can't you sleep either?"

"I can't stop thinking about that man, Jesus. The things we have heard about Him and the great miracles they say He's done; every time I think about it there seems to be more distance between the things I've been taught all my life and the teachings of this man. And now we are on our way to finding Him!" I replied.

"Nik, I've been laying here thinking the very same things. I tell you something burns in my heart when I think of what we are doing. I know that there has to be more to life than what we have been taught about all the gods and myths. There is an emptiness within me that I don't understand. All I know is that I got to find the one they call Jesus and see for myself." said Marco.

When I heard those words coming from Marco, I felt such a reassurance. Not only because he felt the same way I did, but also because he had described so well what was happening with me. There was a power at work in our midst that we had never known. It was a power that we found to be very encouraging. At that very moment it gave me the courage to tell Marco more of my deepest feeling.

"Marco, you probably already know that I'm scared of this voyage. The truth is that I would like to be back home in my own bed right now, but I know that would be a terrible mistake. That same burning you have in your heart is in mine too. No matter what lays ahead of us, I know we have to find who this Jesus is. I'm really glad that you are with me; not only here beside me, but that our hearts are together." I said.

"Ya. Me too, Nik. Now say good-bye to Athens and get some rest. We'll be needing it in a couple hours." he said abruptly.

I knew that was his way of wanting to end the conversation. We had never been able to talk so much about our deepest thoughts. I knew Marco had a tender heart but he didn't like many people to know it. I also knew he was right about needing some rest so I rolled over and tried to find sleep knowing that I had said 'Good Bye' to Athens, at least for a while.

## CHAPTER TWO

# FAREWELL TO ATHENS

"Get up you lazy, good for nothin land lovers! This ain't no pleasure trip. Hurry up and get some food fixed and it better be extra good bein' as it's already late." a growling voice came clearly into our ears and quickly drove any intention of returning to sleep from our minds. As if that loud growling wasn't enough to rouse us, the severe jostling that nearly shook our bunks apart brought us to life in no time. When we were able to focus our eyes we could see by the dim torchlight it was one of the deck hands that had come down to get us about our duties. He looked to be a hard sort of man. I knew he wasn't just talking to be talking when he ordered us to work. However, I had a strong sense that he was attempting to size us up more than he was trying to get his hunger satisfied. He looked into our eyes seeking to find what was giving us the desire to be on this journey. I made a mental note to work at getting to know this man better. I saw in his eyes a glimpse of the same emptiness Marco and I had within us.

Marco and I hurriedly worked to put together a meal. Marco took charge without really knowing it. He had the ability to dig into the task before him with a determination to get it done and done right. He had a fire going in the stone oven in no time and had mixed up a large bowl of batter before I was able to finish getting the salted fish laid out and the coffee boiling. In no time we had hot biscuits and baked fish ready to take up on deck. Once more, I found myself being grateful to have Marco along with me.

When we stuck our heads up through the hatch, the sun was barely rising. The smell of cooking had already told the men that they were in for a better meal than they had been used to getting. That in itself would make our voyage much more pleasant. By the time the last piece of fish was grabbed from the pan, Marco and I had made new friends that I was sure to get to know later. Even Capt. Vitas was unable to hide the satisfaction he got from the breakfast. My only concern this morning was how were we going leave the ship when our voyage ended. I jokingly told Marco that the crew just might hold us prisoner to keep us from leaving. The smile on my face faded quickly when he looked at me with such a serious face that I knew I might have spoken more truth at jest.

As the morning progressed we finished cleaning up after breakfast and helped with some of the work on deck. We both noticed that the growl in the crew's voices was much tamer now. For the most part they were willing to teach us the things we did not already know. It was amazing but I was able to begin building trust and friendship with the one who had came below to get us up. Just before it was time for us to go below and put together the noon meal, I had the chance to get into a conversation with him about the places he had traveled. I learned he had been all over the area around the Sea of Galilee. It was hard to leave to go below. I had so many questions I wanted to ask him but decided to limit it to finding out his name for now. He told me it was Vito and I told him mine was Nik as I stood to leave. His otherwise emotionless face gave way at that moment to a faint smile. I headed for the hatch with a thankful heart for the events of the morning.

The noon meal was to be the quickest of the three we prepared each day. It was to be dried fruit and whatever bread that was left over. Occasionally some dried meat was to be served. Our chores in the galley were quickly finished and I was anxious to get back up on deck. I saw Vito stationed at the rudder. He was straining to keep the ship on course, having to maneuver the ship frequently with the rudder. The wind had now picked up and we were sailing along at a fast pace. Capt. Vitas seemed pleased with the way things were going on this voyage but he remained ever watchful. He was a man who took nothing for granted. Everything was going smoothly this day and most of the task of stowing away cargo and gear had been completed. I was given the job of cleaning the main deck, which I didn't mind a bit since it had been well cleaned on a regular basis. It was a beautiful day to be outside even though it was mid winter. The weather had been exceptionally warm and nice all fall. Most shipping would have been halted for the winter months by now during more normal years, but this year many ships were still making their voyages and enjoying pleasant weather.

It was only a short time before I heard Capt. Vitas order another hand to replace Vito at the rudder. He came over to the water barrel near where I was mopping and found a place to rest. We began talking about the many things involved in sailing a ship like this one. I found it to be most interesting but the afternoon was quickly passing and I wanted to hear about Vito's travels. I decided to make a straightforward approach beginning with a question about Galilee.

"You said you have sailed on the Sea of Galilee. How long were you there?"

I asked.

"Almost two and a half years. I liked working on boats there. They were small and the trips were not long. We hardly ever were more than two days out at sea. But we had to do a lot of hard work loading and unloading. Lots of people there—all kinds. Some pretty strange ones too." Vito answered. "What do you mean by strange ones?" I questioned.

"Well, there were some who had some really different ideas and other folks who didn't care for their ideas. There were a lot of strong differences by the time I left there and I imagine it ain't no better by now. I haven't figured out who was more stranger—the ones with the new ideas or the ones who wanted to keep the old ways." Vito said as he looked off into the distance as if to find an answer to his own question.

"These people with new ideas—did you ever meet any of them? What were their ideas?" I asked, wanting to keep on track and hoping he was talking about the teachings we had heard of.

"I saw this feller they called John once. Now he was a strange lookin character but he had some common sense things to say. He didn't hold back on tellin you what he thought, specially if'n he thought you was doin wrong. I would'a liked to have heard him more but by the time the ship got back to that area he had moved on and someone else took up his teachin. They say this John really liked to wash'em in the river after he teached at em. Strange alright!" he said with a chuckle.

"What about the one who took up his teaching—ever see him?" I asked.

"No, never did. Had to leave and wound up on this ship with Capt. Vitas. I heard later on that what them two fellers was teachin was makin a lot of folks mighty upset. Some said them two had powers that wasn't natural at all. Some even said they had demons in'em." Vito finished saying as he got up to return to work.

Vito had just left and I was quickly trying to finish cleaning that end of the deck when Marco walked up. He had been working on some old nets he found, having got permission from Capt. Vitas. I don't know what he was planning to do with them and, at the moment, I really wasn't all that concerned. I wanted to tell him what I had learned from Vito but it was going to have to wait until later. Capt. Vitas motioned for us to get down to the galley. The sun was getting low on the horizon and that meant suppertime.

We lit the lanterns and Marco began searching for some of the food that was still fresh, wanting to use it while it was still good. He asked me to build a fire in the oven and heat up some water. We were going to make soup. It wasn't long before the aroma was drifting up through the hatch and causing the crew to stick their heads down to encourage the meal along. I began telling Marco what Vito had told me that afternoon. He was interested but I could tell he had something else on his mind.

"What's bothering you, Marco?" I asked.

"Nothing, probably. I just can't help but think someone has been down here besides us today. There seems to be a few things missing. I could be mistaken about it though so don't say anything to anyone yet. Capt. Vitas wouldn't hold for no stealing." Marco answer with a hushed voice.

"I didn't see anyone come down here all day. Is there another passageway anywhere?"

"Only the cargo bay hatch and those steps over there. You been where you could have seen someone come down through them? Marco asked with a growing concern.

"Most of the time I was right by the both of them. I guess someone could have slipped down here if he was quick enough but it wouldn't have been easy for him. How much stuff is missing?" I inquired.

"Oh, just a few things I think. I'm pretty sure I left a few things here this morning that aren't here now. There ain't no rats on board big enough to have carried them off, that's for sure. Well, we had better get this soup served up. Come on and grab those bowls over there and some spoons. Get whatever bread you can find and I'll come back down for a keg of ale." Marco said as his mind returned to his duties as head cook.

"Aye, aye, sir. I'll get right to it." I said giving him a brisk salute and a click of the heels.

We endeared ourselves to the crew once more with a delicious meal and enjoyed some light-hearted conversation with them as well. Time passed quickly that evening and Marco reminded me that we had to clean up once more. He gave me the job of washing up while he started making bread for the next couple of days. As we began our work in the galley, our conversation once more returned to the purpose of our journey. Vito had stirred my curiosity with his comments about

washing people in the river. I was also wandering why people would be so upset at these new teachings. Marco was much more attentive now and wanted to hear every detail that I had heard from Vito.

As our work neared completion for the day we both felt our bodies were ready to give way to the comfort of those lumpy and smelly bunks. It would soon be time to start all over again in a few hours. I hadn't given much thought to just how often people eat until now. With that mind boggling thought I said good night to Marco and found my spot among the lumps and holes in my bunk. Marco just fell into his and didn't bother to fit himself at all.

We laid there for a few minutes and then I remembered I wanted to ask Marco about the nets he had been fixing. I said his name softly so as not to wake him if he were already asleep and he answered with a voice that told me I had about half his attention.

"What are you going to do with those nets?"

"Just wait and see." he answered and drifted off beyond any further conversation.

I pulled up the cover and closed my eyes. Sleep came so quickly that I didn't even have time to think about it. It must have been only a short time later that I was awakened by something falling to the floor of the galley. I laid still, hoping to see if I had been dreaming or if someone was prowling around. I strained to see if I could make out Marco in his bunk. Moonlight was streaming down through the hatch door and made just enough light to make out the more prominent features of the galley. It left a lot of dark shadows. I continued to lay motionless for several more minutes and never heard anything more than the dripping, creaking, and groaning of the ship. Again, without thinking, sleep overcame me and the night passed on without further incident.

Day two at sea began with Marco calling me to rise and cook. He was such a good friend but there were times when I valued his friendship more than others. This was not particularly one of those times. It seemed as if the night had been only a blink in time and now the chores of another day awaited our attention. The best way to get to the end is to take the first step—however clumsy they were.

After we had all the breakfast duties over with and were up on deck doing our work there, Marco motioned me over to him. He looked around checking to see if anyone was within hearing distance and then put his arm around my shoulder, pulling my head close to his.

"I found more things missing this morning and there was a sack of dried fruit on the floor. I know it wasn't there when we went to bed. I thought I heard something last night but I wasn't sure if it was you or what." He whispered.

"Yes, I heard something too but I guess I was so tired that I fell back asleep instead of getting up to see what it was. Something or someone must have been down there with us last night. You going to tell Capt. Vitas?" I asked.

"No not just yet. But I do have a plan in mind. Whatever you do, don't let on like you suspect anything. Don't say a word to me about what we know when we are down in the galley. Try to get whatever rest you can today because we probably won't be sleeping much tonight. Now here's wha—" Marco was saying as I interrupted him.

"You're not planning on us trying to capture a blood-thirsty, food stealing, pirate by ourselves are you? We don't even have any weapons to defend ourselves with except for them old butcher knives! Don't get crazy on me now!" I argued with all the effort I could and still keep my voice down to a level that wasn't heard across the deck.

"Hold on! You are getting all worked up and we don't even know but what it is some animal or something. Now think for just a minute...If there was some cut-throat pirate down there do you really think we would still be alive now. He would have had two nights to get rid of us by now. Just trust me, and besides all we would have to do is yell and there would be at least five deck hands down here in no time." Marco said, trying to offer encouragement to me and perhaps even to himself.

"It's kind of hard to yell when your throat has been slit. You sure you know what you are doing?" I protested once more.

"Sure I do." Now listen—we gotta be ready tonight. We will go to bed about the same as we have been but we can't go to sleep. It is going to be hard but we have to stay awake. If we hear something, the first thing we do is to grab a torch. I am going to keep some coals burning in the oven so just poke it in there to light it. Whatever it is down there will either have to get past us to the stairs or get out through the hold doors. The only other choice they got is to hide down there midst the cargo." explained Marco.

"What will we do if we find someone? You know how much fight comes from someone who gets cornered?" I asked.

"Well, I been thinking on that too. Do you think we can trust Vito to help us and not tell anyone else?" asked Marco.

"I suppose we can. He seems to like us and I know he would want to help protect his food supply and the ones who cook it." I answered.

"Good! Then we will need to let him in on our plan and have him guarding the doors to the cargo bay. He can help watch the hatch too.

It will work out fine because he's on lookout tonight so he'll be up there anyway. Now we had better get our work done and try to get a little rest in before night. We'll talk to Vito after dinner." Marco said as he left to continue his mopping.

The day went on with not much excitement. Our work in the galley already began to take on a routine pattern that helped make the job easier and done sooner. The duties on deck even seemed to take less effort. We had time to get acquainted with more of the crew but we didn't hear any more news about the teachings of John or Jesus. However, we were able to build a good relationship with most of the crew and they became familiar with our interest in learning more of these teachings. In fact we did learn that a couple of the deck hands were wanting to work their way to Israel also.

Evening came and Marco and I both agreed it had been a wonderful day. We were on a ship that had a good captain, the weather was exceptionally good for this time of year, the tension that we feared from the crew was almost completely gone, and we found we had the abilities to do our jobs well. Although we didn't find time for a nap, neither of us felt tired that night. We were even able to spend a little time up on deck gazing at the stars. I looked to the eastern sky and envied the stars that shone over the land there, wondering about the sights they beheld. As I turned my head to look to the west, I found my heart tingle just a little. I wondered if my mother was looking to those same stars, hoping they would provide protection for her son. I could feel my eyes filling with tears and hoped that they would not run down my face, or at least Marco wouldn't choose this time to look at me. My eyes continued to be filled and soon the tears were rolling down and falling off my chin to the deck below. My heart became so tender and I reached a point of not caring if he did see my tears. I had people who loved me and I loved them. Right at this moment our hearts were being connected in a way that was beyond my ability to understand but I was thankful.

After a few more minutes, I told Marco that we had better get below if we wanted to go pirate hunting . He chuckled a little and when he turned to go, I saw in the moonlight the remains of a tear or two on his cheek. As we made our way below, I committed the precious time we had just had to the deep places in my heart. Yes, it had been a great day.

We laid our torches close to our bunks as we climbed into them for the night. Marco carefully checked to see that there were some coals still glowing in the oven and then we began our wait. An hour or more must have passed. I had to fight hard to keep from going to sleep—even succumbing to it and having to force myself to return to listening for any sound that would alert us to the prowler. As I began to imagine what a blood-thirsty pirate might look like, I found it easier to stay awake.

It wasn't but a few minutes more that I heard something back in the cargo. I raised my head just enough to make sure I could hear my best. I was hoping Marco was awake and wondered if he heard it too. Again a faint shuffling sound came from the cargo area. The sound was coming closer to the barrels of food we had been using. I could hear the sound of the old wooden lid being lifted from the keg of salted meat. I knew it was only about twenty feet from our bunks. The only thing that would be blocking the path to where that keg was sitting would be the big table we used to fix the food. I heard a faint sound coming from Marco's bunk and could tell he was reaching for his torch. I stuck my hand out for mine and soon we were both up to our feet with our torches bringing light into the galley. We took a couple of steps toward the barrels and began to make out a figure turning to run. We quickly followed and I stretched out my hand to grab hold of the shoulder of whoever was fleeing. I locked on to that shoulder and pulled it around toward me. At the same time I lunged forward and found myself falling on top of our intruder. Marco was right there with his torch held up to see what was going on. A slight scuffle started but ended when Marco added his weight to hold our visitor down.

Everything happened it seemed in an instant. Now my mind was returning to working in more normal time. My first thought was that I had did it! I had captured a pirate! But pirates are supposed to be much bigger than this one. He sure gave up without much fight. Then I began to get my eyes focused on what was laying beneath me. I saw the back of someone's head. I could feel that the body under that coat wasn't nearly as big as mine. I saw a small hand sticking out from the end of a tattered sleeve.

"Who are you and what are you doing hear?" I demanded.

The intruder slowly began to turn over to face us and I carefully relaxed my hold. As their face turned toward us the torch light revealed that our pirate had turned out to be a young boy. So much for my gallantry. My pride of grabbing hold of a fleeing pirate now turned into hoping I hadn't caused injury to a small boy. We heard the running footsteps overhead and realized that Vito was on his way down to help us. Finally, I looked up at Marco and was astonished to see his face. He was ghostly white and his mouth was open—as if frozen in place.

"What's wrong, Marco. You all right! You look like you seen a ghost or something!" I questioned him without getting any response.

About that time Vito came running up and began surveying the situation. Marco remained frozen in place while Vito and I picked the boy up and began checking him out. He didn't seem to have any serious injuries and he had a sack of food on the floor where he had landed. The old coat was one that had been hanging in the galley for a long time. It was way oversized but it had apparently been giving some warmth to the boy. We tried to question the boy but he wouldn't respond. He just stood there with his head down. By now it was obvious that something was seriously wrong with Marco. Even Vito was staring at him. I left Vito to hold onto the boy and turned to see about Marco.

"Marco, what is the matter with you?" I asked him as I took hold of his arm and shook him.

Slowly he turned towards us and color began to return to his face. After a moment of two he said, "He's my little brother."

"Your brother!" I exclaimed, "How did he get here?"

"I don't know but how he got here but the real question is what we are going to do with him. He can't make this voyage with us and we can't turn back now. "Stephan, what has gotten into you?" he said as he turned to his brother, "What were you thinking or did you even stop to think? Don't you know what this must be doing to our mother and father?"

"I didn't figure it would be any worse for them since they surely would know that we must be off together somewhere. You know I always follow you when I can." Stephan pleaded.

"Not this time, Stephan. We are going to be gone for quite some time and it could be too dangerous for you. I just won't have time to watch out for you and work too. I'm sorry but that is just the way it has to be." Marco said as he tried to understand his little brother's heart.

"Ephesus will be the first place we can put him off. Capt. Vitas ain't never the kinda man to throw anybody over, specially kids. Should be there day after tomorrow. When you gonna tell the Capt. bout the boy?" Vito asked.

"I'll tell him first thing in the morning but I need some time tonight to think about what to do with Stephan. Do you or any of the crew know somebody he could stay with in Ephesus till another ship goes back to Athens?" Marco inquired.

"I don't know off hand but findin a ship goin to Athens this late in the year won't be easy. Gotta be careful bout what ship you put him on. There's some of em I wouldn't even go on." Vito replied.

It was becoming clear that we had a significant problem on our hands. Little else was spoken for quite some time. Marco spent most of an hour pacing the galley floor, deep in thought. All of us were pondering what the best thing to do would be. It appeared that there was no solution that would even be acceptable. Our spirits were growing more disheartened as time passed that night. Finally Vito got up from his seat on one of the barrels and said he was going to his bunk in the crews quarters. He had become just as silent as we were but, as he was leaving the galley, I sensed there was a different working going on in his mind. He seemed to be mauling over something but he wasn't ready to discuss it.

Stephan had fallen asleep on Marco's bunk. His small body only occupied the lower end of the bed. Looking at him sleeping there only served to convince me that we had to do everything we could to assure that he got home safely, even if it meant we had to return to Athens. Our quest to find this man, Jesus, would have to wait until another time. I was just about to announce this decision to Marco when he began to speak himself.

"There is no way we can take Stephan to Israel with us. The trip would be too long and much too dangerous for him. We don't even know how long we are going to be away. Secondly, we don't know anyone in Ephesus who we can leave him with. A ten year-old boy is pretty helpless in a city like Ephesus. That only leaves one choice—taking him back home. Now, I know how important this trip is to you so this is what I have decided. When we get to Ephesus, I am going to find a ship heading for Athens and take Stephan home with me. You can stay on board here and finish the voyage. You kno—" Marco was saying as I interrupted him.

"No, not without you! You are just as interested in making this voyage as I am. If you can't go then I won't either. We'll just have to wait until spring and try again." I protested.

"It won't be that easy. Don't you know what my parents are going to say when I get back with Stephan? It will be best if you are not around—I can assure you of that much." Marco argued.

"I can't go on without you! First of all we both know that the crew has taken to us because of you and your good cooking. You seem to have a way of understanding how people think and act. You can figure them out before they can do or say much at all and by the time they actually say or do anything, you are already ahead of them. I'm just not ready to go this journey alone yet. Maybe I'll find somewhere to stay besides Athens for the winter—we'll just have to figure that out on the way back. It is settled. We are both going to take Stephan back home." I said with as much determination as I had in me.

"We'll see how things are in the morning. Now let's get what sleep we can before we have to be up again." Marco said as he rolled into the bunk that was shared with his little brother.

Morning came soon enough and Marco and I went through the chores of preparing breakfast, leaning more on the habits of routine than on applying ourselves to doing a job we wanted to do. Little was said concerning the events of the night before. Marco seemed a little uneasy and I knew he was planning on what to tell Capt. Vitas about Stephan. I found myself becoming increasingly discouraged by the fact that we would be turning back from our journey. However selfish it was to be feeling this way, the disappointment was there and it couldn't be denied. I knew Marco had to be torn between the disappointment and his love for his brother. As hard as I tried, I was not able to lift my spirits from that state of depression. Silence overcame the galley that morning and we had little to say to anyone as we took the food up on deck.

As the men finished eating, Marco started to make his way to Capt. Vitas. Vito came up to him and brought him to where I was standing. He began to speak to us with little more than a whisper.

"I been thinkin and I just might have somethin figured out. It don't really matter to me if I sail on to Israel or where ever we end up. I'd just as soon go back to Athens for the winter and take a few months off. Now, if you'll let me, I can take the boy back with me and you two can go on. You can trust me with him—ain't nobody gonna lay a hand on him—I guarantee you that. I know what you two are out to find and if you wait til spring shippin time you might be too late to find it. What do ya think?" he asked as he looked us directly in the eye.

We were both taken back by his plan. My mind became flooded with thoughts that seemed to be coming from a hundred different directions. I could tell Marco was stunned. He just stood there looking into Vito's eyes as if to discern what was going on within the man. Finally Marco managed to stutter out an answer,

"I—I don't know—let me think this over. I need to talk to Stephan and Nik"

"Sure. Just let me know what you decide fore you mention anything to the captain. Remember—I promise to take good care of him." Vito assured us.

"I'll get back with you before noon." Marco told Vito as we left for the galley.

Marco let his body fall onto some sacks of grain and held his head in his hands. I could tell he was agonizing over what to do. After giving him some time to think, I began to question him about some of the thoughts that raced through my mind.

"Can we trust him? I know he seems to really care about us and Stephan, but we just met him only a few days ago." I said.

"Oh, my family has kinda knowed Vito for a while. He has been around the fish market for over a year. My dad worked with him for a short time last spring." Marco said.

"That helps some but I still wonder what your folks will have to say when they find out we sent Stephan home with someone else instead of bringing him back ourselves. I think I would be pretty upset if I were in their place." I protested.

"They will be angry alright! But they would be angry even if we took him back ourselves. This way at least, they will have some time to get over it before we make it back home. I wouldn't even think of letting Stephan go with Vito if I didn't think he would be safe. I wouldn't do anything to ever hurt him." said Marco as he got up and paced the floor.

"I know you wouldn't and it's not that I don't want to trust Vito. It's just that we have to be sure we are doing the right thing by going on with our journey. Are we willing to accept the responsibility if something should happen to Stephan? I asked.

"I'd given anything if Stephan hadn't put us in this predicament but the fact is he has and there no changing that. If I didn't have this desire so strong inside me to know what all this teaching is about, I'd say let's take him home. I gotta find out about it! I don't want to go back to the things we've been taught in Greece. There is something in what we have been hearing about that gets in me—I don't know what it is. I just got to find out—I want to be able to help Stephan come to know it too. Do you hear what I'm sayin?" Marco pleaded through tears.

"There's a lot of things about what we have been taught that just don't make sense. I feel that same stirring in me every time I hear people talking about these new teachings. All I can tell you for certain is that I don't want to go on living by ways I know are wrong. I'm glad you feel so strongly about our trip. It helps assure me we are doing right. Stephan is your brother and if you think he will get home safely with Vito, then that's good enough for me." I answered.

We woke Stephan up and told him of the plans. He wasn't happy about it but he knew he didn't have a choice. I stayed with him while Marco went up to find Vito and, after he told him of the decision, they went to Capt. Vitas. Marco explained about Stephan being on board and about the plans for Vito to take him back to Athens when we reached Ephesus. At first the captain didn't say much—he shifted the pipe in his mouth from side to side and made some low noises under his breath. His first words to them was to have the boy brought up on deck. Marco came and called us up.

Capt. Vitas watched us approach him. He waited for a short time and then took Marco aside. The two of them talked and we could only hear an occasional gruff coming from the captain. Marco appeared to be demonstrating something to the captain that was having a calming effect on him. Capt. Vitas looked at Stephan a couple of times as they talked for a few minutes before rejoining us.

"Since you are causing me to loose one of my crew members, I find it necessary to dock your pay to half a day's pay for two days work. What's the boy been eating?" Capt. Vitas wanted to know.

"Sir, please don't dock their pay. I gotta cousin in Ephesus who'd be glad to come on board and he's just as good a hand as me. These fellas been doin a good job for ya. You run a good ship, Capt. and it won't be hard to find men willin to sign on with ya." Vito begged for us.

"We'll have to see bout it later. Now, get back to work all of you and keep that kid out of the way." Capt. Vitas bellowed out as he marched off.

"I think it'l be alright. The captain has to make it sound like he's tough and hard but I know he has a good heart. Just don't do anything more to raise his feathers. He's a good man." Vito reassured us.

We all followed the captains orders and quickly got back to our duties. Marco told Stephan to get below and help clean up the galley. He sent me down to start fixing the noon meal and he went to ask Vito where he could find a long pole. Marco was definitely up to something but he wasn't about to let any of us in on it yet. The morning passed quickly and I had most of the meal ready by the time Marco came below. He helped me finish up and we took the food up on deck.

As we passed out the portions to the crew, several of them started teasing Marco. They were asking him if he thought he was on a whaling ship and they wanted to know why he didn't have a big fish for everyone. All the teasing soon had the whole crew laughing and in a cheerful mood. It was good to see the men happy and Marco was enjoying the whole thing as well. He would just smile at them and let their jokes roll off. I knew Marco and I knew he knew something they didn't. I had seen him smile like that before. He was definitely up to something.

That afternoon I asked Marco what all the teasing was about.

"You know how sailors are—they'll rib you over anything." he replied.

"I know this is more than just 'anything'. What are you up to?" I asked.

Marco looked at me for a minute or so and then began to explain what was going on.

"I found some old fishing nets and asked Capt. Vitas if I could fix them. He said I could and so I figured out a way to pull them along as we sailed. I figured they would surely catch enough fish to be able to pick over and have a fresh meal once in a while. I'll need you to help me pull the net in and see what we got. They should have something in them by now. Let's go see."

I was anxious to see what Marco had made. It was also good to have a change in the routine. Our steps quickened as we approached the rigging Marco had made to hold the net out into the water. We began to pull in the ropes that lifted the net out of the water. The net itself was water soaked and heavy and we had difficulty pulling it in. A couple of the deck hands watched us and again began their teasing. That made us work all the harder. As the net began to come out of the water, we could see it held several good sized fish. The men who had been laughing at us we now silently standing by, trying to see what all was in the net. Their laughter was replaced by words like "Heave" as they grabbed the ropes and helped us pull the net in.

As the net was finally lowered to the deck, we could see we had caught several kinds of fish and a few other creatures as well. Marco began sorting through the catch as quickly as he could—wanting to throw back what he didn't want to keep before they died. Soon he had eight large perch and two or three sword-fish laid out. He also had what he said was a squid put aside to fix. The rest of the catch was quickly returned to the sea.

Capt. Vitas came up and looked over the catch we had made.

"Looks like your plan worked, Marco. We'll be eating good tonight. Now get a couple of the men to help you take down the rigging until we need it again. Wouldn't want someone to think we was a fishing boat."

It a short time we had the poles and nets stowed away and Marco and I began cleaning the fish we saved. He said we had enough for two big meals plus some stew. We had only been at sea for a few days but it was going to be a real treat to have fresh fish. Marco's plan seemed so simple and I began to wonder why the men had made such fun of him. I finally decided to ask about it.

"How come other crews don't try to catch fish and why did they make such fun of you? I asked.

"Shipping crews don't care much for fishermen. Pride has a lot to do with it. Also not many people know how to rig up a net that will work on a cargo ship. Anyway, that's why the captain wanted to take down the rigging for the net. He didn't want some other ship to know that he had let his crew do some fishing." Marco explained.

The whole crew enjoyed a fine meal of roasted fish that evening and Marco was able to walk around the group of men with an even bigger smile on his face. Not only had he showed them he knew how to fish but he had done an excellent job cooking the fish. I think it was the best I had ever eaten.

Our fourth day at sea was not like the previous days. Nearly every crew member had to come down to the galley to meet Marco's brother. It was surprising to see men who had been hardened by life on the sea show such tenderness. Although I hadn't been on a cargo ship before, it was becoming evident that this crew's attitude was much different than most and their spirits seemed to lift each day. The weather remained so pleasant that it was easy to forget that we were into the winter months. The winds continued to move us along at a good pace and we saw several small islands before noon that day. Capt. Vitas figured we would be docking at Ephesus by tomorrow evening if not sooner.

The captain ordered extra men to stand watch. He knew the waters well and didn't want to risk hitting jagged rocks or reefs. He also knew the danger of being attacked by thieves who were known to live on the small islands we saw. They could lie in wait and then quickly sail out to attack cargo ships that were for the most part defenseless. About the only way to defend the crew and the cargo was to be ready for hand to hand combat when the pirates tried to come on board. Capt. Vitas had been in that situation before and knew the cost to both crew and cargo. He decided to purchase a small catapult and placed it on the main deck and had a wooden box made to cover it. The catapult was small enough to be maneuvered easily but it was capable of hurling a twenty pound ball nearly four hundred feet. He had not fired the weapon since it was put on board but he took care to keep it ready. He had seen the piece in action and knew it could take a ship to the bottom if necessary.

Late in the day Capt. Vitas ordered the sails lowered some to slow us down for the night. We also changed course to take us out to safer waters until daylight could offer its protection. Day four passed on without incident.

We were up before light on the fifth day. None of us in the galley slept well that night. It must have been the anticipation of seeing Ephesus and knowing that this might be our last night with Stephan for a long time. We were also uneasy about the possibility of being attacked. I was glad to find work to do to help get my mind on other things. We kept busy until late morning. Capt. Vitas wanted us to take the watch at the bow. They had raised the sails again and we were once more moving along at a good pace. It was just before noon when we spotted two ships sailing toward us in the distance. We sent word to Capt. Vitas and he came forward with his scope. After studying the ships he collapsed his scope and said there was nothing to be concerned about. They were cargo ships and were probably heading for Greece.

When Marco and I heard that we looked at each other and then looked for Vito. We wanted to ask him about the possibility of transferring to one of the ships and getting a head start back to Athens. Maybe we were hoping for too much but it was worth looking into. We tried to find Vito before we had to return to the galley to fix the noon meal.

We were unable to find Vito that morning but we left word for him to come down as soon as possible to the galley. Marco even stayed up on deck for a while longer as I started fixing the meal. Finally he saw Vito and told him about the our plan to see if he could take Stephan with him to one of the ships that was approaching.

"There's a slim chance that they'll come close nough to tell what ship they are. Gotta be careful not to get on certain ones if'n you want to make sure the boy gets home safe. Then we have to hope they'll come near nough to talk with. Lot to hope for. I'd be willin if'n it was to work out. It'd save us at least two days at sea. Let's go talk to the captain." Vito said. "He'll know best."

"Let's hurry!" Marco exclaimed. "They'll be getting pretty close by now"

Vito and Marco hurriedly explained the idea to the captain and he thought there was a good chance of getting close enough to the ships if they could be trusted. He pulled his scope out and studied the first ship that was approaching. After a bit, he lowered the telescope and said,

"Best let this one pass on by. Pirates wouldn't even want to mess with that crew."

While they waited on the other ship to get near, Capt. Vitas took the time to express his aggravation at being troubled with this situation,

"How can a man tend to running a ship with all this nurse-maidin going on? I never seen the like before and hope not to again. Loosing a deck hand and having to stop dead in the water—I'll be the laughing stock of every port around. Is there anybody left on this ship that is still working? I never seen the like!" he grumbled.

As he was finishing his last few words he had the scope raised back to his eye and soon announce that he knew the ship that was coming near. He gave orders for a signal flag to be raised and we saw the other ship signal back. They would be coming along side. Marco came running down the steps into the galley. He grabbed Stephan and hugged him so tightly that I wondered if he could still breathe. Marco told him what was about to happen and had him get ready in case it worked out. He asked me if I could handle fixing the meal by myself but didn't wait for an answer before going back up on deck with Stephan.

Both our ship and the approaching one had dropped their sails. They were slowing in the water and soon glided to a stop within several feet of each other. Capt. Vitas greeted the other captain and began the conversation.

"Where are you headed? " he asked.

"Athens and then on to Sparta for the rest of the winter." replied the other captain. "You going to lay up at Ephesus for the winter?"

"Nope, we're going on east as long as this weather holds." Capt. Vitas replied.

"We wanted to know if you could take on an extra deck hand till you get to Athens. He's got a boy with him we got to get back Sure would appreciate the help and Vito will make you a real good hand."

The other captain turned to talk to a deck hand that had come up to him. After the two of them had discussed something he yelled back to us,

"You say your man's name is Vito?" he asked.

"That's right," Capt. Vitas answered. "Hate to loose him but he has his mind set on helping the boy get home."

"Vito, this is Alexus, your cousin. I didn't know you had a son. Why didn't you tell us?" the deck hand yelled jokingly from the other ship.

"Alexus, that you? I thought you'd still be in Ephesus. Your too lazy to work in the winter." Vito yelled back.

"Come on over captain and bring your man with you and the boy. We'll see what we can work out." The other captain said to Capt. Vitas.

I had joined Marco on deck and he gave his little brother one last hug and told him what to tell his family. We said good bye to Vito and watched them as they were lowered in the skiff along with Capt. Vitas and another deck hand. My heart ached with pain as I watched Marco's eyes tell of the anguish that was tearing inside him. We stood at the railing and watched as the two captains negotiated a trade. Finally Capt. Vitas climbed back into the skiff and the man named Alexus joined him. As the deck hand rowed them back to our ship we watched the sails raise and then billow out on the ship that was to take Vito and Stephan home to Athens. By the time our ship was under sail again Vito and his little friend were just two small silhouettes waving to us.

I knew Marco wouldn't feel much like talking so I went about the task of finishing the meal. I saw Marco reach out and shake Capt. Vitas' hand and thank him for the kindness he had shown. He didn't say anything that afternoon until word came down that we would be sailing into port at Ephesus at sundown. The first leg of our journey was nearing completion and already it had been filled with more adventure than we had ever imagined. What would the rest of the voyage have in store?

# CHAPTER THREE

# STAYING AHEAD OF WINTER

As the red sun was saying farewell to the day and the western sky displayed all the beautiful colors of orange, purple, and gray, our ship dropped its sails and the crew took to the oars to bring us to the dock. By the time we were tied in place, darkness had overtaken the evening. Capt. Vitas told the men that we had a considerable amount of cargo to off load and would be bringing on some more. He wanted to wait until morning to unload so he gave the crew the evening off but added a stern warning to be ready and able to work just after daybreak.

Marco and I went with the men to a tavern nearby where we hoped to find a fresh meal. As we neared the establishment the delicious aroma of food filled the air. Somehow, this fragrance was able to overpower the salty smell of the sea, the fishy smell of the markets nearby, and the musty odor of our clothes. Even though Marco's cooking had been the best many a sailor had ever eaten, it was not the same as a meal made with fresh ingredients. We were also anxious to hear the latest news form the men who had been to other ports in this part of the world. Evenings in a tavern like this one provided a wonderful time for men who had been cut off from the rest of the world. It was not uncommon for these gatherings to go on till the wee hours of the morning. For the first time in my life, I actually felt that I was one of the sailors and they had come to accept me.

After having stuffed ourselves with all the cook would let us have, we scattered throughout the tavern and began sharing our experiences. Great tales were told that night and roars of laughter threatened to bring the rafters down. Some of the men grew louder and more boisterous as they poured drink after drink down their throats. After a while those who were drunk either passed out or left and the room became much quieter. Conservation turned to a more serious nature. We learned that pirates were operating in the waters about two days to the south and they had attacked and sunk three ships since late summer. There was also talk of storms coming to the region and some of the men warned that this spell of late fall weather was about to give way to winter. A few captains had decided to stay in Ephesus for the winter, not wanting to take a chance on getting caught in a winter storm at sea and having to worry about pirates too. We wondered if Capt. Vitas had heard about these reports and what he would do about them. Our concerns were soon to be answered as he came into the tavern and found a table with some other captains he knew. We were sure to have an answer by the time we arrived back at our ship.

Meanwhile, we heard a group of men talking about the teachings we had heard so much of and quickly joined the discussion. They had heard this man, Jesus, teaching people and even saw him restore sight to some men. Marco and I leaned across the table, wanting to catch every word we could. Excitement was building in the both of us and we soon found ourselves interrupting with question after question.

"Are you sure he actually gave sight back to some man? Was there anyone who knew him to be blind before? It wasn't some trick just to get people roused up was it?" I asked, not so much doubting what I had heard as I was wanting to find solid ground to build my hopes on.

"He was blind alright—plenty of people knew him for a long time. That man, Jesus just touched his eyes and told him he was healed and he was. I saw him do it! He had some kind of power—let me tell ya! And he sure could talk. He told people stories in such a way that even us poor people could understand him." one of the men replied.

"What are his teachings about? What is he telling people?" Marco asked the man.

"Well, mostly he teaches about the need to turn away from doing wrong and do what is right. He tells people to treat others with kindness and to care for them. He said people had to be 'born again' if they was to get to a place called heaven. Now that part I didn't understand then and I still don't now." the man answered as he seemed to be searching within to understand even as he spoke to us.

"Who is this Jesus and where did he come from?" asked another man sitting in our group.

"Some say he came from a town called Nazareth but I heard him say he was the Son of God and has been around since the beginning of time. Now figure that out if you can!" said the first man.

"Don't make sense to me! You must have had too much brew yourself." countered the second man.

"All I know is what I saw and what I heard. That Jesus man has some strange powers and he has got people stirred up. They's some that don't like what he's doin' but I'm here to tell you sure as I sittin' here, he's someone whose gonna bring some changes—mark my words on that!" replied the first man.

"What god did he say he was the son of?" I asked.

"Well, best I get it, he says there's only one God and that this one God made the whole world. He says that all the other gods people worship are just made up and people spend their lives believing in them or worship some man-made shrine or somethin—I don't know just how it goes but he's pretty insistent about there bein only one God." the first man answered.

This first man was an older man and we could see he was struggling to comprehend all that he was telling us. He had seen much of what he said first hand and did not understand it all. Now, he was trying to tell it to us and realized how bizzar it must sound. He must have wanted to understand the things he told us as much as we did. I felt compassion in my heart for the man. He was well along in years and wanted to know the truth of what he had heard. I found myself wondering if he would live long enough to find that truth and I had a renewed appreciation for the strength of my youth as I looked into his face and watched as he searched for that knowledge.

"All of this might sound far-fetched but if you really think about it, it is not any more strange than all the stuff we have been taught about the gods of Greece." Marco began to reason. "You men have been around these parts long enough to know how ridiculous some of these teachings are. I'm convinced that if there is something more than this life, it ain't found in one of the gods we have been told to bow down to. Every time I ever tried to question the reality of the gods of Greece, I was told to just accept the fact that they existed and that was to be the end of it. Well, I'm not going to believe in something unless there is more to it than that. Is there any proof that this God is any more real than those Greek gods?"

"Yes there seems to be. Besides the claim that He created the whole world and all that is in it, He is said to have split a sea apart and made dry ground on the bottom of it. All of Israel was able to walk through to get away from the Egyptian army. When the Egyptians tried to follow them, this God closed the sea back and drowned all the Egyptian, horses and all. Another time He destroyed two cities with fire that came down from the sky because they were so wicked. Also He once flooded the whole earth and saved only one man and his family along with some animals so He could start the human race over again because people were so awful. These things and more have been written down by the Jews. It is there history." the old man said.

"But how does that make Him different from any other god? Has anybody ever seen Him?" Marco asked.

"Not actually saw Him but some have seen His angles. Some have heard His voice. And, yes, I remember hearing a story about one time when some priests of some god tried to get their god to answer them. They tried all day and called out to their gods to accept their sacrifice but their gods didn't come. Then a man who belonged to this God called for water to be put on the altar and more water and more until it was drenched in it.

Then he called out to his God to come and burn up the sacrifice that had been soaked in standing water. He did it!" replied the old man, smiling as he told the story.

"Wait a minute! What are these angles? Where did they come from?" challenged Marco.

"I don't know. I guess they are His messengers or something. All I know is I have heard enough about this God and this man they call Jesus that I am convinced that I want to learn more. I have found more reason for hope in these teachings than anything I have ever heard. There is so much that I don't understand but I have been able to take in enough that I know I have found it is something of great value. Angles or messengers— who cares what they are. I am an old man with not much time left. I am convinced that life does not end in death—there is more beyond that. But I'm also convinced that a life after death can be one that is pleasant or one that is torment. I would like to be sure that I find they way to the pleasant one." the old man said calmly and with a slow and deliberate tone.

"I believe you may be right in what you have just said. I don't have anything solid to base my convictions on except for what is working in my heart. I have had such a stirring to find the truth you have spoken of for quite some time. The more I learn, the more I am convinced. We're on to something. Marco, you know it too!" I exclaimed.

"You're right, Nik. Even as we sit here now, it stirs even more." Marco answered.

"You fellas have gone plum crazy. I don't know if it's what you ate or what, but I'm gettin out of here!" said the second man as he got up and left our table.

"What's you name, mister?" I asked the old man.

"Ben, Ben Ides." he answered as he shoved his hand out to us, as if he had just met us. Marco and I introduced ourselves to him and we continued out conversation for a while longer. As we continued to talk, I began to work on a plan to take Ben to Israel with us. I wasn't sure how Capt. Vitas would react to another "guest" on board his ship. I admired the captain and would readily agree that he had already been more than fair, but I certainly didn't want to try his patience. Ben knew a lot of information that could help us greatly, but more than that, I wanted to help him find the truth he sought so desperately for. I decided to privately ask Marco for his opinion about taking Ben with us and wasn't surprise that he liked the plan. We shared our plan with Ben and asked if he would be willing to go if we could get it worked out. After expressing his concerns about heading out to sea this late in the season, he agreed to go if we could work it out with Capt. Vitas.

It was after midnight when we returned to the ship for the rest of the night. Some of the crew had taken rooms at the tavern but we decided to save our money for more needful things. We found it hard to sleep that night and weren't all that thrilled when we were awakened by Capt. Vitas calling all hands up on deck.

It wasn't light yet when we gathered with the rest of the crew to hear what the captain had to say. We noticed a few of the men who had taken rooms weren't back to the ship yet, but that didn't stop Capt. Vitas from proceeding with what he had on his mind.

"You all have more than likely heard about the change in the weather that some say is coming soon and you have no doubt heard about the pirating raids that have been going on. You also know that I am not a man to back down easily but there comes a time when common sense must prevail. I think we can make it to Israel and hold up for the winter there, but it won't be no easy trip for any of us. The only way we can possibly make it is to have a full crew of men who are committed to doing their duties and then some. We won't try to sail from here unless we have willing men for every duty on this ship."

"I am going to give all of you this opportunity to leave just as soon as we have unloaded all the cargo for this port. I won't hold it against you if you decide not to stay on board—it could get pretty rough out there. I know this old ship and I think she can make it through but she will need some dedicated hands to help her. I need to know right now how many of you are willing to head out with us today. If we're going to be short handed, I need to know it now so I can round up replacements or we just won't go. It's up to you—who's willing to go and who wants to stay at Ephesus?" Capt. Vitas spoke.

As he was speaking the rest of the crew joined us on deck. When he finished talking to us, three of the men said they wanted to stay at Ephesus for the winter. Capt. Vitas didn't hesitate long before he gave orders to haul the cargo up from the hold and then he left to seek men willing to replace the ones who left.

"Capt. Vitas," I called as he was leaving, "We met a man last night who might be willing to go with us and he seemed to have the experience we'll need. His name is Ben Ides and he will probably be around the docks somewhere."

"I'll give you a quarter hour to find him and have him back here at the ship when I get back, then I'll see if I can use him." Capt. Vitas said with a sternness that revealed he was more than a little concerned about setting out to sea. "But you be sure to get back here to help unload."

"I will, Captain!" I answered promptly.

I told Marco where I was going and then left to find Ben Ides. I ran down the street toward the tavern, glancing from side to side hoping to see him. I stopped at the tavern only long enough to look inside but he wasn't there. I ran on down the street a little further and saw a crowd gathered. I couldn't see what they were gathered around until I crowded my way through to the middle where I found Ben telling his stories. I found myself filled with excitement one minute and then overcome with doubt the next. Was this man just good at telling stories he made up or were the stories he told true? I found myself wanting to believe him and, at the same time, hoping not to be made a fool of. It was when I remember how badly I wanted to find the truth about the one they called Jesus, that I decided the risk of being a fool was worth the chance to learn the truth.

I grabbed Ben's arm and told him to come to our ship with me if he wanted to sail with us. He got up and left the crowd without finishing his story. As we headed back down the street he turned and yelled to the people who were left standing, "Keep your ears open—you'll hear more soon enough!"

When we got back on board, Ben helped with the unloading. He never stopped talking the whole time we worked. By the time we finished hoisting the last load to the dock, we had been told much about the teachings of both men, John and Jesus. It seemed that these new teachings were based on simple truths and common sense. We learned a good bit about the Jews and their beliefs. I did my best to take mental notes until I had a chance to put them down on paper. Just as we unhooked the rigging from the last pallet, Capt. Vitas came up and had three new men with him.

He had worked out a deal with some merchants who wanted to sell their goods before the spring shipping season came. He had made a bargain that would turn him a hefty profit, provided we were able to reach Israel before winter caught up to us.

He ordered the goods loaded and took care not to load the ship as full as he usually did. He wanted to make sure we made the best time possible and also wanted to be able to navigate shallow waters if needed. We made fast work of the task at hand and were soon ready to cast off. Capt. Vitas hadn't had time to speak with Ben until just before we were ready to leave. Ben went up to the captain and stuck out his hand. "Ben Ides the name, Captain, and I sure would like to set sail with ya if you'd have me."

Capt. Vitas looked Ben over and was slow to give an answer. Finally he asked, "It could get pretty rough before we reach Tyre—You sure you're up to it?" "If you're thinking it's my age that's bothering you, you needn't worry.

Who do you think helped get this gang of yours movin so fast with the cargo? No, sir Capt., you don't need to fret about me. I'll do my part and then some, I'll guarantee." Ben said with all the confidence of a strutting rooster.

"Alright then. Before this voyage is over we'll most likely be needing to draw from your experience. Welcome aboard Mr. Ides." replied Capt. Vitas.

We were soon under sail and headed for Myra if the weather held. Capt. Vitas had chosen a route that held fairly close to land. We would be passing by Miletus, but had no plans to stop there unless forced to. We would be sailing through some passages that were known for their jagged reefs. They had claimed more than a few ships over the years. The winds had picked up considerably since we docked at Ephesus and we were making good time. I was amazed at how the ship handled since we relieved her of some of the cargo.

Marco and I were put to work securing the cargo and didn't have any cooking duties until the evening meal. Late in the afternoon we were sailing along through areas that had hidden reefs and rock formations. Capt. Vitas had doubled the men on watch but didn't want to slow down any until darkness would make it necessary to drop sail unless we reached deep water before nightfall. His years at sea had helped him to know the waters well. He called out to the men on watch to be looking for danger well before they were able to see it. He was truly amazing.

As the sun began to sink in the west, one of the men on watch called out that a ship was headed for us. The ship had came from behind a small island and was now bearing down on us. Capt. Vitas took notice and soon was giving orders to uncover the catapult on deck and make it ready to fire. He took the wheel himself and added more men to watch the waters. Alexus was put in charge of the catapult and Capt. Vitas told Ben to help him. In just a few minutes we had gone from a peaceful afternoon to being ready for battle. The other ship was closing in on us even though we were still cutting a pretty good wave.

It was soon evident that the approaching ship was a pirate ship and they intended to do us in. We knew we couldn't outrun them but Capt. Vitas had a plan as usual. He gave strict orders for the men to keep a keen eye out for danger as he intended to get as close to the underwater reef as he dared, hoping the pirate ship would try to get even closer and tear the hull out of their ship. He was also planning to drive them into shallow water by firing on them. If they tried to avoid the catapult's missiles, they just might turn into a hidden formation waiting for them under the surface.

Capt. Vitas was planning on waiting until the pirates were within 300 feet before firing on them. It was then that Ben spoke up to persuade the captain to let him fire sooner. "Capt., let me get a ball off when they get just under four hundred feet out. If we wait til they get much closer than that, they might be the first to strike. I've launched many a ball from a weapon like this and I know what she can do. If we can attach a plank to her beam she'll throw that ball another sixty feet or so. It won't hurt the catapult as long as you don't put too much stress on the beam. Trust me on this and I'll put an end to that bunch of thieves."

"You've done this before?" asked Capt. Vitas.

"Oh, sure, lots of times and I've put a dozen ships on the ocean floor." Ben answered confidently. "This one will make it thirteen."

"Alright, help him get it sighted in Alexus. It's probably our best hope anyway." Capt. Vitas commanded.

Ben and Alexus turned the catapult towards the pursuing ship and Ben carefully calculated the trajectory, using only his keen sense of distance. As they worked feverishly to tie a plank onto the beam, Ben seemed to be counting as if to measure the distance he was to gain. As Alexus was checking the release mechanism, Ben took effort to selcect just the right ball. When he was satisfied with his choice, he kissed the ball and placed it onto the catapult's arm. Several of the crew stood in amazement as we watched Ben preparing to fire upon our enemies. He was relying almost totally on his senses to know just how to best use this little catapult. We were anxious to see if his senses would be successful in sparing us disaster.

"Everyone get ready—just another minute or two and she'll be right where I want her. Hold her steady if you would, Capt. O.K. Alexus, let her fly!" Ben order.

We stood there for what seemed like minutes watching the release pin fly off, the arm spring upright, and the ball go flying through the air. It appeared that the ball was going to fall into the sea long before it ever reached the pirate ship. Ben watched with the rest of us but he never doubted but what his aim would be good . We watched the ball go tearing through the mainsail on the pirate ship and then we saw wooden splinters flying up in the air. The ball had landed exactly where Ben wanted it to—on the rudder at the rear deck. Not only was the ship without a good sail, she was helplessly floating in the water without any control of her direction. We began to notice that she was taking on water was well and would soon be joining the other twelve ships Ben had sent to the bottom.

"It will be a long swim for those guys to get back to that island—some of them won't make it. That's their doin's though." Ben thought aloud as he watched the effects of his well placed shot.

Capt. Vitas turned the vessel back out to deeper waters and soon was able to relieve the watch as we continued on at a good speed. The crew all congratulated Ben on his good marksmanship. Alexus was truly amazed at Ben's ability with the catapult and they talked for quite some time about all that had happened. Ben speculated that the pirates had been watching the seas from a hilltop on the island and when a ship was spotted, they headed out for the attack. Capt. Vitas stopped to thank Ben for his help and the three men continued their talk about the little weapon. Ben suggested that the captain secure an extension for the beam. The makeshift extension they had used worked but the strain on the ropes holding the plank to the arm would only allow two shots at best. He also said the accuracy would be improved with a fixed extension. This would permit launching smaller missiles but would increase the range considerably. Most of the pirate ships relied on weapons with short range capabilities. Capt. Vitas seemed to be very interested in Ben's idea. Several of the crewmen joked with Ben about the need to improve his accuracy. We sailed on through the night without further adventure. We had passed Miletus without having to stop since we didn't have cargo for there and we had escaped the risk of pirates for the time being. We continued on course for Myra and hoped to reach port there in three days or so. The wind had shifted to the southwest and blew steadily since we had passed Miletus. We were making good time even though we were having to do considerable tacking. We were glad to have the wind to help us move along so swiftly but there was an uneasiness about it. The crew's outward attitude grew more somber each day. Nobody seemed to want to talk about the wind or what it might be brewing up. Marco and I went about our duties as did the rest of the crew. There just wasn't much conversation going on, even from Ben Ides.

It took us another day to clear all the small islands that dotted the sea between Miletus and Crete. The stress of having to watch for treacherous reefs and rock formations had taken a toll on the crew. Even Capt. Vitas displayed signs of weariness and fatigue. Heading out into the open sea helped to relieve the sullen spirits of the men. The wind continued to blow and by the third day out from Ephesus, it was nearing gale force. We were still a good day's voyage from Myra. It would be very risky to sail into port there, if not impossible unless the wind relented. The crew had lowered the sails and we were only using two smaller ones to help keep us moving east. The seas were now rougher than I had ever imagined. Waves were crashing over the deck and everything that had not been tied securely was washed overboard. The deck hands clung tightly to railings and ropes as they made their way about.

Capt. Vitas stayed on deck most of that morning. Just before noon he took the wheel and told us he was turning the ship to shore. He hoped to be able to sail into a cove where the storm might not be so severe. The sky was growing darker and more ominous. We were at least an hour from the cove and it would be a tight race to make safety before the storm reached us in full force. Capt. Vitas order another sail raised. Marco and I watched from the protection of the hatchway as two crewmen struggled with all their might to hoist the sail. Several times it appeared that the waves had pulled them from the ropes they held to tightly. We gained a full understanding of the dedication that Capt. Vitas had talked about back at Ephesus. These men were giving everything they had to the task before them— anything less and they would not have been successful. Capt. Vitas had tied himself to the wheel-post and was fighting to keep the ship under some control.

We heard the old ship creaking and groaning. Water was dripping down into the hold. Some of the cargo was getting wet and most likely would be ruined. It was evident that we would be having to bail water if the storm lasted much longer. Most of the deck hands had come below to safety. They only went out on the deck when it was absolutely necessary. Some of them were helping Marco and me keep the cargo secured and we were appreciative for it since we had our hands full.

Ben came down the steps and yelled above the crashing waves, "There's another storm cloud moving in from the northwest. Just hold on a while longer and then the worst should be over! I'm going back up to check on the captain."

He left and shut the hatch behind him We could still hear the wind roaring and the waves crashing on the deck above. We tried our best to keep the heavy barrels from flying across the hold and crashing into the ship or us. Ropes were breaking almost as fast as we could get them tied. Then we heard a change in the sound of the wind. It was coming from the other side of the ship. It grew even stronger for a few minutes and then began to subside. Before long the waves quit crashing above us. The ship was still be buffeted but not nearly as hard as before. The deck hands began to go up on deck and attend to their duties. We followed them to the hatchway and saw Ben and Capt. Vitas both at the wheel, doing their best to hold the ship steady.

Capt. Vitas gave the command to lower all sails and check for damage. The wind had calmed considerably but it was growing colder as the old ship slowed in the water. The crew reported that we had lost a good bit of equipment, the skiff and quite a few ropes. The little catapult had been driven to the edge of the deck and was only kept from falling overboard by a rope that had gotten wrapped around one of the wheels. Marco helped me look over the cargo for damage and we found that most of it had not been damaged except for a few bags of grain that were soaked and some broken china. There was a lot to be cleaned up but at least there was a ship left under it.

Capt. Vitas was exhausted. He had been injured from the ropes that secured him to the wheel. If it had not been for the help he got from Ben, he most likely would have been seriously hurt of killed. The captain was taken to his quarters and Ben continued to look after him, rubbing liniment on his injuries and binding them up. No one took command but everyone went about their work and began to make repairs and clean up the storm damage. It was a great compliment to the captain and his crew to see the men thrust themselves into the task at hand without orders or supervision.

Capt. Vitas sent word to the crew to drop anchor and spend the rest of the evening and night where we were. He wanted to make sure the ship was thoroughly checked out and also knew his crew was exhausted. A good night's rest would help everyone. We would be sailing for Myra in the morning and hopefully reach port there by noon. We spent the rest of the evening cleaning up the hold. We put the cargo that was damaged the most on the pallet to be hoisted to the deck above and left it there until the captain could decide what to do with it. Marco fixed a stew from some of the damaged food and we had one of the better meals he had fixed in days.

Ben came down to join us in the work, but mostly he came down to talk. It didn't take long before we were once more talking about Jesus and His teachings.

Ben had learned a great deal of the history of the Jews. He spent much of the night telling us about their customs and how the priest, scribes, and teachers held fast to those customs and laws. Ben said that was why Jesus was causing such a commotion—He taught that the religious leaders had focused so much on the laws that they forgot what the laws were made for. Many of the priest were beginning to fear that Jesus would take the people away from them.

We asked Ben about the times he had actually heard Jesus teaching and we found that it only took one small question to get Ben talking for quiet some time.

"There was this one time that I was with a several thousand people. Jesus had been speakin' to us for over a day. We were gettin' tired and hungry but we didn't want to leave because He was tellin' us things we knew were right. We didn't want to miss anything. He was healin' sick people, restorin' sight to the blind, and even brought demons out of some. Well, on the the third day, I think it was, He told his men to get food for the people but they didn't know where to get any since we were way out in the middle of nowhere. A boy there had a basket of fish and bread and Jesus took it and somehow He made it have enough food in it to feed everyone there, I mean thousands of people! There was food left over. I never seen anything like it! Jesus said we must have faith, that we should believe that He was the Son of God and ask for forgiveness of our sins. He promised us a new life. It was more than I could understand at the time and I wanted to find out more but I had to get back to sea. Now, I'm determined to go back and find Jesus so I can have this new life." Ben went on. "I just have to get back there or I won't ever have peace."

Marco and I were overwhelmed at what Ben had just told us. As Ben had not been able to comprehend all that he heard, we were not able to understand all that Ben told us. There were so many questions we wanted to ask but didn't know where to begin. Finally Marco ask him, "What kind of sins was Jesus talking about? And who are we supposed to ask for forgiveness?"

"I think He meant that our sins was somethin' we had done wrong or maybe somethin' we didn't do that we was sposed to do. He said we would feel somethin' inside us that told us we had sinned if we had our hearts right. We are to ask God to forgive us. Now, not just any god but the one God He was tellin' us about.. The One He said was His Father." Ben answered.

"It sounds like such a simple thing to do— this teaching seems so complicated. Is there anything you might have forgotten to tell us?" I asked.

"Oh, there's lots I haven't told ya! It wouldn't help clear things up though— it's all pretty remarkable. There's a lot of people who don't understand—even the men who are His followers. They can listen to Him and then still not get it. But

I'm here to tell ya right now, I've made up my mind that I gonna do my best to know what He means." Ben stated.

"I heard that this man, Jesus was born to a couple in some town of Bethlehem or something like that. If that's true, how can Jesus be the

Son of God? Someone explain that to me!" Marco pleaded. He wasn't being obnoxious with his question; he was really trying to learn the truth of the matter and he was feeling frustrated by things that appeared to be contradicting one another.

"That's a tough one, Marco. There are a lot of people who are asking that same question. Jesus and the people who are followin' Him say that His mother came to be with child by a miraculous work of God. The man Jesus' mother married was not the father of Jesus. That part right there hasn't gone well with some Jews. So now, when Jesus tells them He is the Son of God, it really gets them mad. If things keep goin' like that, I wouldn't be sprised but what there will be some of the Jews wantin' to kill this Jesus." Ben continued sharing.

"Well, that makes it about as clear as mud! How's a person supposed to know what to believe?" Marco said as he got up and paced back and forth as he talked, as much to himself as he was to us.

"I can only tell you what I have in my heart in answer to that, and there's one thing I have learned in my long life—trust your heart more than your head. My heart tells me that Jesus has powers and authority that no other man has. In all I have ever seen or heard, He has never misused either of them. I now choose to believe this Jesus." Ben said with a slow and deliberate voice that revealed his determination.

We had become so engrossed in our conversation that we had lost track of time. We had secured and cleaned the entire hold without hardly realizing we were actually working. Ben had rekindled the burning desire to find the truth of Jesus' teachings and we found it hard to sleep that night. Ben finally ended his stories and left for his bunk. Marco lay staring at the ceiling without saying anything for quite some time. Finally he asked, "You think Stephan and Vito have made it back to Athens yet?"

"They should be getting close, especially if they got any of this wind we had."

I answered, trying to be as encouraging as I could.

"I wonder what my folks will have to say about me leaving and then having the brass to send my little brother home with men we hardly knew?" Marco thought out loud.

"I can't answer that, but I can tell you what I think about Vito. He won't let any harm come to your brother and he's a good man. He will more than likely know what to say to your parents about letting you find what your heart tells you to. He could probably do a better job of it that either of us could. They'll make it. Marco." I assured him.

When morning came, we hoisted sail once more and headed to port at Myra. We didn't have much cargo to put off or take on there but we needed to replenish supplies and replace some of the things the storm had caused us to loose. There was some speculation about what Capt. Vitas would decide to do. Some of the crew thought he would want to dock at Myra for the winter but others knew it wasn't the best port to spend the winter months in. The weather had turned somewhat cooler than we had enjoyed for most of the voyage but it wasn't unbearable yet. We were anxious to know what he would decide but thought it best not to question him about it. We had to be content to wait until we docked at Myra.

## CHAPTER FOUR

# THE RACE CONTINUES

O ur time at Myra was uneventful for the most part. We accompanied the captain as he went to purchase the needed supplies and equipment. Many of the dockside business had been closed for the winter and the town seemed somewhat deserted. It didn't take us long to tend to our business there and we were ready to set sail two hours after we had docked. There was never a mention of spending the rest of the winter months at Myra. Capt. Vitas didn't give any indication that he even considered wintering there and the crew, out of respect for him, followed his unspoken leading willingly.

We didn't have time to talk to anyone around the docks at Myra, so we were unable to glean any more news about the happenings in Israel. Our disappointment at that was lessened by all that we had learned from

Ben. Furthermore, we were getting close enough to Israel ourselves that we were getting anxious to be on our way just as soon as possible.

On the way back to the ship, Capt. Vitas told us to secure a large supply of wood for the old oven in the hold. He gave Marco instructions to keep a fire going in the oven at all times until further notice. Once on board, he told the crew that they would be working shorter shifts on deck as the temperature grew colder. They were to use the galley as a place to stay warm and all meals would be served there from now on. They were given orders to help re-arrange the cargo to allow room for these changes. He reminded them to be considerate of our duties in the galley and not give us any problems. Marco and I were not sure about the already small kitchen being even more cramped for space but we knew we would enjoy the opportunity to talk with more of the crew. It seemed like a good trade—not that we really had any choice in the matter.

The weather held stable but the temperature slowly fell until it was a little above freezing. We had a good breeze that helped the ship slice through the water but it was a biting wind that was seasoned with moisture that chilled us to the bones. The crew became even more appreciative of the captain's consideration for them every time they came below to get warm. Marco did his best to keep an even fire in the old oven but there were times when it seems to devour wood at an unbelievable rate. Capt. Vitas estimated we would be able to go from Myra to port on the island of Paphos in four days, barring any problems. The wind was helping us to move at a faster than normal pace but the wood was being used up by the strong draft as well. At the rate we were going the wood would be gone before we reached Paphos.

When morning came on the third day out we woke to find the galley much cooler than it had been for days. At first, everyone thought Marco had failed to tend to his duties of keeping the fire up. We were soon to find that Marco wasn't down in the galley with us but was up on deck doing something with the vent-pipe from the oven. He was covered in black from the soot in the pipe. He worked on without giving us notice and ignored our questions. He only paused long enough to tell us not to bother the fire in the oven till he got down there himself. I knew that to be his way when he was onto an idea. He would not offer explanation or allow interruption when he set about trying his ideas. He would wait until he had accomplished what he had planned in his head and, once it was working, he would let you in on what it was all about. That was just Marco. He had so much going on in his mind I'm surprised his head could stand the commotion.

When he finally came back down to the galley and got the fire going again, he explained he had put in a baffle to keep the wind from drawing all the heat up the pipe. This would help the galley to stay warmer and the oven would not use near as much wood. We trusted him to know what he was talking about but we were soon to find that he had been right. The galley was soon warm and the fire held much better. There wasn't much Marco couldn't do when he put his mind to it. Once more I was thankful to have him on this journey with me.

When night came that day, we had a good number of the crew with us in the galley. There was a lot of joking going on and some unwholesome stories were being told that were best to leave untold. The mood continued to be light-hearted but we were amazed at some of the men who had taken on an uncharacteristic determination to use vulgarity with every breath they took. We knew that such stories and foul language was not uncommon on the high seas but it was not common to crews that served Capt. Vitas. He was not only a fair man but one who did his best to keep some dignity on board. We were not able to explain what had happened to make these men behave in such a way.

Eventually the conversation turned to religious matters. Several of the crew knew of our intentions to find out more about Jesus. It was on this night that we first witnessed a division among the crew. Some of the men were understanding of our desire to find out more, but a few others found our plans to be nonsense. These men began to ridicule those of us who expressed a willingness to listen to any of these new teachings. The mood in that room quickly shifted from being lighthearted to being filled with tension. Ben did his best to restore harmony by attempting to explain the reasons men from many different parts around the Mediterranean were searching for these teachings. For his efforts, he was singled out to receive the strongest verbal assault of the evening. Seeing that reasoning with them was futile, he sat down and mentally shut out the rest of us. At that point, the only ones willing to speak were the men who insisted on verbally abusing those who did not agree with them. When they failed to raise a response, they would try to increase the volume of their comments. It was then that Capt. Vitas came down the steps into the galley. He put an end to the conversation with one short statement.

"I will not tolerate such behavior on my ship and any man who wishes to continue doing so, will be put off at our next port." The captain then went over to the stove and poured a cup of coffee and then left again. The room remained quiet the rest of that night. The crew knew that this was not an idle threat but that Capt. Vitas meant every word. Even if he was hard pressed to have a full crew, they knew he would not tolerate the kind of behavior that had occurred in the galley. He was a fair man but he was also a firm man who held deeply to his convictions.

Marco and I talked on several occasions about what had happened there that night. We were never able to come up with an explanation that we thought offered an adequate answer. We were able to agree that there was an over-whelming presence of evil in that room that night and the men who the evil presence was coming from had greatly been changed from their normal character. Beyond that, we had no other explanation.

As morning came on the forth day out from Myra, we were told that we would be reaching port at Paphos before nightfall. As Marco and I tended to our morning's duties, we could feel much of the tension from the night before still existed. The conversation that morning was limited to only the most necessary exchange of words needed to get the work done. A little before noon, Ben came down to the galley and offered his help. Being careful to make sure we were alone, Ben told us to be on guard of impending danger.

"I felt such a wickedness last night—it made me cringe inside but I tried not to let it show. I tell you it was powerful! I felt it a couple of time before when I was in Judea. Some people had such a evil spirit in them you could smell it. Once I saw Jesus command an evil spirit to leave a young man. It was a frightful experience, let me tell you!" he said just above a whisper. "The boy went into fits and everyone thought he was dyin'. Finally this spirit came out of him and left. You could actually tell that it had gone. I felt that same presence down here last night. It's in some of the crew for certain. Watch out and try to stay clear of them as much as you can."

"Jesus has power over this evil spirit? It obeyed Him!" Marco asked.

"It sure looked like He did to me. He ordered it to leave and it left." Ben answered.

"How did it get out here in the middle of the Mediterranean to the crew? Did it just come here or has it been here all this time?" I asked without hardly giving Ben time to answer.

"Don't know about all that. I just know there was somethin' evil here last night." Ben said with more seriousness than we had seen before.

As we prepared the meal we hoped the weather would be warm enough to take it up on deck but the captain wanted the men to eat below. We set out the food and soon the crew began to come down to eat. The men came in, sat at the table, and ate without talking. The only sounds we heard was the scraping of spoons on the wooden platters and the bang of the ale cups on the old table. A couple of the men did manage to grumble for more ale but that was all that was said. The tension was thicker now that before. Just before the meal was finished, Capt. Vitas came down the steps and stopped before he reached the bottom. He looked the room over with scrutinizing eyes, stood there for what seemed like an hour, and then went back up on deck without saying a word.

It was around three o'clock when we heard the ship's bell calling all hands to the main deck. The captain himself had rung the bell and was standing there beneath it waiting for the crew to assemble. When all hands had gathered there, Capt. Vitas began to speak to them.

"We will be docking at Paphos shortly. Unless there is a drastic change in the attitude of this crew, I will be putting some of you off the ship there. I don't know what has come into some of you, but whatever it is, I won't stand for such behavior on my ship. It is very clear that a division has occurred among the crew—one that makes it too dangerous to continue our voyage until harmony can be restored. Those of you who have been responsible for this disruption know who you are and I have a pretty good idea who you are. Unless you can convince me that you are willing to get back to working together in unity before we dock in a couple of hours, you will be put off the ship. I'll be in my quarters should any of you want to come to talk this out—if not, well then you have heard my plans. That is all. Return to your duties." Capt. Vitas said as he walked off.

The captain's words had a sobering effect on every man on the ship. We knew he had not used empty words but fully intended to do exactly as he said. That was just the way the captain was. I don't know what the others were thinking but I found myself wondering if I had caused some of the problems we were having. I knew I had not intended to cause a conflict but it was evident that most of the division was over the discussion of Jesus and His teachings. I debated on going to the captain to see if I had been one of those he found troublesome. As the deck hands walked off to their duties, I noticed three of the crew having a discussion that was turning into an argument. One of the three suddenly turned and headed for the captain's quarters. The other two yelled threatening words after him and then went off to their work. I concluded that I was not one who the captain was upset with.

Ben and Marco motioned for me to come with them to the galley. We spent a few minutes speculating what Capt. Vitas would do when we got to Paphos. We hoped he wouldn't want to spend the rest of winter there if he didn't have a full crew. Our conversation was interrupted by a commotion up on deck. We ran up the steps to see one of the two men who had been arguing just minutes ago beating the man who went to the captain's quarters with a large peg from the ship's rigging. The man was in such a rage that he was about to kill the man he was attacking. Several of the crewmen ran to tackle the assailant and finally subdued him. Capt. Vitas arrived at that moment and ordered him to be bound hand and foot until we reached port. The victim had been cut several times on his head and possibly had some broken ribs.

"Get him down to the galley and be careful how you move him. Wrap him up good to keep him warm. I'll see if there is a doctor on Paphos first thing when we dock. Ben, you stay with him and see if you can do anything to help him." the captain ordered. "A couple of you men go find the other deck hand who has been with these two. I want him put under guard until we dock."

Marco and I helped get the injured man below. He was moaning and drew his body up in pain. We tried to keep him still but it was not an easy job. Ben rummaged through some of the supplies we used in cooking and came back with a warm pasty substance bearing a putrid odor. He said it was a poultice to help heal the wounds to his head. After applying the poultice, Ben carefully felt of the man's sides and chest.

"See if you can find something to make a bandage out of. I need to wrap his ribs up fairly tight if we can." Ben said as he finished examining the man.

We did all we could for the injured man and then went up on deck to see if we were getting close to Paphos. We could see tiny lights flickering in the distance and knew we would soon be docking. It would be none too soon for many of us. We had encountered pirates, storms, and cold weather. Our voyage from Ephesus had been filled with danger but to see what happened on this ship today was more frightening than all the other troubles put together. We witnessed men who were once friendly and helpful turn into cold-hearted beings with little or no concern for anything. It was as if their minds had been taken over by some power or spirit.

We docked at Paphos and the two crewmen were taken off the ship and handed over to the magistrate there. Capt. Vitas wasn't sure what would happen to them—sometimes such crimes called for execution and other times the prisoners would be let go. Much depended on the mood of the magistrate and how many people were there to demand justice. I felt pity for the two men. I wasn't sure how much of all this evil behavior was their fault. Was this something they had little or no control of? What if the same evil spirit had come on me—would I have been able to stop it? Once more I found myself with more questions than answers. I hated leaving these men behind and I know Capt. Vitas did as well, but it was a necessary course of action he had to take.

As we wanted to try to make the most out of every day we could, Capt. Vitas ordered the cargo to be unloaded and new supplies taken on while he searched for a medical help for the injured deck hand. We worked until well after midnight and when the captain ordered us to move away from the dock and drop anchor some three hundred feet out. He was unable to find a doctor and told all the crew to stay on board ship, being ready to set out to sea at first light. The captain never did explain why he thought it necessary for us to leave the dock for the night, but most of us knew he was just as concerned about the wickedness going on as we were.

It was a restless night. The injured man kept moaning and we all noticed more noises than usual. I'm sure this was mostly due to the awareness of what the evil spirit had done among us, but I think it was also partly because of thinking what was to become of the two deck hands now in prison on the island. It seemed like daylight was taking its time getting here. Finally we heard the captain calling the deck hands to their duties and the anchor was hoisted up. The sails went up and we were on our way to Tyre. Marco and I worked to make a good breakfast for the men and wanted to do what we could to help restore the harmony that we once enjoyed on this voyage. During the night the temperature had dropped to near freezing and we knew the crew would appreciate a hot meal and strong coffee. Marco had the old oven glowing, making the whole galley warm and comfortable.

This was it! The time we had long been waiting for. Our next stop was Tyre, a city known as the shipping center for the world. When we landed there, we would be able to set foot on the land that held so much hope for answers to our many questions. It was normally a six-to-seven-day voyage from Paphos to Tyre, but this trip was anything but normal. We could feel the excitement and anxiety growing within us each day—not only in us but in several of the crew. Ben was especially anxious to get there. He hardly stopped talking about what he was going to do when he got to see Jesus again. His enthusiasm was contagious and by the second day of this part of our journey, the crew was once more in harmony and in much better spirits.

Late one evening Marco and I were talking with Ben about what to do when we landed.

"I think we should try to stay together, at least for now. Ben is already familiar with the area and we sure could use his help." Marco suggested.

"That makes good sense to me. Not only will we be safer in a group but it will be helpful to know where we're going." I agreed.

"That's fine by me. You two have already helped me in ways you probably don't know about and I would be glad to help you find what you are lookin' for. I know of a couple of the deck hands who want to go along too. But we need to do some plannin' now so we'll be ready when we get there." Ben stated.

"You mean about what to take along?" Marco asked.

"That to begin with. You gotta realize that we could be there a long time. What are we going to do for food and shelter? We need to plan out how to make the most out of whatever money we have." Ben said.

He had just finished speaking when we heard someone coming down the steps to the galley. It was Capt. Vitas.

"I thought I would find you three here. I have a couple of things to talk with you about privately. First of all, Nik, you and Marco have done such a fine job here in this galley, I 've decided to go ahead and pay you what we agreed on. However, since you have been such good help and done more than I asked from you, I want you to have this bonus—it amounts to full pay and a little extra too. Ben, here's yours and you will find that I put in some extra to show how much I appreciate the many things you've done to save this ship." Capt. Vitas said.

We looked at what the captain gave us and were left speechless. It was nearly three times what we expected to get. Those precious coins meant so much to us. We would now have provision for most of our journey. It was beyond anything we had ever expected.

"Thank you, Captain for your kindness. You don't know what this means to all of us." I barely managed to say without breaking into tears.

"Well, since we are one of the last ships carrying freight this late in the season, people are paying well for what we can deliver. Beside that, you have helped us make really good time and you have earned it." replied the captain, "But there is something else I want to talk with you about. I have heard quite a bit about these teachings you have been talking about. I would like to go with you to find out more about them if you would allow me."

Marco and I looked at Ben for a moment and then the three of us began to smile our biggest smile. Once more we realized that this was even better than we have ever hoped for. Marco and I thought we would be making this journey alone in an unfamiliar world and now we would be going with men who offered knowledge and security. It was more than we could comprehend. Just as the evil spirit had caused such fear and misery days earlier, we now felt that a completely different spirit was working to provide for us.

"We'd be honored to have you with us, Capt." the three of us replied, almost in unison.

"We should reach port by tomorrow noon. As soon as we get all the cargo unloaded, gather all the supplies we have left and bring them with us. They'll just go to ruin if we leave them on the ship. Keep it to yourselves what you got paid and let me know when you are ready to leave. Once we finish unloading the cargo, I won't be giving orders. I'll just be one among you—that understood?" Capt. Vitas said.

"Yes, sir." we answered.

But we knew it would not be easy to forget he was the captain. He was not a man who demanded recognition but, because of his fine character, he was a man who earned respect and trust. As he turned and left the galley, we came to realize that the food and supplies that we could take from the ship would allow us to go for many days without spending our money to eat. There were also enough blankets to allow us to sleep outdoors if needed.

Ben and I noticed Marco was lost in another world. We knew he was in the process of coming up with an idea that would serve us well so we left him to finish his work. After a few minutes he turned to us and said, "We need to find some sticks about three feet long. We'll need some twine too—and some of that torn sail over there. If you can find any short pieces of rope we can use them."

He didn't finish speaking before he was up and about his search for the items he needed. It was less than an hour that he had put together a back pack to carry our provisions. Everything he needed to make it was found right here in the galley—sticks from crates, sails, rope, and twine. It was simply amazing to watch Marco work when he got an idea. He could make most anything from most anything.

We managed to finally fall asleep that night but it wasn't easy. It was still cold up on deck and the crew kept coming down all night to get warm. We found it impossible to get the visions of our journey out of our minds long enough to let sleep take over. We had to be content that night to just rest our bodies while our minds whirled with excitement. We didn't know that within hours we would be setting foot on a path that would change our lives forever, but we all knew in our hearts that we could not ignore the burning desire to seek the one the called Jesus.

When morning came, the crew worked to prepare the old ship for it's winter rest. Marco and I worked in the hold to get all the cargo ready to unload and began to sort through the supplies, carefully packing the items we thought we would be needing. Since the captain had made thorough calculations for provisions on this voyage, there wasn't much food left. Marco's fishing nets had helped greatly to make what we had last but there still wasn't a lot to take with us. We did find quite a lot of other supplies that we were grateful to have. We found a couple of small axes that we knew would be useful and some good knives—for provision and protection.

We spent the whole morning working in the hold and galley. Before we realized what time it was, we heard the crew lowering the sails and preparing to dock. When we got up on deck we stopped in our tracks. There before us was the great city of Tyre and beyond that was the land of Israel. Marco and I had never in our whole lives seen so many ships. The buildings that lined the shoreline seemed to go on for miles and the streets that led into the city were filled with shops and people were everywhere. Even Athens, in all its splendor lacked the excitement that this city held.

As we helped unload the cargo that morning, Marco and I both realized that we had been able to complete this part of our journey without harm or injury and we were most thankful. We had been through some situations that could have ended in disaster but we had made it through. We had a warm place to stay and sleep, plenty of food that we didn't have to pay for, and now, extra supplies to take with us. We were also grateful to have Ben and Capt. Vitas going on with us. It was beyond our ability to explain how we had been so well provided for, but the two of us were certainly thankful. Our hearts were pounding inside us that morning in anticipation for what lay ahead of us. The only sadness that day seemed to be coming from deep within Marco. I knew he must be thinking of his little brother, Stephan and wishing he could know for sure that he had made it back home safely with Vito. He didn't like to talk about the matter much but this morning I knew I had to offer some encouragement to him.

"Marco, you know all the rough times we went through on this voyage and how close to real danger we came with pirates, storms, and wickedness. But we made it! You also know Vito was not only a good man, but a capable man. He wouldn't let anything happen to Stephan if it was in his power to prevent it. You need to also remember that they only had a few days voyage to get back to Athens. I'm sure that they made it home safe and are guessing about where we are right now. You just have to believe in your heart that they're safe. That's all I know to tell you." I said, trying to let him know I knew his thoughts and shared his concern.

"I know you're trying to help and you are probably right but I just wish I had something better to believe in." Marco responded and went on about his work.

We had finished unloading all the cargo before noon. Capt. Vitas was dismissing the crew and settling up with them. After that he made arrangements to have the ship secured in harbor for the winter. We would have until late afternoon to get our supplies off the ship before they took it away for storage. We left the ship that morning and went to look over the city. We were finally walking on the streets of the land of Israel. It was just grand!

## CHAPTER FIVE

# ENTERING THE LAND OF PROMISE

B en, Marco, and myself decided to explore the town and as we stepped off the wooden platform of the dock, we stopped to look over the shops that nearly surrounded us. There was a strange feeling in the air, perhaps it was only in our minds, but there seemed to be special atmosphere around us. It was as if a strange, but warm, presence was drawing us—like the aroma of fine perfume drifting through the air and enticing the sensory glands to find its source. I'm sure all of us felt that drawing, but none of us said anything about it. We went on to explore the city.

None of us were hungry but we thought we could catch up on the latest news if we were to visit one of the many taverns we saw. Ben surveyed the area with an experienced eye and suggested that we try a place that had a large group of men gathered in front of it.

"There seems to be a lot of talkin' goin' on over there. Chances are we'll hear somethin' about what we're lookin' for. Let's head that way and just listen for a while." Ben said as he led the way.

We made our way through those standing outside the tavern and slowly worked our way inside. Most of the talk we heard was just normal conversation about the things most people talk about, just to have something to say. We got something to eat and drink, allowing us the privilege of staying around awhile. People were friendly and talkative but there was no mention of the teachings of John or Jesus. I could tell that Ben was getting fidgety and, sure enough, it wasn't long before he was up and said,

"Guess we will have to do some fishin' if we are going to catch anythin' here."

He walked over to some men standing just inside the door and began talking to them. Marco and I watched from our seats as he began to warm up to group of men and soon he had them laughing and talking so much it was hard to know what anyone of them was saying. Then we watched Ben as he carefully began to turn the conversation toward things that had been happening in the area. It didn't take him long to get the subject of the Jesus' teachings. Ben was a shrewd man. In just minutes he had gained the trust of the men he had just met, got them to feel relaxed, and now had them primed to talk about matters that we knew had caused considerable division throughout this land. Ben was a fascinating man to say the least.

"We've just come in from nearly a month at sea and was hopin' to find out what all this commotion is about this man they call Jesus. We have heard talk of him all the way back to Greece. Any of you know much about him?" Ben asked with more innocence than he had a right to.

"Oh, there's plenty of talk about him but you gotta be careful who you go talkin' to. It seems the man has got a lot of people ready to do him in. About the only thing stoppin' them is that he also has a lot of people behind him. A man named John had been spreadin' the same teachin's but was put in prison and then had his head chopped off by order of Herod.

Some figured that would put a stop to this whole thing but it seems to have just made people more determined. Now, they're afraid of a roit if they try to do anything to him and I believe they probably would have one on their hands." replied one of the men.

"He's got the whole country stirred up. The Jews that run the temples and councils are afraid He's gonna take over what they've been doin' and the Jewish people think He's gonna lead them to get rid of the Romans and the Romans are watchin' that they don't have an uprisin on their hands. Whole lot of polotics goin' on." said another.

"What kind of things is this Jesus teachin'? Why are people willin' to follow Him?" Ben asked.

"He claims He is the Son of God and that people should believe in Him. He said anyone who would believe in Him would be set free. Now that is what has set a lot of the Jews against Him—claimin' He is the Son of God." said the first man. "Set free from what?" Ben asked.

"Free from your sins I guess. Anyway that is what I have always heard it was. Some of the people have said He promised them life with Him in heaven. I know it sounds a little far fetched but there is a lot of people who believe Him." said the first man.

"Is there many here in Tyre who believe? Do you know anyone who does?" Ben asked, now with a hushed tone, knowing that he would have a better chance of finding these people if he showed he a willingness to respect their privacy.

"Yes, there are several here but they are very careful about who they talk to about it. The way things are going, somethin's about to happen." replied the second man.

Ben motioned for Marco and me to come over to join the men. He waited for us to come near enough for him to put his arms on each of us and then spoke to the men again.

"These two young men have come with me to find out more about these teachin's and who this Jesus is. We believe there is great value to the teachin's and would like to learn more. We would be grateful if you could direct us to someone who could talk with us. We do not wish to cause harm to anyone but would welcome the opportunity to find out what these people believe in. It is our desire to learn all we can about the One they call Jesus while we are here in this land. I know you might think we are crazed seamen who ought to be actin' like some tough old sea dog, but I have seen too many things in my life not to know that there is more to life than what we have now. You can think what you will of me and these two young men—that don't matter anymore. We're determined to go on with our journey but we sure would appreciate any help we could get on the way. If you would be so kind as to take us to these believers you mentioned, we would certainly appreciate it." Ben stated.

The two men looked at the group of men who had been listening to us talking and then at us. A couple of the men in the group nodded their heads and then the first man who had talked with Ben took us aside.

"I will take you to these people but you must wait until dark. Come alone-just you three. You must not tell anyone who these people are. You could be putting their lives in danger so use great care to protect them. Agreed?" the man said.

"Yes, of course. We wouldn't have it any other way." Ben reassured.

We left the tavern and walked down the streets for a couple of hours that afternoon. There were people from all over the world gathered in that city. We saw merchandise that we had never seen before—much of it we didn't even know what it was. We caught a few comments here and there about Jesus but none that we hadn't already heard. It was soon time to return to the old ship once more and gather our supplies and food. Capt. Vitas was there waiting for us and had emptied all the food barrels. We finished packing the supplies in the backpacks Marco had made and walked off the ship with Capt. Vitas being the last one off. He turned back as if to say 'Good-Bye' to an old friend. We waited for a minute or two as he stood with his back to us. We could only surmise he was waiting for a tear to drop from his cheek before turning to face us. He had always wanted to present himself as a strong man, but that would have been fine with us. Sometimes it takes a strong man to cry and not be ashamed to show it. Anyway, we understood what went on in his heart that moment.

We told the captain about our conversation of that afternoon and of the plans for tonight. He understood when we told him we had to go alone to see these people and said he would wait with the other crewmen who would be going on our journey. He had also been able to talk with some men himself that day and had some things he wanted to share with us. We agreed to meet back at a little shop that offered a bunk and biscuits to sailors who needed to place for the night. It also had a bath house which we all looked forward to.

We had some time until it would be dark enough to meet the man who would be taking us to talk to these believers. Marco and I wanted to try some of the strange foods we saw in the market place but Ben warned us to be careful about what we ate. He knew that some of the food was much more spicy than what we had ever tasted. We gladly listened to his advice after we touched the food and found that the juices had made their way from the food to our hands and then to our face. My eyes were burning and my cheeks felt like they were on fire. Ben led us to a fountain where we did our best to wash the hot juice from our hands and face.

"How can anyone stand to eat that stuff? It would burn your insides out!" Marco exclaimed.

"Some of the shepherds around here can eat it all the time and it don't bother them. They claim it keeps them from ever gettin' sick. I imagine they could probably defend themselves pretty good with it too if they was to get that juice on somebody that was tryin' to harm them." Ben remarked.

"Well, that may be so but they can eat all they want of it, including my share. What do they call that stuff?" I asked.

"Don't know—just know it's best to leave it alone." Ben answered. "We better get goin' to meet our new friend. He'll probably be waitin' by now."

We walked down the street to the tavern where we had first met this man. He was there waiting for us. He waited until we were nearly to him and then turned to leave, twisting around to motion for us to follow him. We went down some narrow streets and made several turns. It was hard to tell what part of the city we were in and would take us quite a while to find our way back with the help of our friend. Suddenly he stopped and looked carefully around the corner of a building. When he was satisfied that no one was watching, he led us to a small house just down the street from us and knocked softly on the door. The door creaked open slightly as an elderly man carefully surveyed us. Suddenly, he swung the door open and reached out to pull us in quickly. His house was dimly lit with only enough candles to see the sparse furnishings. As our eyes adjusted to the darkness, we saw other people in the room with us. There were two other men and two women. All of our host sat silently, looking intently at us for what seemed like several minutes, although I'm sure it was only one or two minutes at the most.

"Please forgive our suspicious behavior. You must understand, though, it is most necessary if we are to remain alive and out of prison. You have been brought here because our friend believes we can trust you. Before we go on with this time tonight, we need your assurance that you will honor that trust." said the man who had let us in.

"You have our word on that my friend. We intend to harm no one and will do what we can to protect your privacy. We are grateful that you have allowed us to come here." Ben answered.

"Fine, fine. Your eyes and heart speaks as well as your tongue. My name is Eli and this is Abijah and his wife and Aroch and his wife. What is it you want from us? How can we be of help to you?" asked the old man.

We could see that our host was a small man well on in years. He was bent over from years of hard work and his hands were twisted and gnarled in the joints of the bones. The others there were aged as well and, more than likely, had been doing much the same work as he had. It was evident that they had spent many years together as we continued to talk with them.

"Well, you see, these two young men here with me, Nik and Marco, are on a journey to seek the truth. I'm Ben and I've been with them quite a while and I can tell there determined to know for certain what the truth is and won't quit until they do. I know they are on to somethin' and I have decided to seek it with them. We are lookin' for people who can tell us information about the teachin's of a man they call Jesus. Your friend here tells us you might be able to help." Ben said.

"There is much to tell about Jesus but we must be mindful of the time. It is dangerous for us to have you here. We will try to answer your questions but it might be more helpful if we were to tell you briefly what we know of Him and then your questions." Eli suggested.

"That sounds good to us." Marco responded quickly, trying to save the precious time we had with these people.

"We have watched this Jesus for over thirty years now. In everything we have seen and heard, there is nothing that has caused us to doubt He is who He says He is. There is much to cause us to believe. We have heard many things said about Him that have not been good but they have all come from those who oppose Him. Jesus has said that He is the Son of God and we believe that is the truth. Is this the truth you seek?" asked Eli.

"That is the main point of it, but we also are seeking to find evidence that will add solid foundation to this truth. We are seeking a truth that will withstand the strongest challenge." I answered.

"That is a lot to be asking for. Most people in this day are willing to accept whatever is popular today and hope for the best tomorrow. With such a determination, I know you will find the truth and you will know its value." Aroch responded

"We first came to know Jesus the very night he was born. Oh, it was such a night! One that we shall never forget! My friends here were with me as we were tending sheep in the hill country outside Bethlehem in Judea. In the darkness of the night we saw such a radiant light coming from the heavens and chasing the darkness from the hillsides. It was such an unusual light in that it shone from all sides, leaving not the tiniest shadow. The sheep were made nervous by it but they didn't run. We could see other shepherds on distant hills as they looked to the light coming from the heavens." Abijah began telling us.

"Yes!" Eli interrupted, "I remember we were all frightened and it seemed that we were unable to move. Perhaps that is the same way with the sheep—I don't know. We had never seen anything like this before or since! And such a stillness came with it. Not a sheep bleated—no wind sweeping down the hillsides. Our dogs came and laid at our feet. You could have heard for miles in that silence—but there was not a sound!"

We could easily tell that the excitement that these men experienced that night was still alive in their hearts as they retold the story. Their faces revealed that they still treasured all that had happened that night. We were anxious for them to continue and didn't have to wait long as even the women were wanting to help tell the story.

"That silence didn't last long, though. We soon heard a faint sound of singing coming from far in the distance. As we looked in that direction we could see some kind of forms approaching ahead of the singing. They moved at great speed and would stop abruptly to speak to those standing out in the open. They came to us and told us not to be afraid. A baby was to be born nearby who would be the One to offer salvation to the world. They said He would be the fulfillment of what had been written long ago.

It was so beautiful and—" said one of the women before she was interrupted by the other.

"Yes, and these ones who came to tell us this news were flying in the air with huge wings. They were much larger than we are but they seemed to just be able to fly and hover above us as if they didn't weigh a thing. They told us we could find this baby in a stable. He would be wrapped up and laying in a feed trough. At the time, I know I didn't catch that part right away. It seemed such a contrast. Here was to be born this wonderful baby that was so important, told to us by these splendid beings we later found out were angles, and then to hear something about a feed trough?" the other lady added.

"By the time the angles had told us what was happening, thousands of other angles, most not quite as large as the ones who spoke to us, came flying just above the hillsides. They were singing praises and crying "Holy, Holy, Holy". They came in waves. You could hear them coming far in the distance and then they would be over us, then went on and their joyous sounds faded into the distance. Then another would come. The sound should have been deafening with such a vast number of voices but it wasn't. It lasted for hours and a peacefulness reigned throughout the countryside. The sheep had all laid down to rest and felt the peace that had blanketed the land. We decided to look for this new born baby. The radiant light that had shone so brightly over the entire land was now becoming more defined. Although the hills were still illuminated by the heavenly light, the source had given its dominance to one star-like light that was hovering low over the outskirts of the nearby town of Bethlehem." Abijah continued with the story.

"We went toward that star and soon found that shepherds from all over the countryside were headed there as well. By the time we reached the edge of town a large group of people had gathered around a small stable. We waited for those in front to move on so we could see but no one wanted to leave. We had to finally work our way to the front of the crowd. When we got there we understood why no one was willing to move away. The baby's face had such a beautiful radiance—we knew He was no ordinary baby." Eli went on. "So we decided that night to keep a watch on this child and see what should come of Him."

"While He was yet a boy, He was teaching in the temple. He had such a kindness and gentleness about Him. He had such a great comprehension of things and yet He was always humble—willing to try to explain in ways people could understand. But there were some who were already jealous of Him." said Abijah's wife.

"This is incredible! I have heard many things about Jesus before, but nothin' like this. Oh, to have been there that night!" Ben said with tears rolling down his face.

Marco and I were thoroughly engrossed in the story we were hearing but Ben was getting something more than either of us were. I think it was, at least in some part, to do with the fact that he had heard Jesus himself teaching and now was getting the assurance he was needing. We both felt he was very close to finding his truth.

"That night was wonderful, no question about it. But for us, even greater times were to come later. Jesus had a cousin, they called him John. He was just a few months older than Jesus and went off by himself to grow up. Some people say he was out of his mind. A few years ago he came teaching that people should turn from their wicked ways and be baptized. He said he was making a way for One who would be greater than he was. John had many followers and helped a lot of people change their lives. Then Jesus came along with His teachings which continued on with what John had been teaching. Well, Jesus had John baptize Him and when he did, some people heard a voice from heaven saying that God was well pleased with His Son. They also said that a Holy Spirit came on Jesus as he came out of the water." Eli continued.

"I was there and even though I didn't hear the voice, I could tell that something happened to Jesus immediately after He was baptized. Something came over Him—an empowerment of sorts. For me, that was all the assurance I would ever need to believe in Him." said Abijah.

"You have used the word baptized several times now. What does it mean?" asked Marco.

"To be baptized is to be lowered into water and then lifted up—washed clean. It is symbolic of having our sins washed away and coming spiritually clean. It also symbolizes that we die to the old self and are born a new person, free of our sin. It is a public act that shows we have made a decision to accept this salvation." Aroch replied, trying his best to help us understand.

"We have witnessed many miracles that Jesus has done which further convince us that He is the Son of God and that He is the Christ that Scripture has told us would come. There are many Jews who do not want to accept Him. Some honestly believe that He is not the Messiah and are holding to the teachings of old. However, there are others who see Him as a serious threat to their position and fear they will lose their followers if Jesus is allowed to continue. They are seeking a way to kill him. Many people like us have had to flee or risk being killed as well. It is getting very dangerous to have any association with Jesus or His followers. We cannot go to the Roman soldiers for help and we cannot seek help from the priest and Jewish officials. All we can do it to just keep believing in Jesus and wait to see what comes from all this. Time has passed quickly. I hate asking you to leave now, but you must. Please understand." Eli said as he came and took Ben and me by the hand.

"We would like to stay the rest of the night and hear more of Jesus, but we do understand your concern for safety. We are grateful for what you have told us tonight. It has been most helpful. What we have seen in your hearts has helped to convince us that we can find it also. Thank you for lettin' us come into your home." Ben said with a great deal of difficulty as he tried to hold back the flood of emotion that was rising within him.

We hugged the old shepherds, knowing that we probably would never see them again in this life. It was amazing how quickly such bonds of friendship could be established. Yet, the word, friendship, doesn't fully describe the relationship that was built in that dark little room that night. It was more like they were our family. We left that house with more assurance than ever that we would be able to satisfy that burning desire in our hearts. We took extra precaution not to be seen until we were safely away from the little house. When we had made our way back to the waterfront, our guide left us. The three of us soon found Capt. Vitas and the other two men waiting for us outside the rooming house. We were anxious to tell the them what we had heard and also wanted to hear what the captain had to tell us, but managed to wait until we had enjoyed our first hot bath in nearly a month.

Ben started telling about our conversation with the shepherds, but chocked up so often that Marco and I had to finish it. Tears came into the eyes of Capt. Vitas as he sat listening to us. It was evident that the things we were telling him was going straight to his heart. The other two men, Alexus and Cirro, were more reserved in letting their inner feelings show. Even at that, their eyes were welling up with tears. It was not because of our ability to tell stories that was having such an effect on these men, but there was a power at work in our little room that was helping all of us to know that each word that was spoken was the truth. What was happening there among us was something that none of us had experienced before that night.. None of us were able to offer any explanation, but Ben, Marco, and I had felt the same power at work as we had spoke to the old shepherds. We finished telling of our visit with the shepherds with care not to leave out any part of it. Ben helped us to be careful not to unload too much at a time on our friends, but to tell them in such a way that they were able to take in what we were saying. I found nearly as much help in retelling the story as I did when I first heard it from the shepherds—I think Marco and Ben did as well.

"There is also some other news we heard today. The one called John the Baptist has been killed because of his teachings. There is much division in the places we will be going into. We must be careful for ourselves and for those who offer help to us." I concluded.

When we had told the last of the news we had, all of us sat quietly for some time, allowing all the words we had heard to fully sink into our hearts. The tears continued to flow for a while longer and then Capt. Vitas finally rose to speak.

"The things I heard this afternoon will seem pale in comparison to what you have just shared with us. I am thankful that you found these people to talk with—I believe it has been most helpful to all of us. Alexus and Cirro were with me when we heard some men talking about recent happenings in Judea. There have been some un-natural things going on—truly remarkable. These events have caused many people to believe and, yet, have caused others to oppose what is going on. We were told that many Jews have left their homes rather than stay and risk punishment for their beliefs. As we continue our journey and meet these people, it will be well to remember they are living in fear. It is up to us to help them feel they can trust us." the captain said.

"That is good advice and please remember that we could be placing those we speak to in more danger. We can learn much from these people—they will most likely be our best source of information. Whatever you do, don't call attention to them." I said as I remembered how fearful the old shepherds were. Just having my mind return to the thoughts of them caused me to once more feel a closeness to them. I was the strangest thing!

"One other piece of news is that there is word that some of the Jewish leaders are making serious plans to kill this Jesus. I hope we get there before that can happen." Alexus said.

"We all do but we must rest now for the journey ahead. Slow and steady is better than haste and regret." Ben interjected. "Best get some sleep while it's still dark.."

The six of us did the best we could to find a place to lie down in that tiny little room. We were all tired—it had been a long day. I know I felt all my strength was nearly drained. The emotional experiences of the day had been exhausting. When I laid down in the spot I found, sleep came almost instantly.

When morning came, Marco and I weren't sure how to act, not having to cook. It wasn't long before all our group was up and ready to head to the kitchen in the back of the place. The smell of hot bread greeted us as we opened the door of our room. Marco had done a fine job cooking on the voyage, but even his best biscuits couldn't compete with the smell of fresh, hot bread. Ben nearly shoved us out of the way to get there first. That was Ben—soft and tender, wiry as a rooster, and bold as a charging bull—all rolled into one. I guess that's why we took to him so.

After breakfast, we sat around the table making plans for the day. It was agreed that we would start walking toward the Sea of Galilee and take our time getting there. It was likely that we would be able to learn more news of Jesus along the way. Capt. Vitas had brought along a small sail that we could use as a shelter if we wanted to make camp and sleep outdoors. Normally, it would not have been safe for us to stay out along the road because of thieves and robbers, but since there were six of us, we could take turns on watch. It was also possible that we would spend time in one of the small towns of Cadasa or Gischia. Alexus spoke up after we had concluded our plans for the day and suggested we take time to give a closer look at this city of Tyre. He was somewhat familiar with the city, being there numerous times before. He wanted us to understand their culture and social life.

"I'm really not interested in learning more about the people here in this town. I think we need to get going on our way." Marco protested mildly.

"I know how anxious you must be Marco, but it will be very helpful to see what has influenced these people and become familiar with their ways. They have come here to this city from all over the world. There is much to gain by spending some time here and the only thing we have to loose is time. I can almost guarantee you that the time we spend here will be more than made up later on. Trust me on this! I've been here and I know what I'm telling you is right." Alexus said in defending his suggestion.

This proposal caused quite a bit of discussion among us. We could see the value in what Alexus was saying but we also shared Marco's desire to be on our way. Alexus saw we were not settled on what to do so he compromised his proposal.

"Alright, you don't want to spend a day here but what about at least three hours? I would like to have more time, but in three hours, I can show you at least some of what you will need to know. If you still feel you must go, we will go. Please, I beg you!" Alexus pleaded.

"Alexus is right in what he has said. We can learn much here. I told you I would not be giving orders on this journey and I won't, but I believe we would be wise to listen to him." Capt. Vitas said.

"Marco, that alright with you? How about you, Ben? I say we let Alexus show us around unless you really have strong feelings against it." I offered, wanting to get this mater settled. For us to be concerned about time, this was not productive use of it.

"Fine by me!" Ben said.

"Ya, sure, but we can leave after three hours." Marco agreed with some reluctance tempering his words.

"Good! Follow me." Alexus said as he stood up quickly, causing his chair to go sliding across the room.

We grabbed our packs from the corner of the room and headed out the door and up the street. Alexus would stop periodically and turn to tell us about the part of the city we were going through. As we went further up the streets, the surroundings changed drastically from that of the waterfront area we had been in. The buildings displayed a lot of the architecture of those we saw back in Greece. Alexus pointed out to us that the Greeks had been very influential in developing the social and cultural background of the city. There was considerable evidence of worship of many of the same gods that were esteemed back in our homeland.

We came to an area of town that was the residences of the aristocracy of Tyre. Alexus stopped on a street corner and waited for us to take in the grandeur of the mansions and shops that lined the streets for several blocks in all directions. He thought it best not to enter this district since we would draw much attention with our packs and our modest attire. Marco and I both thought that even the affluence of Athens lacked the elegance of what we saw before us. The merchandise outside the shops was beyond our ability to describe. We had never seen such wealth accumulated in one place.

"How did these people get so rich?" Cirro asked as he stood in total awe of what he saw.

"Most of them started as traders and merchants—some had shipping companies. Now most of them just take it easy up here all day long and let others make there money for them. You see now why I wanted to show you this? You got all this god worship going on and these rich folks living like kings. Most people don't want to see anyone change the way things are. They got it good and they want to make sure it stays that way. That's why these new teachings aren't going ove so well." Alexus answered and then explained his purpose.

"I can understand why the idol worship is threatened by the things Jesus teaches but why are these wealthy people so against Him?" I asked Alexus.

"Mostly because their wealth hasn't exactly come to them by fair dealings. These people don't like being told they have done something wrong and they have the influence with the authorities to make it dangerous to accuse them." answered Alexus.

"Not all these people are dishonest, I know that from being on the seas with some of them and working for some others. There is a few good men living here but they don't want to stand against those who control the politics. I'm glad not to be in either part. They can have their riches but I fear it will cost them dearly someday." Capt. Vitas added.

"There is one more part of this city I want you to see. We better leave this part now anyway. Follow me!" Alexus said as he swung his pack over his shoulder and walked with a quick pace up the street. He led us to a busy part of town with a lot of people mingling in the streets. Markets and shops lined the wide pavements. Customers were arguing with the merchants, sometimes with such enthusiasm that it appeared that a fight was about to break out. There were groups of people gathered around talking. Children were running through the whole area, chanting to sell whatever was in their baskets. Most of them darted from one person to the next, stopping only long enough to get paid for whatever they had. Shop owners and market vendors kept a sharp eye out for the young businessmen, since they chose to replenish their supply of goods from the crates and baskets they found conveniently lining their way.

"Why do these kids take these things so openly? Aren't they afraid of getting caught?" ask Marco.

"Many of them do this to survive—they have no home and no one to provide for them. If they get caught, well at least they have a place to stay for a while. They are very fast and not easy to catch. Also they have gained the favor of many people in the crowds. They get to buy food and such for less than the merchants charge and, some of the people see it as a way to get even with the merchants who aren't always fair in their dealings." Alexus offered in answer.

"Where do these children come from? From what we have seen of this city, there should not be so many children without homes." Ben surmised.

"There is a section of the town that you haven't seen. It is where the people live who do much of the work in this region. They spend their lives laboring for barely enough to survive on. Those with families, well, they are often forced to live off the land or do what they have to in order to stay alive. Many children and women die and the families usually lack the means to bury them properly. It is a pitiful life and I would rather you not see this part of this great and powerful city. Once you have seen how these people live, you will never be able to get the images from your mind. It is such an insult to humanity to have this tremendous display of wealth and yet have children struggling just to stay alive only blocks away. That is why I wanted you to see this city. These people and many more like them fill this land. The poor have little hope of ever getting out of this poverty and the rich feel like their wealth will last forever. That is one of the main reasons why there is such opposition to change. The rich don't want to lose their advantage over the poor. It makes me sick every time I think about it." Alexus said in a way that revealed he was more tender than we had ever thought.

"That is the way life is all over—the rich get richer and the poor do the work. Why do you let it upset you so much here, Alexus?" Cirro asked.

"It is different here. Perhaps there are more extremes, but the main reason it bothers me so is that the religious and government leaders take part in this injustice and favor the rich while they oppress the poor." responded Alexus.

"He's right about that. That is why there is so much opposition to the teachin' of Jesus and John. The poor see hope in them. These priest and religious leaders cater to the folks that can support them financially." Ben interjected.

"Let's be careful how we talk about these people. Sure there is injustice and wrongful dealings and there is, no doubt, a shameful poverty here. But it is never wise to lump people into like bunches. I've always found there is good and bad in all kinds and if you give them enough time, they'll show which they are." Capt. Vitas advised.

"Maybe so, Capt., but I seen enough here on my other visits to know it ain't right. I wanted you to see so you could understand what these people are going through. You need to know why there is such strong opposition and to be careful who you talk with about Jesus. Someday, I want to do something to help change the way this city is." Alexus said in rebuttal.

"You are a good man, Alexus, and I didn't mean to sound harsh. We want to see the same thing but we must work together, drawing from each other's strengths and overcoming our weaknesses." Capt. Vitas said as he placed a reassuring hand on Alexus' shoulder and squeezed it to show he did care for him.

"Your tour has been helpful, Alexus. We have learned much today that will help us on our way. Unless you have more to show us, I think it would be good to get out of here and find a place to camp for the night a few miles down the road. We have a couple of hours of daylight left so we can find a good place to stay." I suggested.

"We've seen enough and it is a good idea to find a camp before dark. Let's get going." Alexus replied.

We left Tyre on a southwest road that led to Gischia. There were people going and coming on the hard packed road. We often had to step off to the side to let carts and wagons pass by us. Some people would smile and nod their head as they passed by but others would not even look to the side to acknowledge us. There were a couple of garrisons of Roman soldiers who did take notice of us. About two to three miles out of the city we found a sheltered spot off the road some distance and made camp there. As the sun went down in another glorious display of color we were glad to have a fire to warm ourselves by. Marco, with his fondness of cooking, soon had our supper in the making and some of us found time to take a much-needed rest.

Our smoke and the smell of food must have drifted out to the road as we saw some people approaching our camp. Capt. Vitas rose to greet them and I noticed that Marco reached for the knife he was using and made sure to keep it within reach. Cirro and Alexus had slipped their hands under their blankets and I knew both men held their weapons ready if needed.

"Hello!" said the captain as he reached out his hand to them. "Welcome to our humble camp." One of the men who seemed to lead the way shook hands with Capt. Vitas and spoke something we didn't understand. He smiled as did those with him and we responded with nods and smiles.

"Would you like to stay with us for a while?" Capt. Vitas said as he turned and swept his hand in an effort to help them understand they had been asked to join us.

"Our father doesn't speak your language but he said we would be honored to stay the night with you. We have camped here in this place many times before. It is a good place to stay. We are on our way to Tyre to trade our goods there." spoke one of the younger ones.

"Tell your father we are glad to share our camp with you. Make yourselves at home." Capt. Vitas offered.

The visitors all bowed to us and then proceeded to unpack for the night. They brought some food over to where Marco was preparing our meal and offered to help by putting their food along with ours. Marco and one of the young men worked together fixing food that soon had our mouths watering. Without being able to communicate with words, the two of them seemed to understand each other well. I began to talk with the one who had spoken to us and learned that this group was a family of three sons and their father. They made a living from weaving blankets and rugs and, sometimes fine cloth when they could get the materials. We talked until it was time to eat. Just before Marco called for us to eat, this new friend, Joel, mentioned that he had camped here one evening when a man named Jesus and some of His followers had stopped to rest with them. I wanted to hear more about this but I knew we would have to continue our conversation later. I have never found it in me to turn down an invitation to eat. Ben and I had our wooden spoons poised over our plates and ready to unload their savory, steaming contents when one of the young men announced we should all wait until we had offered a prayer of thanksgiving. The leader spoke words we once more failed to understand and then Joel spoke, asking a blessing on our meal. When he had finished, he motioned for us to commence eating. We enjoyed a meal with such taste—one cooked over an open fire and one with flavorings I have never tasted before. I don't recall ever eating such a satisfying meal in my life. After we had helped clean up, Joel and I resumed our conversation. I was growing very curious about why his family had stopped us to pray for the meal. Not knowing any other way, I just came right out and asked Joel why they did it.

"It is something our family has felt led to do and it has been taught to us to do this by the scriptures. I remember that we used to do many things like this since I was old enough to remember, but now we do them because there is something prompting us to want to do these things. It is like a little voice inside us giving directions. We are still amazed at this wonderful happening—it has only recently been like this! It started not long after we became believers of Jesus." he answered with more information than I had expected and with reasons that I found hard to comprehend.

"Do all who believe in Jesus get this inner voice telling them what to do?" I asked, probably with a lack of proper manners and with my mouth still hanging open as I finished speaking.

"Well, it's not so much that this voice tells us what to do, but it is there to give help to us when we have need of it. From those we have talked with, not many have experienced this voice within them. I don't understand it all, but this I know; hearing this inner voice has provided all the evidence I need to know that what Jesus teaches is the truth. No one can ever convince me otherwise." declared Joel with an assurance in his tone that I knew he meant every word he said.

"You mentioned earlier that Jesus once stopped here on this spot. What was He doing here?" I asked.

"He was on a journey that was to take Him through Tyre and on up to Sidon, trying to reach people with His teachings. He said He had heard about the oppression of the poor in Tyre and wanted to offer them hope." Joel responded.

"We just came from there and it looks like they still need a lot of hope. Was He able to help them?" I questioned.

"I think some. He tried to help a lot of people but some just refused to listen to Him and others want His help but don't really know how to get it. I know for myself, I had to take hold of it like I really wanted it. Then it seemed like something started working in me. It is hard to explain but, once you feel it, you want everybody to experience it too." Joel explained.

"My friends and I have traveled from Athens to come here to find out about these teachings and more about Jesus. All of my life I have been taught mythology and a lot of idol worship. It was so empty to me. I know that there is a greater power at work in this world. I want to experience what you have told me about." I continued with Joel.

"You can! Just believe in Jesus—that He is the Son of God and He wants you to be His." Joel exclaimed with a joyous face.

"I want to but there are some things I have to be sure about first. It's not that I doubt what you have said—it is just this is so important to me. I have to know these things without the slightest doubt left in my mind. Do you understand what I am saying?" I replied.

"Yes, I think so. I had doubts myself for a long time, but they are gone now. Something happened and now I just know—it is hard to explain. You will know yourself when it happens to you." Joel said as he tried to encourage me.

"How is it that you are so fluent in our language and the rest of your family isn't? You hardly even carry and accent." I questioned Joel, sensing we had taken our conversation about Jesus to the point where we both knew enough had been spoken. The rest would have to come on its own.

"I lived in Tyre for two summers, staying at my uncle's house in order to learn the language. Someday, my father wants me to take over our business but we have already found that being able to communicate with others has been most helpful in selling our goods. My brothers know some of the language but they are reluctant to use it. Father is set in his ways and says he is too old to change now." Joel answered.

"Was it hard for him to accept Jesus? From what I understand there are many Jews who do not want to accept His teachings." I asked Joel.

"Not really. He seemed to know it was right in his heart and that was enough for him. There are a lot of Jews upset with Jesus and it is often dangerous to speak publicly. There is serious talk of them trying to have Jesus killed. My family is not going to take part in the Passover week because there is too much turmoil. Father thinks it is better to be away during these days." responded Joel.

"Well, it has been great to visit with you. I am glad you joined us to camp here. You have been very helpful to us. We had better get rest now." I said as I got up to spread my blankets out under the canvas sail that blocked the night air. The heat from the fire was doing a good job of warming the shelter. We made enough room there for our guest as well.

As we were turning in for the night, Joel's father called for his sons to join him. They spoke quitely together for a moment and then sat silently with their heads bowed. Their father carefully took a flat piece of bread from his pack along with some meat that had been prepared for them, some herbs, and a few other things to give to his sons. Then he held up a wineskin and spoke a few words before he passed it around to the sons also. After they had eaten and taken a drink from the wineskin, they prayed a short prayer and then went quietly to bed. As I watched them, I became very curious to know what it was all about. Surely, they weren't hungry after the filling supper we had. No, this was more of a ceremonial meal. Joel had also mentioned an event called Passover which I wanted to know the meaning of. I found myself thinking of more questions than I would ever have time to ask. But all this would have to wait until morning. I was tired and, somehow, it didn't seem right to bother Joel after their prayer time. I would try to narrow my list of questions down to just a few and get them answered in the morning.

# CHAPTER SIX

# MIDNIGHT AT NOON

The next morning we awoke early and hurriedly prepared something to eat before we broke camp and headed down the road. Our friends spent time to themselves in prayer and talking. Our group made quick work of cleaning up camp and getting packed. I began to get anxious about leaving before I had a chance to talk to Joel. For some reason I didn't understand, I felt that it was vitally important to know the significance of this Passover event. Joel must have noticed my anxiety as he spoke to his family and they ended their conversation to speak with us before leaving.

Hands were shook and friendly faces did what they could to overcome the language barrier. Joel took me aside after he had acknowledged the others. We began talking rapidly to each other, knowing time was short.

"My father is having difficulty about not being in one of our temples for this Passover. He knows that many things are not right but deep in his heart, he fears that tragedy may be near. He has desired to obey God all his life and, now that he has chosen to avoid Jerusalem this Passover, he is troubled." Joel said with a voice that showed concern for his family.

"What is this Passover and why is it so important to you?" I asked

"It is a feast that Jews have observed since our people were set free in Egypt hundreds of years ago. It symbolized how God delivered us from captivity and it has been observed since. Now, people from all over Israel come to the temple cities to participate, out of traditional duty mostly. My family feels it is a time to honor God by remembering what He has done for our people." Joel answered.

"Is that what you were doing last night with the food your father gave you?" I asked.

"Yes, we did what we could to observe the Passover. This is only one of a very few times my father has not been in the temple to celebrate this event. He said he just could not go there this year, since he cannot accept what the priests are doing. But I must be going. My brothers and I need to reassure our father he has made the right decision in this. I have enjoyed our time together and I hope you find all that your heart is seeking. Please be careful—I have an uneasy fee—well, just be careful." Joel replied.

"We will. Thanks for all your help. I have learned much to share with my friends. I hope your father can find peace with his decision. Maybe someday, we will meet again, but if not, then you have become a friend I will not soon forget." I said as I gave him a hug and waived to them.

I had much to tell my friends of what Joel and I had talked about. I was still talking when we had gone a couple of miles down the road. Ben and Capt. Vitas both seemed very eager to understand what Joel had told of his experience. I found it hard to explain and knew Joel must have felt much the same as he tried to tell me. I did my best to share with them all that I knew and hoped that would help them. We made good time that morning and didn't meet too many people along the way. In fact, we began to notice that it was almost too quiet.

Ben calculated we were about four miles from Gischala when Alexus and Cirro asked when we would stop for the noon meal. Our walk this morning had been across rolling hills and we found that our sea legs weren't used to climbing. We had covered several miles and maintained a steady pace, but the muscles in our legs began to cramp and get sore. Most of us wanted to stop to rest but Capt. Vitas told us that might not be the best thing to do, since the soreness would set in. He encouraged us to keep going on, even if we had to slow down. Alexus now let it be known that his legs ached more than his empty stomach. Cirro laughed at him and we found the effort to keep going for a few more miles.

It was nearing noon when we decided to stop to eat. We found a place where the sun was warming the dry grasses of a slope. It felt so good to take off our packs and lay back on the warm grass. Capt. Vitas had been right about our cramping muscles. They still hurt some but we had walked much of the soreness out. As much as we all liked to eat, we found it hard to end our resting in the warm sunshine. We chewed on dried meat and hard biscuits as we talked over the many things we had learned since coming to shore in Tyre.

From where we were sitting, we could see the town of Gischala. There were a few people out tending to their affairs. I found myself wondering what life was like there in that town. My mind was whirling with thoughts of our journey. We had been able to talk with many people who had much to share about Jesus. I was mentally trying to fit all this information together and then tested it to see how it agreed with what was feeding this strong desire in my heart. Even though I was resting physically, mentally I was soon exhausted. I turned to look at Marco and his face revealed that he was, more than likely, as deep in thought as I was.

The peacefulness of the place and the warmth of the sun soon had part of our group dozing off. Marco and I were getting drowsy as well. We were soon brought back to being fully awake as we noticed that a strange darkness was overtaking the country side. At first, it was like clouds had gathered to block out the sun, but then the darkness that swept over us became even darker yet. We began to talk with one another, having doubt as to what time it really was. Alexus thought we surely must have slept through the afternoon and now, nightfall was upon us. Cirro agreed and tried to tell the rest of us not to be so confused. Ben sat up but remained silent for a while. He studied the sky and listened to the surroundings. Capt. Vitas had one of the most serious looks of concern that I ever saw on him. Marco moved over to where I sat and we whispered quietly about what we thought might be going on. We all noticed that it had become extremely quiet. Not a bird sang, the wind wasn't whispering in the trees—nothing but the sound of our apprehensive breathing. All of nature must have recognized this strange occurrence.

"It's probably just one of them eclipses that happens from time to time. If this ain't night yet, then that's what it's got to be." Alexus tried to explain.

"I hate to disagree with you, Alexus, but this isn't an eclipse. It's too dark for that. I have never heard of anything like this, and I sure haven't seen anything like it. I'm telling you, something is going on!" Capt. Vitas countered.

The darkness remained upon us for what must have been two hours or more. We thought it best to stay where we were until we could know what was happening. It was too dark to travel safely, even though it must have been early afternoon. I almost hate to admit it, but I seriously think everyone of us was too scared to move. Time seemed to crawl as we waited for something to happen. Would it get light again before nightfall really came? Would it ever get light again? Will someone come along to let us know what is happening? Is there anyone anywhere who knows what is going on? How long should we set here waiting before we leave to find out what has happened? All these questions went through our minds. It seemed like we had been there for hours or even a day when Ben motioned for us to set still. He listened intently and soon we all began to pick up a faint rumbling in the distance—coming from the south. The rumble became stronger and it wasn't long before we felt the earth shaking underneath us. A few rocks began to roll down the hillside around us and the trees swayed back and forth as dead branches fell to the ground. The shaking and rumbling lasted for a moment or two and then the stillness that had engulfed the land returned. The only sound that could be heard was the clatter of small stones as they finally came to rest. All of us sat absolutely still for several moments, partly afraid to move, but also listening intently for whatever might be happening next. After a while, we noticed that the darkness was giving way to light once more. The sun didn't return to shine down on us, but it grew lighter and lighter. Sounds could once more be heard in the trees but there was still a hush over the land. We continued to listen and looked toward the nearby town to see if anyone was out.

"I believe we should gather our things and get down to that town while there is light enough to travel. We don't know for sure what time it really is and, besides, I want to find out what went on here." Ben suggested with such confidence that we pretty well knew it would be useless to disagree.

"Sounds good to us." Marco added as he moved about to pick us his pack.

It didn't take us long to reach the outskirts of Gischala and we found people were out looking for an explanation just as we were. As we walked by houses, we saw people peering out from cracked doors and watching us from behind pulled back curtains. The moment we looked their way, they quickly shut the doors or dropped the curtain to keep from being seen. Fear had taken a firm hold on these people and it was certain that they weren't likely to trust us strangers. Those who had ventured out in the open were just as suspicious of us. As we neared them, they would scurry to be near their homes. We walked past a few homes when Ben suggested we stop and attempt to talk to some of those who were watching us.

"Do any of you know what happened here? Why did it get so dark? Do you understand us? We mean you no harm." Ben spoke loud enough to be heard.

"I doubt they can understand you, Ben. Let me try with some of the words I learned from Joel. If we try to us motions to communicate, they might think we had something to do with the darkness and earthquake." I offered.

I did my best to recall a few words. Apparently it helped to ease the suspicion and a couple of the village men came closer to us. They passed their hands through the air to indicate the darkness that had came over us. They continued to describe what they saw with all kinds of motions and then led us to a house on down the street where we were presented to man we assumed to be the leader of the town. He looked at us intently without saying a word. After a short time, Capt. Vitas spoke gently and reached out his hand to the man.

"Nik, try to tell him we mean no harm—we just want to know what has happened. See if we might spend the night here." Capt. Vitas asked.

I began telling the man what the captain had said and must have been able to get at least some of the message to him. As he responded, I could gather that he offered a place in the rear of his house for us to stay in. Through our broken words, I could tell that it was unlikely that anyone in this village knew why it had been so dark. We thought it would be best to spend the night and see what tomorrow would bring.

We didn't talk much among ourselves that night. I think the events of the day had left us shaken and we were still on edge. I know in my heart, something of great significance had occurred this day. I was unable to determine if it was something to be joyful about or if a great tragedy had taken place. I do know that the heavy curtain of fear was lifting from me and, for some strange reason, hope was rising in its place. I wanted to ask Marco if he was experiencing these feelings, since we had often felt so alike many times before. Unfortunately, an opportune time did not come and an unusual quietness reigned until it was broken by the sounds of heavy breathing and an occasional snoring. These answers, like those we so anxiously sought all afternoon, would have to wait until another day. Sleep finally came to give the mind rest.

We woke to the light of a new day streaming in through the window. It was as if there was a newness in the air—a time to begin anew. I felt it in a strong sort of way. Some of the others may have as well, since they seemed to be eager to get on our way. I can offer no explanation for why I felt this way, not even in the most vague sort of way, but there was such a definite stirring in my heart that I knew it had to be true. Oh, I wanted so badly to be able to verify this with Marco.

We ate breakfast with our host and his wife after we tidied up our room and then attempted to express our thanks as best we could. It is amazing how well people can communicate with their facial expressions. Even though we were not able to speak many words that were mutually understood, it was evident that the man who had offered his home to us had become close to our hearts. We were never to know his name or any more about him but there was a heart felt connection made that night that would probably last our lifetimes. Looking into the man's eyes as we left brought to mind the many times we had encountered strangers who had become dear friends by the time we left. It was more often than coincidence, far greater than chance, and more intense than most social connections. There was a distinct and definite thread being woven around us and through those people we met on our way to the truth. I found great hope and inspiration in this very fact and it kept my heart stirred.

I was able to walk along beside Marco as we made our way to Bethsaida on the northern shore of the Sea of Galilee. We had planned to take a boat south from there and then make our way down the Jordan River. It had been quite some time since Marco and I had been able to talk about the deepest feelings in our hearts. Since we left the old ship, we hadn't really had any time to be alone. Inwardly, I think I may have felt we were drifting apart and it bothered me. Marco had been my best friend for many years, in fact, I can't remember ever being without him. It was good to have time to renew our bond of friendship.

As we talked, I found that Marco had also sensed a renewal as we awoke this morning. He had no better explanation for it than I did, but it was there. He also shared my eagerness to get on with our journey and had noticed that he found reason to have hope, hope that was greater than before. If I were asked to describe what we saw along the way that day, I would not be able to do so. Marco and I became so engrossed in our conversation that we hardly noticed the others in our group, not to mention any sights we passed by. If we met anyone on the road, I was unaware of it.

We were both soon in high spirits. It was as if we had found a treasure map to follow and now we had discovered the landmarks the map used to indicate where the treasure was hidden. We knew we were on course and not far from finding the answers we had long been seeking.

"You think we ought to let the others in on this? I feel kind of selfish about keeping it to ourselves." Marco asked.

"Yes, me too. Yet, this is all so strange. If we try to explain it to them and they haven't felt what we felt, how can we get them to believe us?" I replied.

"Don't forget who we are with. Ben and Capt. Vitas have just as much driving them as we do. Alexus and Cirro may put on like they are rough and tough, but we have both seen the compassion in their hearts. I think that makes a man a whole lot more understanding in any situation. Besides, we can start by asking them if they noticed anything this morning back in that house in Gischala. If they didn't, we can just let it drop for now. If they felt what we felt—well, then we won't have to worry about them understanding all this, will we?" Marco reasoned.

"Marco, you can smooth things out better than any man I know. I guess I got so caught up in what all this means to me that I forgot how the others must feel. Have I told you how glad I am that you came with me on this trip?" I said.

We were just about to let the others in on what we had discussed when we heard Ben call out from a ways behind us.

"You two plannin' on goin' on without us? Send word back when you get there and tell us how it is!" he yelled out.

We stopped and turned to notice that we were over a quarter mile ahead of them. Apparently we had quickened our step and shut out the rest of the world as we had talked. Marco and I had been able to get into our own little world, at least for a while and it was good. We waited for the others to catch up to us and decided it was a good time to rest and eat. While the others ate, Marco and I began asking about what they had felt in the last day or so. It didn't take more than that to get them talking. Ben was first, as usual, to tell us what he thought about all that had happened. When he started to tell how he felt something different in the light coming in through the window at the man's house, Capt. Vitas interrupted by finishing what Ben had started to say. Ben sat there nodding his head so enthusiastically that we thought it might come off. Alexus and Cirro just sat with there mouth open and the remains of the last bite of food, lying practically chewed, on their tongues. By the time we finished telling them all that we had talked about, the whole group was ready to get up and run the rest of the way. Such hope! What more reason could we need to go on? We were all so encouraged by the things we shared. We laughed and reviewed the experiences we had on our journey. Finally, as the reality sank in of just how awesome our trip had been, we became more solemn—knowing that a great power was working in our midst. Our laughter quickly gave way to silence but the hope remained. It was then that Cirro began to speak with a voice broken with emotion and, at times, barely audible.

"Before daylight this morning, I saw one of them angles like them old shepherds told us about. It wasn't near as big as what they saw but it must have looked just like them otherwise. It stood there in the air and reached out to me saying, 'Come to me, Cirro. I want you to come to me.' At first it really scared me and then I got so I wanted to go to him. Then it was gone. I thought I was just dreaming and have been thinking about it all morning. I didn't want to say anything cause I wasn't sure what you'd think. I know I was awake. I know I was! What's this all mean?" Cirro managed to get out between long periods of weeping.

"There has been much to understand, too much to comprehend. The only thing I can tell you for certain, Cirro, is that we are on the way to finding understanding of all this. I am certain of that—more so now than I was this morning when I woke up. Another thing that I have found to be of great importance is that what we do with the understanding we find is vital to how it will affect us. For example, take the awareness that we all had about this being a new beginning this morning as we woke—if we had not shared our thoughts with each other, much would have been lost, possibly forever.

And you, Cirro, had you not told us about seeing that angle, you may have convinced yourself that it was only a dream and we would not have benefited from what you saw. Truth and knowledge are only useful if you apply them to your life. I have found that to be evident in many of Jesus' teachings." Capt. Vitas spoke with a comforting and assuring voice.

As we finished eating, doing so not out of hunger but because we knew our bodies would need energy replenished; we also tried to digest all that had been said. There was much to consider. Capt. Vitas' words kept going through my mind and I knew he had spoken with wisdom. We found our enthusiasm to get up and run had been tempered with patience and knowledge. Finally we had all our packs on and returned to the road. We had another four to five miles to go before reaching Bethsaida. We met a few people on the road that afternoon but didn't have opportunity to talk with any of them. Other than finding the country-side filled with beauty, our journey that afternoon was un-eventful.

## CHAPTER SEVEN

# BACK ON WATER

The dew of the evening air was settling around us as we entered the streets of Bethsaida. Although the town had some size to it, there was not much activity going on as we made our way down the streets. Those people who were out looked at us with a sense of uneasiness. We soon noticed that when we stopped to try to talk to them, other people would move towards them as if joining together in defense. It was certainly evident that tension was reigning high and trust was scarce in this city. When we came near a group of men standing outside a building that must have been a tavern or meeting place of some kind, they came shouting at us with sticks in their hands. As we moved on quickly, Ben remarked about how he figured something must have really scared these folks and Alexus quickly agreed.

"Let's cut off up here to the right and make our way back out of this town for the night. It don't appear we are too welcome here. We'd be better off out with the wild creatures than to risk beddin' down amongst these people. I'd sooner trust a room full of drunken deck hands as I would tryin' to sleep here." Alexus suggested as he led the way around the next corner without waiting for approval from the rest of us.

"Might as well!" responded Capt. Vitas. "Friendliness don't seem to be one of their strong points. Maybe they'll be in a better mood tomorrow."

"If I remember right, there is a place just up in the hills outside of the city where I stayed once when I was here. We'll be safe in the rocks up there. We can make a camp up against some of them rocks so we won't have to worry about them comin' up from behind us a least. If they want trouble with me, they're goin'a have to do it face to face. Sure don't know what's got 'em so on edge but it's plain enough they are." Ben said and then continued talking to himself in short phrases which showed his irritation with the town's people.

We made our way out of the town without any more encounters and found the area Ben had remembered. It did offer good protection from intruders and had a nice view of the Sea of Galilee. There was enough of a breeze coming up the hillside that we were glad to get a fire going to help take off the chill. Since we had landed, this was the first night we were alone. On other nights we had stayed in someone's home or had others camp with us. This night was different from most other nights on our journey. Our group was quieter than usual and I had a feeling of loneliness that had not been there before. I didn't even have a desire to talk with Marco about it. As I laid there looking up at the stars in the night sky, I felt so small and helpless. Oh, I had certainly been able to make the voyage from Athens and even did a decent job as a deck hand and galley mate. I came from a family of prominence and had been well educated. I had been able to hold up to doing my part on this journey and even felt like I had done as well as the more experienced men who were with us. Not bad for a young man on his first time away from home! Then why did I have this feeling of being nothing? I kept staring at the stars. They seemed so far away and there were so many of them. How could something be so enormous? Does the sky ever end? Where did it all come from?

These thoughts all came racing through my mind. So many questions without answers. Then I remember what my new friend Joel had said to me about Jesus wanting me to be His. How did my mind go from wandering about the starts to thinking about what Joel had said? I started to question my sanity for a moment. Then I began trying to figure out how someone as big and powerful as God or His Son, Jesus—how could He even know I existed? I am just a speck of dust in this universe. How could He want me to be His? Why would He need me?

For the first time since I had left home in Athens, I found tears rolling down my face—not just a single tear making its way down across my face; but a flood of them. I wasn't sure why I was crying. I wasn't scared and I don't think I was home-sick. The tears seemed to come rolling out of my eyes so profusely that I wondered how there could be any more left inside me. I tried wiping them away the best I could. I sure didn't want the others to see me like this. As I tried to regain control of my emotions, I realized that these tears weren't tears of emotion. They were tears from the heart. At that very moment I realized just how broken I had become in the past few moments. Left to myself, I would not or could not be anymore than a person walking on this land, living for a while and then to die. I would not be unlike those town's people who had only a short time ago wanted to harm us for little or no reason. I could be like all those swarthy seamen who live for the day because they have no hope for a tomorrow. In fact, they have no hope at all.

I had found a great truth lying there under those twinkling stars. I knew that I would never find the Truth if I relied only on myself to find it. I had to let Truth come to me. Suddenly the tears started flowing again. This time instead of tears that seemed to be emptying me, they were more like tears of overflowing joy. I found myself not caring who might see them. Something had happened to me! I felt it deep in my heart! I wanted to tell all the others but they were finally asleep. I had to tell someone though, so I quietly moved over to Marco and gently woke him.

"Marco, wake up! Marco, it's me. I have to talk to you and it can't wait. Come on! Wake up!" I said as I continued to shake his arm.

"What's wrong? Is there someone out there? What is it?" Marco asked as he tried to come to being fully awake.

"No. No, there is no one bothering us. It's alright but I need to tell you what just happened to me." I whispered to him in hopes of not waking the others.

"What are you talking about? Can't you just tell me in the morning? " Marco questioned.

"No, I can't wait any longer. I have to tell someone and you are the best someone I know. Let's try to slip over to those rocks so we don't disturb the others."

I suggested.

We very carefully moved several feet away from the other men who were sleeping and nestled up against some rocks so that we were nearly facing each other.

Marco turned to look back at the blanket he had left behind as he held his arms in his hands, having noticed the chilly night air.

"This isn't going to take long I hope? Now what is it that can't wait?" Marco said with a strong hint of irritation in his voice.

"We can never find this Truth we seek because we just don't have the power to do it. Those stars up there! Don't you see—we can." I was beginning to say when Marco stopped me.

"Nik, you must have been dreaming or something cause you aren't making any sense. What does the size of the stars have to do with us finding truth? Is this trip getting too much for you?" He asked in hopes of finding out what must have been wrong with me.

"All those stars up there—where did they come from? Who made them?" I asked as I grabbed Marco by the arm and turned him so that he was looking up at the same sky I had seen only moments before.

"I don't know for sure. God I guess. All I know for sure is that the gods we were taught about didn't make 'em." He replied.

"Alright, now, if God has the power to make all that huge sky up there, how can He even be concerned with us—with me in particular? What am I that I should matter to Him?" I continued to ask.

"I'm supposed to know the answer to that? You still aren't making any sense to me and it's getting cold here. What are you getting at?" he replied impatiently.

"My point is that He does care about us. There is plenty of evidence to prove that if you will think back to all the things that have happened on this trip. Now, if God, who has all the power to make stars and everything else, can take notice of someone like me—well I find that pretty exciting. And another thing— Remember Joel from the other night? He told me that Jesus want us to be His." I told Maroc, hoping he would be able to grasp at least part of what was stirring within me.

"You said something about not being able to find the truth. What do you mean by that?" Marco asked with a tone that showed he was letting his irritation give way to a desire to understand what I had experienced.

"Well, it seems to me that this Truth we are seeking is far beyond our ability to comprehend, at least by our own efforts. That is what I was trying to tell you about the stars and all. This Truth is more than we can ever find by ourselves. When we realize that we can't do it on our own, and really have a sincere desire for it, then that Truth will come to us." I said.

"What makes you so sure you got this all figured out right? How come you talk about God one minute and then about Jesus the next? How do you know Jesus cares about you? You're telling me some pretty strange stuff here!" Marco asked.

"All I can tell you is that I felt Him working in me just minutes ago. It's something I have never ever felt before. Marco, I just know! I felt like I emptied everything out of me and then I felt like I was filled to overflowing. I don't understand all that has gone on but I know we are so close to knowing the Truth." I said as I tried to finish the words before the tears came and I choked up.

Maroc reached out to offer me comfort as he tried to comprehend all that I had told him. I truly felt his friendship at that moment. I knew he understood why my tears flowed so freely and, even though he hadn't shared in my experience, he proved himself faithful. Once more, I was glad he was with me on this journey.

(Saturday night)

After a few more minutes we carefully made our way back to our blankets and tucked them around us to hold in what warmth we still had in us. The night was chilly and the rocky camp site proved to be more than a little drafty. It was well into the night when Marco finally went off to sleep. I know it must have been at least an hour or more that I laid there recalling all that had just happened. It seemed like only a short time before the others were stirring around the camp and attempting to make breakfast. I noticed that Capt. Vitas was not moving about as he normally did and he kept his blanket pulled over his shoulders as he sat near the fire Alexus had made.

As we sat together eating our breakfast, plans were made for the day. Ben suggested we head straight for the boat docks to see if anyone was willing to help us cross the lake. It seemed like a good plan and we hurriedly gathered our belongings, being anxious to leave Bethsaida.

We reached the water front in short order and found a fisherman working on his nets. Ben began to make conversation with the man but got no response from him. Finally, Ben offered to pay the fisherman to take us across the lake.

"What you go over lake for? Where you from?" Asked the fisherman in broken language.

"We're heading south. Came from Tyre and it's been a long walk. Can you help us?" Ben replied.

The old fisherman looked us over with scrutinizing eyes and waited a couple of minutes before he finally spoke again. "Where in south?"

Ben returned the old man's look and he hesitated before he spoke. "Jerusalem."

"Jerusalem!" Yelled the old man. "Jerusalem! Then you get. Go!" He yelled as he waved his gear at us and began coming after us. As he came he yelled to his friends and we soon found ourselves being chased by several men. We walked as fast as our dignity would let us and found that it wasn't fast enough to get away from our followers. We left our dignity behind and ran along the coast hoping they would give up and let us be on our way at a more respectable pace.

We had ran several hundred yards before the old fisherman and the others gave up the chase. Just as we were slowing down and trying to catch our breath, we heard someone calling out to us. "Over here! Come on down here." Yelled a man as he motioned for us to come to the dock where he stood.

At this point, we were willing to go to anybody who wasn't wanting to do us harm and we accepted his invitation.

As we approached the man he said, "You must be strangers here in town and ain't found it to be a friendly place."

"Not the least bit friendly at all!" Marco answered before any of the rest of us could say anything.

Well, I figured so," said the man. "It's getting so that it ain't safe to be seen in this place unless you've lived here all your life. Was you fixin' on getting a boat to go out on the lake?"

"Yes, but what has got these people so riled up? I really think they meant to do us harm." Ben responded.

"Oh, I'm sure they did. What with the Jews making a commotion in the south and the Romans getting worried about uprisin's, well these folks are tryin' to make sure nothin' changes for them. They want to be left alone. Sad though—just a few loud mouths gettin' word started and then helpin' to keep things stirred up and, let me tell you sure as I'm standin' here, things is mighty stirred up." The man went on to tell us. "Where you wantin' to go to if you don't mind me askin'?"

"We would like to head down the Jordan as far as we can. Jerusalem is where we hope to get to." Ben told him.

"You tell them fellers that you was goin to Jerusalem? Why, It's no wonder they was aimin' to club you." he said, interrupting Ben. "Hurry up and get in! Untie the ropes so we can be on our way! It won't even be safe for me here now that I been talkin' to you."

We were soon on our way, having stored the docking ropes, and soon had the small sail filled with a gentle breeze. The small fishing boat glided over the water's surface with ease and we could see the men we left on shore fade into tiny specks as we headed out onto this magnificent lake.

"Sir, we deeply appreciate your willingness to help us, but I'm afraid we failed to come to an agreement on how much you want to take us along and just how far you are planning on going. I also want to apologize for not introducing ourselves." said Capt. Vitas in his most cordial way. He then proceeded to introduce each of us to our rescuer.

"Well, I'm pleased to meet all of you and my name is Artemis. I was plannin' on sailing to the south end of the lake to try fishing there for a while. We will most likely stop there unless I get a feeling to go on. I don't suppose you'll owe me anything for the trip unless you just want to. It's just not in me to make money off people. Guess that's why I'll always be a poor fisherman. Now, why is it you want to get to Jerusalem?" Artemis asked.

"Have you heard any talk of a couple of men named John or Jesus? I asked him before allowing time for any of the others to answer him.

"Just some. Seems like those two end up bein' connected somehow to all the accounts of trouble I hear. They must be doin' something to stir up folks down that way." Artemis replied.

"Well, they are the reason we are going to Jerusalem. We want to find out more about them." I continued.

"You won't be learnin' much from the one they call John cause they done killed him and from what I've been hearin', they're wantin' to do the same to that Jesus. Best be careful who you go askin' bout them or you might end up that way too." Artemis warned with a tone that showed genuine concern for us.

"Thanks for the advice but we're willin' to take some risk. From all we have learned so far, their teachin' is worth riskin' quite a bit. We knew that John has been killed but we also know that his teachin' is goin' on still." Ben responded.

"What are these teachin's about? How far have you all come to get here?" asked Artemis.

"Our journey started in Athens just as the last ships were to set out before winter. We landed at Tyre and have made our way here." Marco was answering when Artemis interrupted.

"I'm from Corinth! Haven"t been back there for three years now but that's my home. Imagine meetin' folks from back home clear out here!" Artemis went on.

"These teachings you asked about—Well, they are about living a life here and now so that you can have life eternal when your life here is over." Marco started to explain.

"Say that again now! I think you done lost me for we even got started." Artemis again interrupted.

"Their teachings are about a God who made this whole world and made us too. They teach that if we believe in the one they call Jesus and try to do what He teaches, then we can be with Him in heaven some day. It's not an easy thing to explain." Marco went on.

"What makes Him different from the gods we have back in Greece? Don't they have powers to take care of us?" asked Artemis.

"From what we have learned so far, Jesus and John's teachings are that all other gods are just myths, made up by men. They have no power at all. They teach that God made everything and has power over everything. He is the only God." I offered, trying to help Marco explain.

"Say what! The only god? How can that be?" protested Artemis.

"We don't know how but that is what we are seeking to find. We have seen much and talked to many who have helped us to gain knowledge about this. Even now, we have come to know much that makes it hard for us to accept teachings about the gods and mythology we were taught at home. There is something at work within us that is changing our hearts. We don't understand all that is happening but we have great assurance that we are on the pathway to knowing the truth in all this. You are welcome to join with us if you like." I said.

"I'll have to do some thinkin' on it and let you know." Artemis answered as he turned to guide the rudder and adjust the sail. He had just been bombarded with ideas and teachings that must have left him not knowing what to believe in. We knew he needed some time to think, recalling how we felt when we first encountered some of the same teachings we had just shared with him.

As it became quiet on the small boat, we noticed Capt. Vitas was leaning in the corner of the boat, his blanket pulled over him and shivering,. his face was covered with sweat. His breathing was becoming labored and shallow.

"It appears that drafty night up in those rocks has given him lung sickness. There's not much we can do but keep him sitting up and warm. Don't reckon anyone's got a bottle of ale or something strong to give him to help break up that stuff?" Alexus asked.

"Don't have any drink but let me try this on him." Artemis replied as he dug in a small wooden box for a small jar of dark looking paste. He loosened the captain's shirt and began rubbing the paste on his chest. Capt. Vitas coughed some and turned his head away, trying to escape the terrible smell of the dark paste.

"I know, Capt. It don't smell so good but you got to take it into your chest. It's helped me get over a whole bunch of ailments and hurts. I'm afraid it's all we got to help you. Besides, it'll wash off—someday." Artemis said as he continued to care for the captain.

It was nearing noon-day as we continued across the lake. Capt. Vitas was sleeping on and off and we began to see signs that the paste Artemis had rubbed on was working. We had figured our voyage across the lake would be about fifteen miles. The morning breeze had helped us to make good time but now the air was calm and our pace slowed considerable. Even though we all had an eagerness to be on our way, we knew this slow and easy trip across the lake would allow Capt. Vitas time to rest and, hopefully, recover from his illness.

"Will you be able to sail down the Jordan, Artemis, or is this boat too large?" Ben asked.

"The boat wouldn't be too big for this time of year, but the river can only be navigated by the most darin' of sailors. There are rapids and swirls almost as soon as you get into the river from this lake. Only fools and the like would ever try to make it down the river, especially durin' the high water times of the spring. The Jordan falls nearly seven hundred feet in the first ten miles. Might be able to take a skiff once a person gets on down the way—past the worst water. It would be iffy at best." Artemis informed us.

"Are there any roads that run along the river?" Cirro asked.

"A few but they are plagued with both rough terrain and rough men. I wouldn't recommend takin' that route." Artemis answered.

"What would be your recommendation then?" Ben inquired.

"You probably ain't goin' like what I'm about to say but, if we turn west now and head for Tiberias, you'll find yourselves on a main road that will go way down south. It won't be as direct as you want but it safer and probably let you make better time. It won't be near as hard on the captain as those hills and step climbs along the Jordan. Plenty of towns along the way too. Could be you'll be able to learn more of what you're lookin' to find along the way." replied Artemis.

"This trip is taking a lot longer than I figured on. How much longer do you think it'll be till we reach Jerusalem?" Cirro asked.

"Once we land at Tiberias, it will be between eighty and ninety miles to Jerusalem." answered Artemis.

"That could take a week or more. Any faster way there?" Cirro again asked.

"It's about thirty miles out to the Great Sea at Ptolemias. From there by sea to Joppa and then forty miles back by road to Jerusalem. If you are in such a hurry, why didn't you sail on to Joppa from Tyre to begin with?" responded Artemis.

"The captain had cargo for Tyre and he wanted to leave the ship there for repairs. If we had went on by sea from Tyre we would not have learned much of what we now know. I believe it's all been for the best." Ben answered.

"I figured as much. You'll more than likely learn a whole lot more on the road on your way to Jerusalem. Guess I'll make the turn for Tiberias unless you want otherwise." Artemis said as he began leaning into the rudder.

The rest of our journey across the Sea of Galilee was a quite one with not much conversation. Only Marco, Artemis, and myself remained awake. It didn't seem long before we heard voices coming from the shore. We began talking louder to awaken the others before we docked. Artemis assured us he knew several of the men who would be around the docks, but we were still uneasy about them, not forgetting our treatment earlier in the day.

We tied up the boat and were greeted by several men who called Artemis by name. They were friendly to us as well and Artemis warned us not to mention our desire to head for Jerusalem. He thought it would be best not to invite any trouble if we didn't need to and his thinking seemed to make good sense. We made our way to a market place where we purchased some fresh food and looked over the town. Artemis stayed with us and we all tried to persuade him to come with us on our journey. At first, he acted like he was considering coming with us, but by the time we were ready to head out of town for the evening, he had decided to return to his boat.

"I'm an old man now and I figure most of my life has been lived. I've always tried to treat people right and don't know as I ever harmed even one person. That ought to count for somethin', the way I see it. No, you all go on without me." said Artemis.

"You've been good to us, but what makes you feel you have to justify your life to us? Do you know more about why we're going to Jerusalem than you have let on?" questioned Marco.

"I suppose I know a whole lot about why you're goin', but I'm not sure it's for me. You'll be fine. Just keep on goin'." he replied.

"I really wish you would go with us, Artemis. I think there is more to this teaching than just doing good and living right and I don't want you to miss out on it." I pleaded with him.

He looked at all of us with a warm smile and waved to us as he turned back to the docks. I could not get beyond feeling that he had made the wrong choice. I wanted to grab him by the arm and beg him to reconsider but I didn't. It was then Capt. Vitas called out to him.

"Artemis, wait! We want you to have this." he said as he held out some coins in his hand.

Artemis turned around and paused for a moment. Capt. Vitas moved towards him, recognizing that it would be hard for Artemis to return for the money. He held out his hand until Artemis placed his beneath it and took the coins. They shook hands and held the firm embrace for a time, eyes locked on each other. It is amazing how much can be said without words or motions when hearts are connected.

"We will be making camp a few miles down the road for the night if you should change your mind about joining us. You are a wise man and I'm sure you will know what you need to do. Thanks for the medicine—it has helped much. For now, good-bye my friend." said the captain.

We followed the evening sun westward from the town and made our way along the road from Tiberias. There were other people going and coming along the hard packed roadway. I found myself thinking how good it was to be with other people for a change. My mind began turning back to life in Athens and I wondered what my family was doing on this evening. I wanted so badly to know if Marco's little brother, Stephan, had made it safely home. I wanted to know if my mother was still crying herself to sleep at night. How were Marco's parents doing? When would we see them again? So many thoughts came rushing in that I completely lost awareness of where I was or what I was doing. It was only when Marco grabbed me by the arm and called out my name that I came to realize I was back on that road with my friends. We were well out into the country by now and the sun was nearly below the horizon. Once more, we enjoyed a beautiful sunset with a sky full of orange, red, and purple colors broken only by the newly budding branches of trees reaching up to take in life from above. Such magnificent displays served to bolster my hope of finding the One who created this beauty. I knew in my heart that the fantastic sunset we had seen could not have come from the work of any of the gods we had worshiped back in Greece. There simply had to be more to life and I had every reason to believe that we were getting closer to finding it.

"That looks like a good place to make camp up there on the left. Plenty of cover from those pines and we can tell if someone is comin' up on us. What do the rest of you think?" Ben spoke up, breaking quite a long silence.

"Looks fine to me." Alexus agreed.

"Try to rake up a nice thick bed of those pine needles for Capt. Vitas to sleep on. We want to keep him warm and dry as we can. He's been doin' fine but we don't want no set-backs do we Captain?" said Ben.

"I appreciate your thoughtfulness and I certainly don't want to slow us down by getting sick again. It looks like you have picked a good place to camp. If you don't mind, I think I'll go on to bed now and rest. I still feel tired and chilled from time to time." Capt. Vitas replied.

"Go right ahead, Capt. Do you want us to fix you somethin' hot to eat? Won't take long." Cirro asked.

"If you have any broth, that would be good." Capt. Vitas answered.

"Comin right up!" Cirro replied.

I found this to be incredibly amazing. Here was a seasoned sea captain being waited on by men who had taken orders from him, sometimes orders that left these men feeling bitter or angry. Now, they were treating him like he was their own father, or perhaps, even better. What was it that made these rough and tough seamen turn into kind and considerate caretakers? What benefit could they gain by showing such concern for this man? After giving the matter much thought, I concluded it was probably a combination of different things, the greater being that Capt. Vitas had earned the respect of these men. He had treated them fairly and kindly. Now, they were returning his kindness. Another reason was that these men's hearts were changing. It was a change that could be seen almost on a daily basis. I had expected the Truth we sought to change our lives, at least to some degree, but I was perplexed to understand how these changes could happen before we even found this Truth. An even greater question in my mind was how I was changing. I definitely knew something had changed inside me only twenty-four hours ago—there was no doubting that. But what could the other see in me? Was I going through the same kind of changes they were? Had they noticed any change in me in the way I had seen them changed? Unanswered questions and thoughts too deep for resolution—but I was only 18 years old. How could I be expected to know answers to matters like these? What I did know for sure was that I was tremendously encouraged to know my friends and I were being drawn closer to knowing the Truth.

Once more, Marco brought me to reality and announced it was time for us to turn in for the night. What would I do without such a friend to help me?

## CHAPTER EIGHT

# THROUGH THE STORM

We must have been more tired than we thought as we slept well past daybreak. Breakfast was fixed and camp was nearly cleared when we noticed a man coming up to us. In the early morning light we could not tell who this man was until he was nearly upon us.

(Monday Morning)

"I think that's Artemis! Don't it look like him?" Ben asked as he tried his best to see who was approaching.

"Could be, but what's he doing out here this early? He would have had to start out in the middle of the night to get here this early. Alexus wondered aloud.

"Maybe so, but you can ask him when he gets here. No doubt about it! It's him." Marco said.

"Good mornin' to you all!" Artemis said as he walked up to the remains of our campfire. "See you have gotten soft since you left the sea and turned into late risers. Sun's been up nearly an hour now."

"Well, has all them years of fishin' made you silly enough to go roamin' about in the middle of the night? You must have been up three or fours hours to get here by now." speculated Cirro.

"Actually, I haven't slept at all since we parted last evenin'. I went back down to the docks and talked to some of my friends for a while. I just couldn't get what you all said out of my mind and then I knew what I had to do. You see, there is somethin' I haven't told you that I think is really important." Artemis said.

His answer to Cirro took us somewhat by surprise and we became more serious as we anticipated hearing what he was about to tell us.

"Yesterday morning when you came runnin' up to my boat,—it wasn't just some accident that you found me. In fact, it was almost like I was there waitin' on you." he began to explain but was soon interrupted by Alexus.

"What do you mean, waiting on us? How could you know we were coming?" Alexus wanted to know.

"Five days ago, I heard a voice or somethin' in my head tell me that I was to take some men from Bethsaida in my boat where they wanted to go and that I was to go with them. Now I ain't been one to drink much and have never heard anythin'like that before in my life. To tell you the truth, it scared me half to death. At first, I didn't know what to do about it so I just put off doing anythin' and then I heard it again. This time I was told to get into my boat and wait. Now, this was yesterday morning and I figured I had better do what I was told, so that's what I was doin' when you came up. And when you started tellin' about lookin' for this God—well, I just about wanted to jump in the lake to get away from you all. It was just gettin' too much for me, let me tell you. You was sayin' things that I had heard others talk about and I figured you either had to be right or else into somethin' I wanted no part of. Then all the things you was sayin' to me last night as we left—I knowed you was right but I just couldn't get myself to go with you. I really wanted to but I just couldn't. I walked around for three or four hours tryin' to get it off me but it wouldn't go. Finally, I knew I had no choice but to sell my boat, take care of some business, and then, find you. So, here I am." he explained.

"You mean you heard a voice tell you to pick us up and take us across the lake? Was it loud? What did it sound like?" Marco asked with a volley of questions.

"No, it wasn't loud,—just a clear voice tellin' me to do these things. It was just like somebody talkin' to me except it was inside my head. With all the things I've been hearin' bout, well, I just know there is things to be found out. I'm ready to go with you all to see what's what." Artemis went on explaining.

"Well, you're sure welcome to come along. I know you'll be able to help us know where to go, but I got a feelin' you got some pretty good ideas concernin' these teachin's we're hearin' about. Anyway, it's good to have you. Now, maybe I will have someone to talk to." Ben said as he went about gathering up his belonging.

"We're all glad to have you, Artemis, but the day is getting away from us. We need to be on our way." Capt. Vitas reminded us.

We gathered our belongings once more and kicked out the fire as we headed back on the pathway to Jerusalem. There seemed to be an unusual quietness among us we made our way down the road. I know my mind was diligently working to comprehend the depth and wonderment of what Artemis had told us. What encouragement I found in knowing that a great power was working to make sure we were helped on our way. Artemis' story would have been unbelievable to most people, but we had experienced this super-natural intervention before. It was not so much in unbelief that we were quiet, but more so, with reverent awe and appreciation. Knowing that the Truth we were seeking was working to help us along the way was not only comforting, it was downright overwhelming.

"You been down this way often, Artemis? Do you know bout how far one town is from another?" Ben asked.

"I've been down past Jerusalem a couple of times—even went out to sea from Joppa once. I guess you could say that I got a pretty good idea of the lay of the place." Artemis answered.

"If my recollection is right, we should be able to camp on the far side of Nazareth tonight. I figure its about seventeen or eighteen miles from here, so we ought to be there early this evening." Capt. Vitas commented.

"I don't feel as sure as you do about that, Capt. I'm pickin' up the smell of some rough weather comin' in. I can feel it in my bones too. I'd say by early afternoon we could be gettin' wet if we haven't found shelter by then. I'll be keepin' my eye on the sky cause I don't want you rained on til you get to feelin' better." Ben commented as he scanned the sky for the clouds that would prove his predictions right.

"Let's just keep putting one foot in front of the other as often and steadily as we can and hope to get as far as we can before we have to contend with that. Your kindness is appreciated though. Thank you, Ben." Capt. Vitas replied.

We did just that. One foot in front of the other. It was strange, but I noticed how talking about each step we took drew my attention to the very sounds of our steps. Sometimes you can hear sounds and not even notice them at all. Yet, when something or someone makes you aware of them, you cannot seem to escape them. At least they broke the silence that overtook our group as we made our way to Jerusalem.

As noon approached, the sun was nearly obscured by clouds that were coming in from the west. A balmy breeze was picking up and it was getting quite warm for a change. Ben kept watch on the sky and we noticed he kept squeezing his elbows. After some time, Marco decided to ask Ben about it

"What's the matter, Ben? Your arms bothering you?"

"It's gonna be a rough one, I'm tellin' ya. All my joints are achin'. Just wait and see." Ben replied.

"You could be right. There is something unusual about the way the air feels, that's for sure." Marco answered.

We continued on our way and soon came to the town of Sepphoris. We found the crossroad that indicated Nazareth was to the left so we made our turn and headed south once more. Just outside of the town we came upon a peaceful looking spot with several trees scattered around, so we decided to rest there for a short time. It was a good place to rest and we were surprised to see a number of people come by. For the most part, they appeared to be going about the business of getting goods from one place to another. It didn't take long before Ben was up pacing and checking the sky again.

"We had better get on our way before Ben wears us all out just watching him." Capt. Vitas said with a gentle laugh.

"Laugh now if you want but you had better hope to find somewhere to get in when this storm hits. Mark my words!" Ben retorted.

Almost in unison we got to our feet and slung our packs over our shoulders to continue our journey. As we made our way south toward Nazareth we began to notice that the people we met along the road had a more sullen expression on their face than those we had met earlier in the day. No one in our group said anything but it was apparent that we were all taking notice of each person we met. A few of them would nod or even speak a word or two to us—others wouldn't even look up to indicate they knew we shared the same road with them.

"Best just to smile and nod to 'em. No use tryin' to figure out what's makin' 'em so unsociable." Ben commented.

"That's good advice, Ben. There's something about the way these folks is actin' makes me feel like we're headed into somethin' worse than this storm that's about to break loose. Let's keep movin' and try to make it to Nazareth ahead of this weather. It should be less than a couple of miles." Artemis said.

We had only gone about a mile when we felt raindrops. At first they seemed almost pleasant. I found myself sticking out my tongue to catch them. They tasted so fresh and cool—even with a bit of sweetness about them. Their pleasure was to be short-lived as the scattered drops rapidly turned in to a steady rain that soon had us soaked. The wind also was picking up and the sky grew darker.

"If I remember right, there is a small cave just ahead in that ridge off to the right. We better try to hold up there until this has passed on by!" Artemis said as he led the way toward the rocky hill he had pointed out.

By the time we reached the dark hole Artemis had remembered, hailstones were falling almost as fast as the rain and lightning was striking trees just off to the west of us. The cave had a large overhang of rock above it that gave us shelter from the hail but the lightning was striking dangerously close to us. We all moved quickly into the dark hole that was only dimly lit when the lightning flashed nearby. It wasn't easy to make our way into the cave since the floor was covered with rough stones and wet, slippery mud. Even with the storm raging outside, the cave caused our voices to seem like we were yelling.

"We should be far enough in now to be safe. Best not try to go further and risk falling. Everybody all right? You all make it in?" Artemis asked. "Just sit tight and we'll be fine now. It's gonna' take this one a while to move on over."

It was now fairly quiet in the cave except for the clashes of thunder and occasional howl of the wind blowing across the cave opening. The safety and security of the cave must have caused us to calm down because we were now talking just above a whisper as we checked to see if we were all accounted for.

The storm began to grow even more fierce. The wind blew across the mouth of the cave so strongly that mist from the rain was coming back in nearly as far as we were. Then, suddenly the storm seemed to stop. It became so quiet outside that it seemed not to be natural. Marco started to make his way out to see what was going on. As he brushed past Ben, he felt a strong hand grasp his arm.

"Don't go out there! She's not done yet. She's just got started!"

Marco stopped in his tracks. I can't say what was going on with the others but I know for a certain that there was a lump in my throat that was about to strangle me. I'm not sure but I think I heard some of the others in our group gasping for air. Then for what seemed like several minutes, there was not a sound to be heard except for the heavy breathing of brave men who were now scared speechless.

"Ben, you can let go of my arm now." Marco said with a weakness in his voice that showed he was hoping it was Ben who had a hold of it.

' "Sorry Marco, but that ain't me. I'm over here." Ben answered with a quiver in his voice that I had never heard before.

"Artemis?" Marco questioned, this time with a tone that was made stronger as fear began to grow.

"Not me! I'm back here behind Ben." Artemis assured him.

"Well, let go and tell me which one of you said that!" said Marco with anger rising in his voice.

"It wasn't none of them. I'll let go of you but just stay put! I mean you no harm." said the same voice. "That storm out there is fixing to tear things up good. I've seen them before. Just stay—"

"Who are you and how—? I started to ask

"My name is Nathan and I was wise enough to seek shelter here before I got drenched as you all are. You nearly knocked me down as you came barging in. No harm done though and this cave seems to have enough room for all of us. Beside, I can't ask you to go out in a storm like this one so we might as well make the best of it. Now, there are six of you—is that right?" the stranger asked.

"There are seven of us but how could you—" I start to say but was cut off by this new man, Nathan.

"Would any of you by chance have a candle and flint in those packs you are carrying? he asked.

"I think we might have what you need. Marco, you and Nik see if you can find some. You are a very astute man, Nathan. We do apologize for intruding into your cave but then, I assume this isn't your cave or else you would have had your own candle and flint—am I right?" asked Capt. Vitas in a manner that let Nathan know we were not going to be subjects of his domineering attitude.

Before anything else could be said, the wind screamed across the opening of the cave with such force it nearly pulled us out of the cave. We heard trees snapping and thunder once more clashed through the skies. The storm raged intensely for several minutes. The rain was being blown far back into the cave but we didn't want to move because the rocky floor was now even more dangerous to step on. Finally the fury of the storm subsided but the rain continued to pour down.

Marco helped me look for the candles and flint when the storm let up. Marco's flint rock was too wet to work but mine seemed to be dry enough to try. We soon had two candles burning which lit up the small cave we found ourselves standing in. As our eyes grew accustomed to the dim light, we noticed a few small pieces of wood that someone had been using for a fire just a few more feet into the cave. I knew we needed to get Capt. Vitas dried out and kept from getting cold. We used the candles to get a nice fire burning and could finally see each others faces once more.

"We'll need to get more wood to keep this fire going. I'm going out to get some while there is still enough hot fire left to dry out what I bring in." Marco said as he made his way out into the rain.

"I'll help you, Marco." I said as I followed him out.

"May I have your candle? I want to see where this smoke is going. It seems to be drawn back into the cave further. I want to see what is back there." Nathan asked.

Ben gave him a candle and the two of them made their way back into the cave. Marco and I soon returned with enough wood to last a few hours. We didn't have time to tell the others what we saw outside the cave before Ben and Nathan returned from checking out the cave.

"We won't be able to stay here, in fact, we need to leave now." Nathan reported.

"We don't need to take Capt. Vitas out in this rain. Mister, you're not makin' it easy for me to take a likin' to ya. I think—" Alexus stated to say.

"No, Alexus. He's right. We need to get out now. This cave is a part of a stream that will soon be overflowin' from all this rain. We can't stay here." Ben interjected to stop any arguments that might be building.

"I noticed an old barn just back up the road toward Nazareth. It won't be the best but I think it might keep the rain off. Do you have anything to hold out to keep a couple of these burning logs from getting wet? Maybe the captain could carry them and be kept from getting too wet " asked Nathan.

"You sure are one to give orders but the thing is—you seem to be makin' good sense. I reckon we had better listen to him. We got to get out of here, that's for certain." Ben said as he pulled one of the old sails from his pack.

We left the cave and stepped into a world that looked much different than the one we saw only moments ago. Trees were twisted and broken. The tiny new leaves that showed promise of spring were now scattered all over the ground. We had to climb over fallen limbs and tree trunks as we made our way to the road. From the looks of the trees, I was wandering if the old barn would still be standing. There wasn't much that was left untouched by the storm. We even found a wooden plank with a ships name on it. Capt. Vitas recognized the name and said it would have had to come all the way in from the Mediterranean. That was hard to imagine but this had been some storm.

"I think that should be the barn over there." Nathan said as we stepped over what looked like the last tree in our path.

It was remarkable! We had just walked out of a tangled mess of limbs, uprooted trees, and splintered trunks and found ourselves standing in an area that was apparently untouched by the storm. The old barn was standing there waiting for us to come into its shelter.

Our group made its way to the old barn and found it to be fairly dry inside. We cleared a place on the dirt floor to place the glowing wood Capt. Vitas had carried and soon had flames leaping out to warm us again. For several minutes our conversation was centered on the storm and the damage it had caused. However, the subject abruptly changed when Nathan asked us where we were going and why we were traveling in a group?

"We're headed south and we are together cause we want to be, not that it should be your business to know." Ben answered with in a sharp tone that said more than the words he spoke.

"No need to be offended. I was simply asking where you were going because it has become somewhat dangerous to be traveling in certain areas. There has been a lot of conflict, especially around Jerusalem. It doesn't take much to get killed if you say the wrong things to the wrong people. If you was one of them who followed Jesus, you will have both the Jews and the Romans out to do you in. That's all—." Nathan responded but was interrupted by Marco.

"What do you know about Jesus and His followers?" he asked quickly.

"Not a lot, personally. My brother, Thaddaeus took up with Him and became one of his closest friends. As for me, I think they were all too unstable to be trusted. Even Jesus's family thought he was crazy. I tried to get Thaddaeus to break away and come with me but he wouldn't hear of it. I'm heading up north to get away until things settle back down." Nathan answered.

"Then you do know something about him?" Alexus retorted, hoping to corner Nathan into telling us more.

"What I can tell you about him and those who follow him is that nearly every word they speak makes them enemies to those in charge, be they Jew or Roman. The one called John was killed some time ago and now, there are serious rumors out that some are plotting Jesus's death. My own brother insists on remaining with Jesus and his men in spite of my warnings that he is in great danger. He has told me that the teachings of Jesus are of great value to him and he is willing to die for them—-those teachings hold no such value for me and, therefore, I chose to protect my life and avoid any association with my brother and his friends. I suggest that you do the same if you value your lives." Nathan replied.

"I suppose much depends on what factors one uses to determine the value of life. Perhaps you have peace with your decision but, as for me, your advice will not provide contentment. The rain has stopped now and I think we should be on our way. Thank you, Nathan, for sharing the cave with us and telling us about this shelter. We will hinder you no longer than necessary." Capt. Vitas said with a noticeable courtesy that hinted of a strong dislike for the advice Nathan had given.

"It is late in the day and since you have already found shelter and have a warm fire going, please stay and let me be on my way. I will have no problem finding another place for the night. I travel with light baggage and a light heart." Nathan countered as he walked out of the old shed and made his way back toward the road.

"Can't say I'm sorry to see him go." Alexus said after waiting until Nathan was out of hearing.

"Oh, there is sorrow in it but each person has to make their own decisions." Capt. Vitas replied.

We considered leaving the old barn and trying to travel on before nightfall. We still had a few hours left before it would be too dark to see. Before we could gather our things, a strong northwest wind began to blow and the temperature started falling. Winter had returned to chase away any thoughts of spring, at least for the present. We busied ourselves with covering a doorway and open window to stop the cold air from sweeping through the little shed. Although it was still cold in our home for the night, we had succeeded in stopping the drafts. Great care was taken to keep Capt. Vitas warm and protected.

(Tuesday Morning)

Morning came with a bright sunrise and the winds had died down considerably. It was still very cool but the sun helped us to get an early start on our journey. It only took just over two hours before we were walking through the streets of Nazareth. We were all anxious to make up for the time we lost during the storm so we purposely stayed near the center of the street and kept our pace steady—hoping to avoid any further delay.

"Isn't this the town Jesus was from?" I asked as we continued on.

"Yes, it was his hometown but he wasn't treated very well when he visited here awhile back." Artemis answered.

"I can believe that from what I've heard about this place. It ain't a town known for its high moral values." interjected Ben.

"To me, it looks like a nice town for the most part. This street down this way has a lot of small shops on it. Hold up for a minute! I want to go down there just for a few minutes." I said as a grabbed hold of Marco's coat.

"What are you looking for? Let's not stir up more trouble." warned Alexus.

"Just let me have a couple of minutes to check out something . It has been said that Jesus grew up working in his father's carpentry shop here in Nazareth. I want to see if it could be down here. I won't be long, I promise." I begged.

Without waiting for their approval, I dashed off down the street , leaving my companions standing in disbelief. I ran past three or four shops and soon came to a small wood shop that was closed. Next to it was little store with an old lady selling cheese. I did my best to communicate with her and was finally able to learn that the wood shop had indeed been the one Jesus grew up in. I started to return to my friends but was held captive for a few minutes by the articles that hung on the walls of the shop. I wondered how many of them Jesus had actually made with his very own hands—the man who is God.

"Nikos! Come on, we must be on our way." shouted Marco as he brought my attention back to the present.

I rejoined my group but remained rather quiet for a time as I struggled to understand how someone who is supposed to be God could also be a man who worked on wooden tools and furnishings. I found myself wishing I could have brought one of the items off the walls of the shop to keep— just in case Jesus had really made it.

"We'll be well down into Samaria by the end of the day if we can keep this pace up." Artemis said. "There will be some long stretches between towns. Long as we got what we need on our backs, we should make good time."

"Only thing I need right now is a donkey's back to be on. My feet are goin' to be worn down to nubs by the time we get to where ever it is we're goin'." Cirro commented.

The sun was well on its way to meet the western horizon when we decided to stop to rest and eat for the first time that day. It was only after we sat down that we began to feel just how tired we had become. Alexus offered to start making something for us to eat as he stood watch in order for the rest of us to take a short nap. After walking for eight hours without stopping, it wasn't long before sleep overtook us. It seemed like only a few minutes before Alexus was rolling us around with his big foot in a effort to wake us up. The first words I heard him say were something about Roman soldiers. As I tried to let his words register in my brain, I could see the soldiers coming toward us. There were about nine of them and they were armed with swords and spears. The commander of the men soon singled out Marco and myself to be his focus of attention.

"Where are you from? he demanded from us.

"We are citizens of Athens, sir." I replied.

"What business do you have here, being so far from Athens?" the commander asked.

"These men are part of my crew. They have sailed with me to Tyre and we are looking for new shipping business as we wait for spring to come. My name is Capt. Vitas. Now, how can we be of help to you?" the captain interjected.

I could tell he had stepped into the conversation in an effort to prevent the soldiers from intimidating us into giving out more information than we needed to. He was a shrewd man and he had now countered the soldiers confrontation by putting questions to them. He was masterful at that. I could tell he already had three or four more questions waiting to be asked. He knew most people in authoritative positions don't like being asked questions. Either they will abruptly stop your attempt to question them or they will, and this is the more normal response, become so uneasy at even being questioned that they will leave quickly.

"Then what are you doing this far inland?" demanded the commander, attempting to ignore Capt. Vitas' question.

"Well, there is merchandise in other places besides the coastal cities to be traded. Now what is it that you might be looking to find?" Capt. Vitas continued.

The commander glared at Marco and me for a moment as he pondered what Capt. Vitas had said.

Without even turning his eyes from us to answer he said. "See to it that you tend to your business and don't let me find you poking your nose where it don't belong. I won't be so friendly next time."

The commander slowly turned toward Alexus, Cirro, and Ben; looking us over as if to imprint our faces into his memory, but he avoided looking at Capt. Vitas and Artemis. Finally he clutched his hand to the handle of his sword and walked off, leading the others with him.

"How did you know you could get rid of those men that fast, Capt. Vitas?" Marco asked.

"I didn't, really. I just figured there was a good chance that I could beat him as his own game. You see, he seemed to have such an attitude of pride and power about him—especially with eight other men behind him. Now if you can ever get at that pride in a man like that—well he won't want to let any of that go. It was more important for him to leave us with his pride intact than to find out about us. But, let me warn you—be careful about it. I can get away with it most of the time because I act like a naive old man and the biggest nuisance you ever run into. It's got me out of trouble a many a time." Capt. Vitas replied.

We spent the remainder of the night at the spot where we had stopped to rest. Our plan was to be up all the more early to get a start on our way.

(Tuesday Night)

# CHAPTER NINE

# HELP FROM THE PAST

L ess than two hours into our journey the next morning, we came upon a small settlement of Ginae. Several people were gathered around two men who were excitedly telling about something. Our curiosity was too strong to be deterred by the threat of more angry natives, therefore we found ourselves standing at the rear of the gathering, looking for an opening to move closer and find out what the excitement was all about. The words we heard next gained our full attention. We were able to understand much of what was being said and Artemis knew enough of their language to help us with what we didn't know. He didn't hesitate to ask a man standing next to him for help in getting the rest of the story.

One of men continued speaking, "I'm telling you I've been dead for over forty years and my new friend here for over a year. We were buried in the hills just this side of Emmaus. I swear what we are telling you is the truth! We both just came out of the grave!"

"You must be insane! No one comes out of the grave—especially after that long of time." protested one of the crowd.

"Think what you want but I'm telling you what happened. There was a great earthquake that seemed to have woke me up. Next thing I know, the stones over my grave are taken away and up I come. I don't even remember getting up. I just came up!" the man tried to explain to those around him.

"Just recently we've heard of people coming out of their tombs but this was only after a few days—not for more than a year-or forty years! Your flesh! It doesn't show any decay!" commented another of the crowd.

"Were there any witnesses to your escape from the grave?" asked another.

"Yes, but you're missing the importance of all this. We are here before you, having been dead for all this time and we now are speaking with you. Where is your faith? Can't you believe us?" countered the other man.

"We are trying to understand so we can believe. We need to know what has happened so as to know what to believe." protested another of the crowd.

"My friends, you only need to believe to understand. I wish I could help you, but, ultimately, that is something only you can do. All I can do is tell you of what I know and have seen." replied the second of the two men.

As I looked around to see where my friends were, I was amazed to find that all our group was now at the front of the crowd surrounding these two men. Our complete attention was hanging on every word and, with the emphasis that was placed on believing, we had to hear more. Other people in the crowd began talking and debating with each other about what they had heard. I noticed that the two men who claimed to be back from the grave were examining the crowd, trying to assess their response to all that was being told. At first, they caused me to feel skeptical about the way they were measuring their influence with the people. It was only after I noticed tears starting to roll down the face of the second man that I was convinced that their story was genuine. It wasn't only the tears but the heart that was revealed behind those tears that assured me of their sincerity.

After having time to talk among themselves, the crowd now returned their attention to the two men.

"Are you the only two people to come back to life?" asked one.

"No, there have been many others as well. All over this region, I have been told." replied the first "What do you think caused your grave to be opened—and those of the other as well?" asked another.

"It seems all the graves were opened just after a huge earthquake and an unusual darkness in the middle of the day—" the man started to answer but was cut off by our very own Ben.

"What about this darkness in the daytime? What do you know of it.?" Ben asked with a sense of urgency.

"Yes, tell us what it was or what it meant." chimed in another in the crowd. "Oh, haven't you heard about the death of Jesus?" asked the first man.

"Of Jesus!!! Is he dead?" I asked.

"Yes, he was put to death just as all this happened, the earthquake, the darkness, and our return to the living. I thought you would have heard by now. Many people in Jerusalem are mourning His death and many have lost hope. But we are here to tell you not to give up hope—this is not the end." he answered.

This news caused another round of discussion among the crowd. Most of the conversations were kept just above a whisper. Our group gathered over to one side as we talked about what Jesus' death might mean to our journey. Even though we had heard many people tell us that plots to kill Jesus were being planned, it was still hard to believe. Just to think of all the un-asked questions that would not be answered was a great disappointment to me..

"Do you think we still need to go on to Jerusalem?" Ben asked. "If He ain't there then what's the use of goin' there?"

"There will be many people there who knew him and have talked with him. They will be able to help us. I think it would be foolish to turn back now." Capt. Vitas replied.

"Don't be so disappointed." said the first man as he overheard us talking. "The Jesus you look for may have been put to death, but it wasn't a death that could hold Him. It has been written that God would send his

Son to be given over to death for us—only to defeat death and sin. The One you seek can still be found."

"How would you know so much about this Jesus? You've been dead long before He was born." argued one of the crowd.

"The Word of God tells us much about Jesus. If fact, it says He has been right there with God from the beginning—and just a few years after my death, God sent Him to be born among men. It was my body that was dead—not my spirit." he responded.

"I don't believe anything you've said. In fact, I think you are out of your mind and I won't listen to any more such nonsense." declared one of the crowd as he turned to leave and several others followed.

"Do you know what is going on in Jerusalem now? Are Jesus' followers in danger?" Marco asked.

"I really can't answer that since we decided to head north to escape the turmoil. I, for one, am not eager to return to the grave just yet." replied the second man.

"Forgive me for asking again, but I must admit, I am more than a little confused by what you have told us. You're saying that Jesus was with God from the beginning, then He was born as a baby here in this country, has been killed, and now is alive! How can this—" I started to ask but was cut off by the man.

"Yes, it is a lot to comprehend. But it is all for a purpose and not just some accidental chain of events. What has happened in the last few days will change mankind from now on. The Way of salvation has come." he answered. "Now go on your way for you are soon to embrace the Truth you seek."

For a couple of moments we stood facing the two men, more correctly we stood looking into each others eyes and continued a conversation without words. We could see into their souls that they had already found what we were searching for and they saw into our hearts that we would be coming into a fullness of our desire. We parted their company with a handshake and a smile.

As we continued on our way towards Jerusalem, a somber mood overtook our group. It was very difficult for us to imagine anything good could come from Jesus being killed. I know that I had my heart set on meeting with Him. I wanted to be able to learn as much from the tone and emphasis of His words as I would from the words themselves. There was so much to learn about all those we had met on the way just by watching them as they shared with us. I wondered what His eyes might have revealed to us as we looked into them. That opportunity, if it ever existed, was now gone forever it seemed. One thing, however kept coming back to my mind. It was what the man who had come back from the grave said about Jesus still being alive. I pondered on this for some time before deciding to ask Marco his opinion on the matter. By this time we were probably five miles down the road.

"Marco, what do you make of what we have heard from those two men? Do you believe all they have told us?" I began asking.

"I guess I do, but, you have to admit, part of what they said puts a strain on accepting it." he answered.

"If He was really put to death, do you think He has come back to life again?" I continued.

"If those two could come up from the grave, who is to say that Jesus couldn't have done it as well?" Marco replied.

"I know, but my mind is bouncing back and forth. I get to the place where I believe everything that was said today—even to the point of getting excited about it, and then I find myself getting angry at the thought of another myth being presented. If I tried to explain all this to our friends back in Athens, they would say that it sounds no different from the stories about any other god we were taught about there." I said in an effort to explain my thoughts to Marco.

"Well, that's the difference right there! See, every time we have encountered any of these people who have talked with us about Jesus, we have had something happen within us that helped us to believe. That wasn't the case when we talked with our friends about back in Athens, in fact,—and I know you have had this happen to you—it was just the opposite. Something inside us rebelled at what we were taught. It was as if our inner being was rejecting it. Not so with what we learn of Jesus. Think on that, now! Don't that make sense to you and help your mind to stop bouncing?" Marco replied.

"Can you say you believe in all this without any doubt at all?" I asked.

After looking at me intently for a moment as he thought over his answer, Marco said, "Without a doubt at all!"

"I wasn't meanin' to be listenin' in on your private talk, but I couldn't help hearin' a lot of what you had to say and I want you to know that what you're feelin' is exactly what's inside me." Ben spoke up . We had been so engrossed in our own little world for a time that we had not noticed the others in our group. When we looked back at the rest of our group, we could see that they must have been in the same struggle as we were and were now ready to believe with us.

"I think that man was right back there when he said we would soon be embracing the Truth. You two young men have extraordinary hearts— hearts of courageous leaders. I wouldn't be at all surprised if we discover what we search for before we reach Jerusalem." Capt. Vitas said.

"I'm not so sure you ain't already found it." Artemis added.

Those words from Artemis took my mind instantly back to the night we had camped in the rock above Bethsaida and how I had felt such a stirring in my soul. I remembered those beautiful stars and how God had created them and how He must have known me. I really hoped I had found the truth I so desperately wanted, but I was left unsure of it. Why couldn't I know for sure? What was yet missing? Was there more that I should do to be sure? Was someone else to do something to help me? All these question came racing through my mind without settling down to rest long enough to give individual thought to. As badly as I wanted to agree with what Artemis had said, I knew in my heart that there was something yet to find.

We traveled on in silence for a while. The weather had returned to being more spring-like and the sun provided ample warmth to us as we made our way south. Our shadows were falling behind us as we begin to talk about stopping to eat. We found a grassy area off to the side of the road and removed our packs. The soft grass we sat on felt so relaxing that I felt tempted to sleep rather than bother eating. My mind was still whirling with questions and theories. I found mental exercise could be even more exhausting than physical labor. Deciding that it would be best to be prepared for the afternoons journey, I half-heartedly reached into my pack for some dried meat to chew on. I continued with my thinking until I heard Marco asking me something. I had to clear my mind for a second to come back to reality. I saw that Marco and myself had settled down a little distance from the others and I had to ask him what he had just said.

"I was wondering if you had noticed we haven't been talking among ourselves nearly as much as we used to. Cirro and Alexus haven't hardly said anything for days now." he repeated.

"I've noticed. It seems you and I haven't said much to the others either. I guess it might be because of hearing about Jesus dying and all. We have learned a lot and it has given us much to think about. I know its been causing me considerable effort to understand all that is going on with our group." I replied.

"I know, but it seems we are drifting apart from what we once were. Especially Alexus and Cirro—it's like they're still walking along with us but, in a sense, they are growing more distant." Marco added.

"What do you think we can do to get us back to where we were?" I asked him.

"I guess the only thing I know to do is to make time to really talk with one another. Find out what has been on our hearts. Remember when Cirro shared about what happened to him a few nights ago? We need more of that. It really helped me to know what was going on in the rest of us. It gave me encouragement." he answered.

"Fine! That's settles it! Tonight it is." I said with a voice that grew in volume and I got up and made my way amongst the others in our group. "We will be making camp tonight early enough to allow us plenty of time to just be together. No visitors, no new friends we meet on the way—just us. Marco and I will do the cooking just like we did on the ship. So let's get picked up and on our way. We need to make a few more miles yet today."

After I finished my impromptu speech, I found myself wondering what I had just said. I was giving orders to Capt. Vitas! I had assumed the command of our group, if it was only for the moment. This was not like me at all. What came over me, I do not know. It just seemed it was the right thing to say at the time and I saw no value in waiting for a better opportunity. I wanted to apologize to my friends for abruptly ordering them to follow my command but, for some reason, I felt that it was best not to do so. Before I had much chance to look around, all of the group was getting up with their packs swung over their shoulder and headed back to the road. I turned to Marco, looking for his reaction to what had just happened. His only response was a shrug of the shoulders and a big smile. We were on our way once more.

Our walk throughout the afternoon kept up at a brisk pace. Ben, Artemis, and Capt. Vitas started us out by leading the way. It wasn't long before Alexus and Cirro moved up to the front of our ranks and led us for most of the afternoon. It was early evening when we came around a bend in the road and saw a rather large city built on a hilltop. Artemis told us it was Samaria or, as Herod decided to call it, Sebaste. It was such a beautiful sight! The whole city was setting on a huge mound with rows of houses and buildings arranged in concentric circles. The late afternoon sun made the western part of the city gleam with a brilliant whiteness that contrasted the shadows of the eastern side. We paused for a while as we stood surveying the city before us. Even when we continued on our way we all kept gazing at the beautiful city. We had not seen any like it since we had left Greece.

Before we got too close the outskirts of the city, I began to look for a good place to make camp. I soon noticed a grassy slope several yards off the roadway and pointed in that direction as I told the group that we would be camping there for the night. I wasn't sure what caused me to know even what to look for in a campsite and why I should be the one to choose it, but there was certainly a definite sense working in me that this was to be the place and that I needed to tell the others. It was beyond my ability to explain why it was important and it was growing increasingly difficult not to obey the leading I was feeling.

"We'll have a good place hear for the night, being at a good vantage point from the road and we can make shelter among these trees with the sails. It should be pretty comfortable. If the rest of you will set up for the night, Marco and I will go look for whatever we can find in the way of something fresh for our supper. We should be back shortly." I said as I reached for an empty sack in my pack.

There I was giving orders again! It was beyond me what was going on. I was as much taken back as anyone. Even Marco mentioned as we headed out to look for food about how assertive I had become.

"I know we talked about how we needed to be drawn back together but you are taking this really serious. Do you have something in mind or want to tell me what is going on because you are not acting like yourself." Marco stated.

"I can't say that I have anything specific in mind except that I feel it is important for us all to get together this evening to share our thoughts and tell what is happening within each of us. We both know much has happened since we set foot in this land. We need to review the things we have learned from those along the way and go over our own personal experiences. I think it will help us understand much and will bring encouragement to all of us. I know I have had struggles with believing all that has occurred and questioned my own sanity. If our friends have been having to deal with that, I want this night to be of help to them. As for my bossy attitude, I can't explain that. It just seems like I feel compelled to make sure get this all done." I tried to explain.

"Oh, I'm not saying you are wrong—it's just so unlike you! Actually, I think you have a very good idea with this. I'm anxious to get back and get started." he answered.

We quickly found some greens and some roots to take back with us. By the time we return to camp the others had stretched the rope and canvas to make a nice shelter and had a fire going. The coals were just right to cook the roots we had found and we soon had the meal ready. The fresh food we had found made our supper one of the best we had eaten since we had landed in Tyre. I noticed that the casual conversation during the meal was more than it had been in several days. It was my hope that we could keep the same openness of heart going on into our time later in the evening.

(Wednesday night)

# CHAPTER TEN

# A LOOK BACK

As the last bites of our meal were being eaten, I began to grow more apprehensive about what to say to start off our discussion for the evening. I kept looking for an opening that might present itself. The others in our group continued to make casual conversation and small talk, but even that was tempered with an uneasiness amongst us. I could feel words starting to form in my throat and somehow catch before coming out. I could not understand why I was having such a struggle with this. I knew I was still confident about the need for such a time of sharing. I was being buffeted in a way I had not known before. Finally, I threw off the restraints that tried to pull me down and choke back the words I wanted to say. I tossed a stick I had been twisting in my hands into the fire and rose to my feet, saying,

"I know you all must be nearly as nervous as I am , but I can't let this night go by without trying to get us to the place I know we need to be. I'm not talking about some city or location. I mean a place where we know we want so badly to be, a place that will give us inner peace. I know you probably think that I am acting strange or different form what you know me to be, but I can't help that. What is stirring in me is too strong to just let it pass on by. I don't really want to be standing here before you saying these things, but I must. I'm certainly not comfortable in doing this, but my comfort is insignificant in comparison to what may be at stake here tonight."

"Nichos, maybe you don't feel like yourself, but I can tell you are on to somethin' You just keep goin' and say what's on you mind." encouraged Ben.

"Ya, that's right." added Alexus.

At first I was taken back by Alexus' words but then quickly felt tremendous help from them. He gave me an affirmation that I was headed in the right direction. I felt help welling up with me that I hadn't known before. It was like a strength rising up to give me more ability to work than was beyond my own power to do. I was increasingly becoming aware of a wisdom to know what to do and say that exceeded my own mental abilities. Had it not been for this tremendous power at work in me, I would have been so overcome with the awesome nature of it that I would have collapsed in my own weakness.

According to everything I knew about myself, I should have been speechless by now. Not so!

"Everyday since we have come together, we have experienced things that have given us encouragement and help to know that we have set our hearts on something that can provide a hope to us that most of the world does not know of. We have been put together for a common purpose of seeking a truth and that Truth is Jesus. When we started out, Jesus was a name that was associated with a teaching that held more hope than any other teaching to this day. Tonight, as we are gathered here, Jesus is no longer a name tied to a teaching. He has become so much more than that. He is hope, truth, and; I can't speak for you as to this specific quality; but as for me, He is a marvelous power working in me at this very moment. *I can feel Him in my spirit and even in my bones!!! He is real!!*" I shouted.

Capt. Vitas and Ben were weeping and Marco stood up only to fall to his knees and burst out crying. Cirro and Alexus sat with their eyes closed and heads tilted back, as if they were ready to take in whatever was going on around us. Artemis was looking to the heavens with a big smile on his face and his arms outstretched.

This was not what I had planned on saying tonight. I was more surprised than all the rest by what I had just said. It was only hours ago that I had confessed doubts about believing all the things we had heard of Jesus. Now, here I was, shouting my unshakable faith in Him to friends.

"It is so wonderful!! I want you all to have what is in me just now!!! I wish I could reach in and hand it out to you. I can't though. That's just it! I can't give it to you! You have to take it for yourselves. Aretmis, remember that voice you heard telling you to take some men over the lake? Believe in that!! Cirro, what about that angel you saw beckoning you? Get up and go to it. All of you, believe in what you have seen and heard here in this land. It has been the Truth. I can tell you, I have found it!!!!! I put my trust in Him. I can feel Him.. It is just like that night back in those rocks under those wonderful stars. How can He have so much love for someone like me?" I cried.

I was soon on my knees and then face down on the ground, crying harder than the rest. How can a young man feel so empty and yet so full all at the same time. As I lay there on the ground feeling humble and unworthy of what was happening to me, I noticed a peace sweeping over my mind. I found I was no longer trying to analyze and understand what was happening. I only wanted to let Jesus do what He wanted to do in me—to let Him pour into me and wash the things out of me He wanted out. I'm not sure how long I stayed on the ground. Time suddenly lost its relevance. As I began to become more aware of the others around me, I remembered the words of the two men who had returned from the grave.

'*The One you seek can still be found.*'

"He can be found!!! He can be! I've found Him!!!!" I shouted as I got up and ran about the others. "You can too!"

"Nik, what is it? What is happening in you?" Marco excitedly asked.

"Oh, Marco, if I could only tell you. It is so much more than I can find words for. I can feel such a warmth rising up through my body and if just seems to be so full that it is spilling over everywhere. I don't know how to describe it or know what it all means, but one thing I am sure of, *it is Jesus doing something in me!*" I answered, having trouble getting the words out while crying and being most joyful.

"Do you know for sure it is Jesus and not some other power working? How do you know it is Him?" asked Ben.

"Oh, I know sure as anything! If you could experience what is happening inside me, you would not have any doubts left at all. I feel Him in me!" I replied.

Capt. Vitas and Artemis were weeping as if they knew what I was telling them was absolute truth. Alexus and Cirro sat quietly listening to all that was going on around them. It seemed they wanted to be certain that this event was really God working in our midst. They seemed to want to be included in what I was experiencing but their skepticism held them back. Marco was now jumping around me as he held onto my arm and pulled me to him with his other hand. In fact, it was Marco's enthusiasm for me that cause me to realize that I needed to be careful not to put myself ahead of the others. I felt led to hold my exuberance back so as not to distance myself from the others. I wanted so desperately to get them to the wonderful place I was in. In my mind, I determined to get a firm grasp with one hand on what I had just experienced and reach out with the other to pull my friends in with me.

"This evening was supposed to be one for all of us. I still want it to be. I want you to share what is in your hearts and to know what your thoughts have been for the last several days. We have all had many things come before us that would be beyond belief had we not found solid grounds to build a trust to prepare us for them. It is important that each of us have an opportunity to tell what they feel. We can be an encouragement to one another." I said as I tried to quite down enough to talk plainly.

"What has happened with you has been a great encouragement to me. We're not far from what we have been seeking. It may very well be right here now. We just—". Artemis said with a broken voice, being unable to finish what he had started to say.

"What happened to you or what did you do to find Jesus just now?" asked Cirro. "Is there a special thing you have to do—like finding a key or saying something special?"

"All I know is that I was believing with everything in me that Jesus was all people have said He is and that He could still be found. I couldn't stop thinking about the other night up in those rocks when I saw those stars and felt how much He must care for me—just a tiny speck in this vast universe. I guess you could sum it up by saying I just believed in His love and gave my heart to Him." I replied.

"Nik and I want us all to be in this together. I know how strongly he feels about each one of you. He wants to make sure all of us hold together until we all find this Truth we desire so much. I think I understand what he meant when he said he can't give it to us. That gift is not his to give. I've know Nik long enough to know that he wants all of us to have what he's found. You can be sure of that." Marco said with a confident boldness that was meant to disperse any doubt.

"You're tellin' it right, Marco. In fact, I can't ever recall knowin' any young men with as much character in them as you two have. When someone I can trust like you tells me somethin', it's a lot easier to believe." Ben said.

"I've spent many years out on the sea and I've always trusted the nature of it to help me know what to do. Now, over the last months there has been a growing emptiness that assures me there is a lot more than nature that controls the sea and the men on it. That has drastically changed over the last day or two. Where the emptiness was, there is a solid trust. Where I have believed in nature, I now believe in the Creator of nature. I too, have put my faith in this Jesus and He has now filled my heart. He is alive in me!" Capt. Vitas shared.

"That's wonderful, Capt. Isn't He is just like what so many people have told us He would be!" I said as tears began rolling freely down my face. I was filled with such joy at knowing Capt. Vitas was having the same marvelous experience I was. My eyes were fixed on Capt. Vitas as I waited on him to continue describing what was going on in him. After a time, it was apparent that he wasn't going to say much more. He just sat quietly with his head tilted to the heavens and his eyes closed, letting tear after tear run down his face. It was easy to see that he had a full appreciation for the great work that was going on in him.

"Alexus, how are you and Cirro doin'? Neither of you has had much to say lately." commented Artemis.

"Hasn't been much reason to talk. There's been a lot of things happen— some of them pretty remarkable. I guess that is just it—they've been so strange and all that I just don't know how I feel about them. I've been doing a lot of sorting out in my mind. I can't speak for Cirro but, as for me; to be completely honest— I'm beginning to feel like I don't fit in." Alexus answered.

"Why do you say that? Have we done something to hurt you?" Marco asked.

"No, nothing like that. It is just that you all seem to be getting more out of this than I am. Maybe I just don't have it in me." he replied.

"Oh, it's in you all right. Alexus, remember when you showed us that part of Tyre with those little children living in poverty? That tells me you have the kind of heart that God can use. I've seen that tenderness of heart many times on our journey. Don't give up now—just press in harder." I said both as encouragement and as a gentle rebuke.

"That's about the way I've been feelin' too. It just seems that a lot of the things that is happening to you guys don't get to me. I don't feel the things you talk about and mostly I feel left out. I don't think it's your fault or anything, but, maybe we weren't supposed to be makin' this trip with you." Cirro commented.

"I don't believe that for an instant. We've been through too much together to even think that way.

I can't say why you haven't felt like a part of the things that have happened lately but I know for certain that you have contributed a lot to this journey. Both of you are important to me and the others." I protested.

"I don't mean this to sound harsh or hurtful, but you both need to quit feelin' so sorry for yourselves and put your shoulder into findin' what you desire and desirin' to know the truth. To be blunt about it, you ain't been doin' much of that. With me bein' the last to join up with you, I don't know you as well as the rest but I'm tellin' the truth to ya. I want you to be right in it with all of us but it takes tryin'. Real hard tryin'." Artemis said, looking Alexus and Cirro straight in the eye as he spoke to them.

"By the time things get to me they seem to have lost something. I just don't feel there is much there to get hold of." protested Cirro.

"Remember the night you saw that angel beckoning you? At first you said you were afraid. Then you wanted to go to it but didn't. Then it was gone. You need to have a trust in you for these things and don't hesitate so long. Be ready in your heart." I suggested.

"How can you be sure that these happenings are from God and not some evil spirit trying to trick us? You got to be watching out before jumping into things, especially when you are dealing with spirits." Alexus pointed out.

"That is why it is important to keep the things of God fresh in your mind and heart. Those things that are genuine, the things we know to be true; live in them every day. Then, when something comes along that is not of God, you will quickly know it." answered Capt. Vitas.

"Well, I clearly remember that deck hand who went crazy because some evil spirit got a hold of him while we were out to sea. I saw enough then to know I don't want no part of it. If it's all the same to you, Capt., I believe I'll take time to make sure before I go jumpin'." Cirro replied.

"It is a good thing to use caution, but too much of it can cause you to miss out on a lot. Getting to know this Jesus is something I sure don't want you to miss out on." countered the Capt.

"It is getting late and unless any of you have more to say, we probably should get some rest. We will be getting close to Jerusalem in a day or two. As we get closer, it will be more likely that we meet people who know more about Jesus and can tell us what is going on. It's quite possible that we might run into some of His disciples. Now, is there anything else before we finish here?" I asked.

"I just want to say that I feel it is mighty important that we keep open to one another—that way, when one of us is havin' a struggle about somethin', the rest of us can be there to help. I trust every one of you here and I don't want to see anybody left out. That's all I have to say tonight." stated Ben as he stood up to leave our gathering and prepare his bed for he night.

We quickly broke up our little meeting and made our beds under the canvas. Marco put a few more pieces of wood on the fire and soon had the warmth of it making our shelter quite comfortable. I was very tired but knew I wasn't going to be able to sleep for quite a while. I was still overwhelmed with all that had happened to me this night. I was still feeling a warmth rising up in me. It just kept coming and spilling over.

Sleep must have overcame me sometime in the night for the sun was well up when I awoke to hear considerable stirring around in our camp. I was astonished to see that my friends were already packing up to move out. I had slept through breakfast and not even heard them. When the others saw I was finally awake, they began to give me a hard time about missing breakfast and not helping with the morning's chores. I knew they were only teasing but I was still embarrassed by it all. I began to quickly gather up my blankets and other things to put in my pack when I noticed something in the bottom of my pack. As I reached in for it, I suddenly remembered the writing pens and paper I had stashed in my bag before leaving home. I was completely amazed that I had not remember it before now and became aggravated with myself for not thinking to record many of the events of the journey thus far. I began to think back on all that had happened on this trip. My mind was soon whizzing past picture after picture as I recalled some of the events. My aggravation began to subside as I realized there hadn't been much time to do any writing. I promised myself that I would make an earnest effort to record every part of this trip at the very first opportunity. I was also thankful that they were firmly embedded in my memory.

"Not that any lazy guy that sleeps through breakfast would deserve it, but there's a couple of meal cakes layin' on those rocks over there. You might as well eat them before some critter gets them." growled Alexus

His gruff voice captured my attention away from my thoughts of writing. Even though he tried to sound rough and uncaring, I found great hope in knowing that he cared enough to save me some food. I noticed that sometimes the gruffest sounding men often had the softest hearts. I was sure this was the case with Alexus. I hurried over to the rock with the cakes on them and began eating them. I was only on my second bite when the full realization of knowing Jesus came back once more. It was wonderful all over again! I was so thankful for everything—my friends, the food, the beautiful sunshine, the fresh smell of the air,—all of it. I was glad to be alive—inside and out.

As I finished eating and started to put on my pack, I noticed that Capt. Vitas and Artemis were not around. I quickly asked if anyone knew where they were and Ben said they had walked off together for a look at the city. I decided to go look for them and soon saw them kneeling, side by side as they looked over Samaria. As I got closer, I could hear them talking. I was about to shout to them that we were ready to leave when I noticed that they were not talking to each other, but to God. There they were—the two of them—just talking to God like He was right there with them—like they had known Him all their life.

Oh the joy!! It started to overflow again. I wanted to run right up there with them and get in on the conversation with God, but felt held back from doing so. This needed to be their time with God. Next I wanted to run back to tell the others, but, once more felt stopped from doing that. This news was not mine to tell. Not being sure what else to do, I just sat down where I was at and let the joy continue to overflow. I began to be thankful all over again for what I had just seen. I was thankful for being stopped from running off and spoiling Capt. Vitas' time with God and for not blurting out news that was not mine to tell. I was just so thankful for everything. Almost before I knew it, I was talking to God myself. We were having our own conversation. I'm not saying that I could actually hear Him speak to me but I could tell in my heart what He wanted me to know. I had a most definite assurance that the very thing that had stopped me from barging in on Capt. Vitas and telling the others was God working in my heart. Now that is enough right there to get excited about. It is beyond my ability to explain and I knew if I tried to tell the others about all that was going on in me right now—well, they just might believe me now. It didn't matter at the moment what they thought. This was my time with God. He was touching my mind and my heart in ways that I had no idea anyone could. It was more than I could even imagine. I just quieted myself and let Him do His work.

The sound of Marco's voice brought my attention back to the present situation. He and the others were standing nearby waiting on the captain, Artemis, and me. I wondered how long they had been standing there, but decided not to bother asking. It really didn't matter.

"Should we go over to get Capt. Vitas and Artemis or wait until they're finished with whatever they're doing?" Marco asked.

"No need to do either. We're ready to go if you'd be so kind as to hand us our packs." Capt. Vitas replied, having overheard us talking.

We had just began to head on down the road when Capt. Vitas turned around to face us.

"Nichos probably already knows, but to let all of you know—Artemis has put his faith in Jesus this morning. He and I have just had a wonderful time with Him." Capt. Vitas said with a huge smile and then he turned to continue on the way.

"I figured it wouldn't be long. I'm mighty happy for you, Artemis." Ben said.

"That goes for all of us,—Right men?" Marco added.

"Sure enough!" Cirro answered.

We made good time that morning and there was certainly a definite improvement in the moral of the whole group. I noticed a lot of conversation going on and there was a sense of excitement about it.

The part that I found the most encouragement in was that Cirro and Alexus had renewed their enthusiasm For the first time in many days, I was the one who was quiet and just a little withdrawn. In fact, it didn't even occur to me that I was being silent since there was so much going on inside me. I began to recall a dream I must have had during the night. It was about some women weeping as if their hearts were nearly fatally broken. I couldn't make sense of what it meant but I just kept on thinking about how Jesus was working in me. It was like I was talking to myself and Jesus all at the same time. It was such a wonderful morning.

Before we realized how far we had gone, we came upon the town of Sychar. It must have been at least ten mile from where we had camped last. Our journey had been a smooth one that morning and we had been so preoccupied that time had passed quickly. It was probably near two in the afternoon as we stopped on one of the streets of the town. People were going about their business and we were not being scrutinized as much as we had been in other places. Ben noticed the aroma of bread baking nearby and proceeded to find the source. We took a few steps to follow him as he disappeared behind stacks of goods that lined the narrow streets.

"Might be best for us to wait here for him. If it's food he's looking for he'll find it and be back pretty quick. He'll be alright." Capt. Vitas advised.

As we waited for Ben to return we looked over the street we were on. There were several tables set up selling goods of all kinds. There was a lot of trading going on and most of the booths were stocked with a variety of foods and articles that had been taken in exchange for other merchandise. It was the first time since we had left Tyre that we had seen so much business going on. It was certainly exciting to watch all the trading take place. The wonder of all this began to give way to a growing curiosity as to why people were freely doing business here in Sychar when most of the towns we had traveled through were quiet, if not even nearly deserted in the market places. I must have been wandering about this enough to be talking aloud to myself because Ben came up to offering an answer to my thoughts.

"I can give you a pretty good guess as to why this place is doin' a boomin' business. There's been a whole lot of people leaving Jerusalem because all that's been goin' on. Lots of them want to get rid of their things so they can travel light and they're needin' to get things they need to move on. It's a real feast for the merchants here. They're buyin' low and sellin' high. If people's goin' north, this is the first place to do much tradin' outside Jerusalem. There's plenty of 'em takin' advantage of folks, that's for certain." Ben explained.

"There will always be opportunist I'm afraid to say." Capt. Vitas commented.

"Well, just maybe there is an opportunity to pick up some food and things at a good price. If you all don't mind, let me have go at a little tradin' of my own." Artemis suggested.

"I'll go with you just to help make sure these fine merchants want to share their good fortune." added Cirro.

"Well, I guess; but stay back unless I let you know I need you, cause I'm gonna' do some fast talkin' and dealin'. I won't be cheatin' now, but I'm gonna' make sure the opportunity stays on my side." Artemis replied.

The rest of our group found a place to sit down to rest for a while. It was intriguing to watch all that was going on around us. From time to time we saw Ben and Artemis darting through the streets going from shop to shop. Just to see the exuberant way the two of them moved about with all the energy of a couple of young men was enough to stir my desire to explore the town.

"Capt., let's go tell Ben and Artemis to meet us back here later. I really would like to see what all there is here. This place is different from the others we've been through. It seems safe enough to me." I suggested.

"It does appear to be more hospitable. I reckon it will be alright. The hardest part might be just catching up with those two bargain hunters." Capt. Vitas answered.

"Let's all try to meet back here before sundown. Whoever sees Artemis, Cirro and Ben, be sure to let them know. I want to head down this way to look over this end of town." I said to the others.

"I'll go with you if it's alright." Marco said.

"You two go on but be careful. This may be a friendly town but there is more than likely a few in it who wouldn't think long about wackin' you on the head to get whatever you might have. I will stay with Capt. Vitas." Alexus replied.

Marco and I made our way down the narrow street, stopping occasionally to look over merchandise, some of which we had never seen before. After a while we came to the end of the shops and the street turned into a well trodden pathway that led out through the country. Just at the edge of the town we saw a small house, unusually well kept for such a homey place. Two ladies were out front talking to each other as they trimmed some vines in the yard. When we heard the name of Jesus coming from their conversation, it was all it took for me to stop to listen for more. We weren't there long before the ladies noticed us. I knew it was not the custom there for women to talk with men, but I needed to find out what these two ladies knew of Jesus. I approached them slowly, trying to communicate the best I could with them. Marco followed behind me.

"Hello. I overheard you speaking of Jesus. Can you tell me about Him? I asked.

"Why do you want to know? Who are you?" they replied.

"We are from Athens on our way to find out what is true. I heard you speak the name of Jesus. Do you know Him? We mean you no harm—only to find out more about Him." I continued.

Both ladies looked us over without saying another word for a couple of minutes. Then they looked at each other, and without a word, turned towards their home. One stopped just before entering to turn back to motion for us to follow them inside. I turned to look at Marco for some reassurance and he shrugged his shoulders and started walking towards the doorway.

"There is something about the two of you that lets me know we can trust you. This is my sister Martha and my name is Mary. We knew Jesus very well indeed. He was a very dear friend and a wonderful teacher. He even brought our brother back from the grave. A wonderful man—That's why they wanted to kill Him. He was becoming more and they were becoming less." she began to tell us.

"Why are you so interested in Him? Athens is a far away place. You must have traveled a great distance in search of this truth you speak of. I take it you must think our Jesus holds some keys to finding this truth?" Mary continued.

"He may very well be the Truth. That is why we are here imposing on you and your sister. It is of great importance to know all we can about Him." I replied.

While Mary was talking to us, Martha was sitting across the room, listening to us at first, but then she seemed to be off to herself. She began to whisper words that were barely audible to us and then she grew more vocal until she was speaking with a voice that demanded to be heard.

"He came to us to love us and show us all that God wanted us to be. He came as gentle as a shepherd. He only wanted to help but they feared Him. They struck Him, beat Him, nailed Him to a beam and hung Him up to die—beaten and bloodied beyond belief." Martha spoke out.

She began to weep, quietly at first and then more freely. She rose to her feet and took a broom which she swept the earthen floor with. Her weeping soon turned to morning. She let the old broom fall from her hands and dropped to her knees as she let out the most forlorn cry I can ever remember hearing. I could feel the agony of heartache and suffering of this lady embedded in her outcry. Her pain was such that it filled the room and flowed into my own heart. Apparently, Marco was also experiencing her grief and his faced was covered with tears.

Martha continued to weep and cry as she knelt on the floor. Mary knew she would have to continue telling us what Martha had started even though she was crying herself.

"We were both there when they took Him. They led Him through the streets, making Him carry that heavy beam after they had nearly beaten any life out of Him. I don't think I ever saw a man so humiliated and scorned. He didn't resist or try to escape. Even on the cross, He showed compassion and tenderness." Mary told as she struggled to get out the words between her own tears.

"Who was it that did this to Him—The Romans or the Jews?" I asked.

"It was the Jewish leaders who were behind most of it. Of course, they used the Romans to carry out the terrible part of it. Can you imagine what it is like to see someone you love and care for beaten and torn open—then to be nailed to a cross and left to die ever so slowly? It's such a horrible thing—" Mary managed to answer before her voice gave way to crying.

"His own mother was standing right there at the foot of the cross watching the life drain from His body. She was helpless to do anything for Him, yet even in His last moments He wanted to make sure she was cared for. He asked our friend, John to look after her. Can you imagine what it would be for a mother to see her son tortured so? Can you comprehend the love of a son for His mother?" Mary spoke in broken words, trying to let us know what had happened that day.

Martha's wailing was quieting down some and she was now more involved in what we were saying. She wiped her face with her hands and picked up the old broom, making a few strokes with it before leaning on it as she began talking to us.

"They thought they had won the victory and that He was dead and gone. Well, He's gone sure enough! That grave couldn't hold Him. When they went to tend to His body on the third day, the tomb was empty! He spoke to one of the women who had come to care for Him and told her to tell his followers to meet Him in Galilee. He has conquered death!" Martha shouted.

Mary come over to put her arms around Martha and they both wept on each others shoulders for a time. I must have become very pale, for even in the dim light of the small room, Marco could see I was having difficulty.

"Are you alright? What's wrong with you, Nik?" Marco whispered as he placed his hand on my shoulder to turn me towards him so as to get a better look at my face.

My appearance must have been such as to really upset him. I knew I was being seriously jolted on the inside. I tried to gain enough strength to utter a few words to Marco to let him know what was going on. It would have been easier to just speak in a normal tone than to try to whisper now, but it felt it was important not to disturb the two ladies just across the room.

"Marco, I just had a dream about this very thing this morning. It was about these two ladies crying with this grief that is affecting us even now. I saw it all before as we are seeing it now! The agony that you hear was in my dream this morning!" I tried to explain.

"Stop it Nik! You couldn't have! This—this can't be-" he whispered back. He was looking me straight in the eye and his hand was trembling as he grasped my shoulder even more firmly.

"I did and this *is* happening! Just trust me and listen." I said.

Mary and Martha were still weeping but turned their attention to us once more. Our conversation must have been loud enough to remind them of our presence.

"Forgive us for our rudeness. We didn't mean to ignore you, it's just that our hearts are so—" Mary started to explain when I stopped her.

"You need not apologize, ma'am. Your pain is such that we can feel it also. You did say that He was not to be found in the tomb? He spoke to someone?" I asked abruptly, only to realize how insensitive I must have sounded before I even finished asking the question.

"Yes, it was empty and He spoke to a woman named Mary telling her to let his disciple know where to meet Him." Martha answered.

"We heard He came back from the grave. We also heard that some arose from the grave when He died on the cross. Is that right?" Marco asked.

"It is indeed! That was some day! Never heard of one like it ever before. It was so scary and horrible. No one knew what make of it. Before it was over, even the Roman soldiers were afraid." Mary stated.

"He is going to meet with His followers? Does that mean He will be here from now on?" I questioned.

"We don't know. We just don't know. Some much has happened and much more has been made of it. One group tells people it means one thing and then others say it's another way. We only know He is alive and wants to meet with His people." Mary answered as Martha reached out to comfort her by taking her hand.

I thought it best not to mention anything about my dream to the ladies since they seemed to have quite enough to handle. I was also anxious to get back with the others in our group. My mind was busy calculating how long it would take Jesus and His followers to make it to Galilee, what road would they be taking, what would be the chance of meeting them, had we already missed them, and so on. I was torn between wanting to rush out to get back to the others and staying to hear more from the ladies. There was such a kindred spirit forming amongst us and I appreciated the

goodness of it. For some reason I felt these two women were like family
to me. The desire to stay soon gave way to feeling the urgency to be on
our way. I thanked the ladies for their hospitality and for helping us, then
tried to assure them that comfort would come to them. Reaching back, I
took Marco by the arm and practically pulled him along with me as we
left. I think he must have still been stunned by all that had happened in
that little home.

"Come on, Marco. Let's hurry up and find the others. We need to
find out if anyone here knows if Jesus or His followers have came through.
Imagine that! Going to where we just came from. Wouldn't you know it?"
I muttered.

Poor Marco must have been even more befuddled by my goings on.
He just tried to keep up with me without saying a word and that wasn't like
Marco. When he wanted to be more clear about something, he wouldn't
hold back on asking question after question. We were soon back into the
more busy part of town and, in my hurry to find the others, I must have
ran into a dozen or more people, spinning and knocking them around.
Marco was just far enough behind that he was the one who got the angry
looks and verbal rebukes. I soon caught sight of Ben and made my way to
him. Cirro and Artemis came up just as I was beginning to speak.

"We just spoke with two women who were there when they put Jesus
on that cross. They told us much but the most important things is that
Jesus told His followers to meet Him in Galilee. We have to try to find
out if they have already passed this way or if anyone knows where He may
be now! We need to hurry and find Capt. Vitas and Alexus. Come on!
Let's go!" I shouted as I was already on my way up the street in search of
the rest of our group.

"Marco, do you know what in the world he is talking about? I tell
you, sometimes that young man truly amazes me and other times he just
downright confuses me." Ben said with all the clarity of a man just being
released from a whirlwind.

"Only some of it, Ben. Only some of it." Marco answered.

We made our way through the streets without knocking any more
people around and soon our group was once more reunited. I led the men
to a cluster of trees, hoping for a place where we could talk freely. With
Marco's help, I told the others what all had happened to us in the ladies'

house and about the dream I had that very morning. The longer I talked, the more anxious I became about possibly missing the very One for whom were searching. I tried so desperately to convey the broken-heartedness and the anguish of the ladies. Everything seemed so vastly important to me and I was afraid that my friends weren't getting the full impact of it. I must have become quite emphatic in attempting to describe it all because Capt. Vitas began to interrupt in an effort to slow me down.

"Nik, now listen to me. If your dream holds so much importance—if your running into those ladies—if all these things have been ordained for you, for us, then tell me this. Do you think God would arrange all this only to disappoint us?" he reasoned and without letting me have a chance to answer, he continued. "If we are destined to meet Jesus, I'm quite sure we will indeed. If we're not, then look at what we have been given. Think of all the people we have met on our journey. Think of what they have contributed to our search for truth. We must be careful not to overlook the gift in our search for the giver."

I looked at Capt. Vitas, taking in all that he had just said. As I weighed his words, they seemed to grow in strength and value. There was so much wisdom behind those words. I began to feel somewhat ashamed for not realizing this myself. The zealous spirit of my youth had just been reigned in and gently guided back to a respectable balance. He was able to accomplish all this with a loving kindness that was absent of any bitterness or anger. I began to see a growing mound of gifts, all of which I felt most thankful for.

"Did either of the ladies say of they had met anyone coming from Jerusalem since all this has happened, any of Jesus' followers?" Alexus asked.

"I don't know. They didn't say if they did. I didn't even think to ask them, though." I replied.

"It might be a good idea to find someone who could say if they have came through here. Those two ladies might be the best place to start. If they don't know, maybe they can direct us to someone who will know." Ben suggested.

"Do you think the women will mind you coming back to talk with them some more?" Capt. Vitas asked.

"From the way they showed how much Jesus meant to them, I doubt they will mind helping us. I think it might be our best chance of finding out more. Don't you agree, Marco?" I stated.

"I think they will be glad to help us. They didn't seem be as afraid as other people we have met before. We can at least try." answered Marco.

"It might be good for you to come with us, Capt. We have told them about our journey and they probably would like to meet you." I suggested.

"Fine, I would like to meet them, myself. It would be best though if the rest of you stayed back so as not to overwhelm the ladies. Let's all head back that way and we'll find a place for you to wait." the captain answered.

We made our way back down the street of Sychar toward the ladies house. We came upon an inn where several men were gathered around, loafing for the most part; and decided this would be a good place to leave our other men. They might even have the chance to pick up some information themselves. The captain, Marco, and myself then continued down the lane toward the ladies' house. I found myself trying to figure out what to say to them when we came to their door. Several lines ran through my head but none sounded right. It was almost like I was trying to manipulate the women with carefully selected words. I had flash backs to my days in Athens where that was a most common practice. A person there couldn't be certain if someone was being honest of if they were simply basting their motives with sweet sounding words to get what they wanted. I knew that wasn't my intent here and I was even sickened at the thought of being that way with these ladies. I simply wanted them to help us if they could. I must have been muttering about all this because I was brought back to the present by Marco.

"Just ask them if they can help us, Nik. Don't make so much of it. They trust us." he said.

"Yes, I know, Marco. Honesty has proven best so many times on this journey. I shouldn't have had to be reminded." I answered.

"This is the house up here, Capt. I hope they're still home." Marco said.

There was an unusual anxiety rising up within me as we stepped up to the door and knocked. It wasn't an anxiety that comes from fear but one of expectation, and I didn't know what to expect. For some reason I felt we were near the threshold of learning why we all had such a common desire to this Truth. I took a deep breath and swallowed as if to firmly implant this anticipation in my soul as I reached up to knock.

Martha answered the door and wasn't at all surprised to see us. She simply turned and waved us in as if she had been waiting for us to show up. Mary came in from another room and both women welcomed us back.

"Ladies, this is Capt. Vitas. He is our ship's Captain and one of our group. We invited him to come with us to meet you. His wisdom has been of great value to us on our journey. As you have said Jesus was your friend, the Captain is ours. We have returned to ask your help. It is not our desire to put you in any danger by talking with you, but, perhaps you might know things that could really help us. You have already helped immensely by all you told us this afternoon. Please feel free to ask us to leave at anytime you think it best." I explained.

"We thought you might be back. There is such a hunger in your souls. We will be glad to help with what we can." Mary replied. "Now, what is it you wish to know?"

"Well, first of all, do you know if any of Jesus' followers have came through here yet? Has any one seen Jesus around here? Is this the road they would take to Galilee?" I blurted out.

"Oh, my! So many questions. Let's set down—I can see this might be a while." Martha said as she motioned toward some chairs by the table. "Followers—now what do you mean by followers—those who follow His teachings or those who followed Him—His close ones? His disciples they call them."

"Well, either ones. Of course, we would be most interested in knowing about His disciples, but we would like to find anyone who knew Him and could tell us more about Him." Marco replied.

"This is the main road north to Galilee but that doesn't mean it's the only way. No one has said they have seen Jesus around here. Now, remember too, that Jesus wouldn't necessarily have to walk anywhere to get to Galilee. We haven't heard any reports about His disciples coming past either. There have been several of His followers in town though— even Jesus' mother." Mary continued.

"His mother? Is she still here?" Capt. Vitas asked.

"I saw her yesterday. She was with one of her sons. He wanted to get her away from all this. He never did take to Jesus and His ways—even thought He was near insanity. He might mean well but I think he just don't want to be associated with Jesus. Did we tell you Jesus asked John, one of His disciples to take care of His mother? Well, he don't want their mother cared for by John or any of his friends. I'm afraid you will have a hard time talking to her with him around." Martha answered.

"Is there anyone else here in Sychar that was there in Jerusalem to see all that? Did Jesus have any people here who were His disciples? I questioned.

"At one time, He had followers all over the place. Why, when He brought our brother, Lazarus back from the tomb, He had thousands of people hanging on every word He said. But when things got a little rough—well His popularity dwindled. I can remember times when He would be walking along and the crowds would be so thick you could hardly move. One time I heard that the crowd was so packed that some men went up on a roof to let their crippled friend down to Him to be healed. The priest and the Romans began making it hard on anyone who claimed friendship with Jesus. By the time they nailed Him on that cross, there weren't many left who would publicly acknowledge Him.. So to answer your question—Yes, there are people here who saw what went on, but not too many are willing to talk." Mary replied.

"It became more difficult for us to stay in Bethany where we had lived for a long time. We moved up here and traveled back to Jerusalem as often as we could. Because of what He had done for our brother, Lazarus, we had to move up here for fear of our lives. They tried to destroy everything they could to stop what He had started." Martha inserted.

"I've noticed you haven't mentioned Jesus' father any. Was he there in Jerusalem with his wife and son?" Capt. Vitas asked.

"You mean Joseph? No, he wasn't there. Life has been very hard on Joseph. You see, some people think he really is the father of Jesus and don't want to believe any other way. For that reason, they treat him with disrespect for having relations with Mary before they were married. Others despise him for staying with Mary and raising a son that isn't his. Still, some of the religious leaders hold him responsible for the way Jesus does. Even his own family is divided concerning Jesus' ministry. Joseph has chosen to busy himself with his carpentry work and do the best he can to stay to himself. Mind you now, he is a good man and loves his wife dearly; but he wishes to be left alone." Martha answered.

"Has it always been that way with Him? Marco asked.

"No, not always. He spent many hours teaching Jesus how to work with wood and brought Him up under Jewish traditions. It was only when Jesus began to speak out and begin His teaching that the pressure increased on the family. That was when he decided to escape all the criticism." Mary added. "Now, he moves around from place to place, finding an empty building to do his wood-working in. When he feels people closing in on him, he'll move on. But he always does what he can to help his wife, Mary—he just doesn't want to be with her when she's with followers of Jesus. He is a very private man."

"Do you have any suggestions about finding some of His disciples around here?" Capt. Vitas asked.

"I think you might have the best chance of meeting them down in Jerusalem. We've heard they come together in a upstairs room somewhere in the city. From the latest we've heard, I don't think they have left for Galilee yet. That would be my first place to look." Martha answered.

"Do you have plans to travel to Galilee or anywhere else to see Jesus? We can see how much you think of Him." Marco questioned.

"Martha and I haven't given it much thought, really. Somehow, it doesn't seem so important that we actually see Him again. We both have so much if Him in our souls and that is like having Him right here with us now. I would hate to say we would never go but who can tell?" Mary replied.

"We have imposed on your kindness and hospitality more than we have any right to. We appreciate all you have done to help us and will always remember the kindness you have shown us. There is much more in my heart I wish I could share, but somehow I don't feel it's necessary to speak what is already evident. Our hearts seem to have been connected in ways that exceed my understanding. I can tell you this: You will always be remembered with deep gratitude and an affection that binds kindred spirits. It is time for us to be leaving now and make our way to Jerusalem. Thank you once again. Marco—Capt." I spoke as I motion toward the door.

Once again I felt like I was giving orders to those superior to me and had stepped our of my character. It knew deep within there would not be a time when we had learned all we could from being with these two wonderful ladies and there might not be a good time to leave. It was just time to be on our way and also, it was not in the best interest of the ladies to remain there any longer. Not only were we going against the social culture of speaking to them, we were also putting them in danger should word get out of the subject of our visit.

Mary and Martha remained seated as we headed for the door, but Mary suddenly jumped up and ran towards us. She hugged me first with such an embrace that made it hard to inhale and then moved on to Marco and Capt. Vitas. Martha was close behind with her own hugs—hugs with even more constriction than Mary's.

I felt so much feeling from those hugs—feelings that were free of wrongful desire, free of possession or dominion, free of obligation. There was such a feeling of purity and genuine love flowing between the independent hearts beating within our chest that I knew had to be coming from our relationship with this Jesus we sought. I found myself wanting to stay to enjoy this precious gift a while longer, but there was a working in my spirit that let me know this gift could be easily tarnished with my own self-centeredness if I allowed it.

There were tears rolling down all our faces as we left that home. I can't speak for what Marco and Capt. Vitas had going on in them but I can tell you I had not known such capacity to love someone ever before. It was a different kind of love—one which was given without obligation or cause. Not much was said as we made our way back to the others waiting at the inn.

"Did you learn anything from your visit?" Alexus shouted as we walked up to them. "You must have found out something for as long as you've been gone."

"It was time well spent. I believe it would be fair to say we learned a lot more about why we're here than about where we should go. Those are two very special ladies." Capt. Vitas replied

"That they are!" I answered. We need to make our way to Jerusalem as soon as possible. Did you find anyone here at the inn who might have seen Jesus or His followers?"

"I overheard a couple of men talking about some people from Jerusalem who had came through here two days ago. From the run of their talk, they didn't think much of them. I figured it best not to ask any questions—just kept my ears open.

It seems there is some division amongst the town—just like its been most of the way here." Alexus said.

It's probably to late to start out yet this evening for Jerusalem. At least we know a little about this place and I think we can find a safe place to stay tonight. If we leave early tomorrow, we should reach Jerusalem before noon Friday." I suggested.

"I noticed a quite looking' place back up the street where we could stay the night. I, for one would welcome a real bed and a roof over my head tonight, what with the rain comin'." Ben stated and he turned to make his way to the place.

"It don't look like rain, Ben. Not a cloud to be seen. A bed does sound mighty good though." Cirro replied.

"Don't sleep with your feet out the winder unless you want them to get wet. Rain's a comin'." Ben retorted.

# CHAPTER ELEVEN

# THE HOLY CITY.

I t must have been just after mid-night when we heard rain on the roof
. Most of us were too tired to bother saying much about it with the
exception of Marco. We heard him tell Cirro to get his feet back in
and shut the window. That brought a chuckle to all of us. Rain was still
falling when we woke up just after daylight.

"Might just as well rest a while longer—this rain gonna be around
for some time yet." Ben muttered from under his blanket.

"It beats me how you can tell so much about the weather, Ben. I don't
recall you ever bein' wrong once." Alexus said.

"It's all in the bones, men, all in the bones." Ben answered.

"Well tell your old bones to dry up. We need to get on our way." I joked.

"You tell em'—I'm goin' back to sleep." Ben replied.

The rain continued until almost noon, coming down had enough that
we didn't want to try to start out in it. We cleaned up our room and made
our way downstairs to the lobby of the inn. There was considerable chatter

going on among the people waiting inside out of the rain. We were able to pick up several bits of information. Probably the most important piece of news was that Roman patrols were being increased and that the Jewish leaders were seeking men who could help stamp out those determined to follow Jesus' disciples. We also learned that this job was becoming more and more difficult since the disciples were more determined than ever to carry on His teachings.

We had eaten well the day before so we decided to make do with a breakfast of bread and dried fruit. The extra rest and growing enthusiasm had our group primed for a fast paced journey. It was still sprinkling when Ben told us it was time to set out. He guaranteed us we would be dry the rest of the day if we could manage to step between the raindrops that were still coming down. So off we went.

The rain had refreshed the countryside and fragrances from blooms filled the air. Spring was well on its was and new life was breaking forth all around us. It seems that a spring rain has a way of unlocking nature and letting it fill the air. It was turning into a beautiful day with distant hills shining brightly in the sunrays that drove back the clouds. I would often get lost in admiration and appreciation of such wonder. Even here in this land that was cluttered with large rocks and sparse vegetation, there was enough new life coming forth to capture my attention. I must have been thoroughly enjoying the scenery and fresh air for quite some time because we had traveled five miles before Marco directed my attention back to the group.

"How are we going to answer anyone who stops us wanting to know where we are going? With those Roman soldiers out on patrol, there's a good chance we will run into them. We need to know what to tell them." Marco said.

"You have a very good point, Marco. Shows you do a lot of thinking ahead. Might I suggest that we tell them we are headed for Jerusalem and then on to Joppa to find work on a ship for the summer. It wouldn't be lying to them entirely because I have been doing some thinking ahead myself. It could be that I might find some old friends of mine that will be setting out to sea before long. Anyway, I got some strong feelings about going there when we are done here." Capt. Vitas answered.

"That sounds like it will satisfy them Romans. Have to admit though, I'm kinda surprised to hear you talking of leavin' already." Ben replied.

"You're not planning on leaving us here in Israel after getting this close are you?" Cirro questioned,

"Now, hold on—Hold on. Don't mistake what I just said as meaning that I was leaving anyone. First of all, I feel a very deep commitment to this group. I will be a part of it until we have all reached our goal. In my heart I know that some of us may well have already reached that goal, even though they haven't realized it fully. At any rate, we must be very near the time when we will all have found what we have sought. Then, secondly, my life has been changed and I am anxious to begin living these changes out in my daily life. Things that were important and took most of my time seem to have lost interest to me. I'm not sure, at this point, that I even want to command a ship again. I'm certainly giving serious thought to the matter. And now, thirdly—we must be convinced in our minds that we are all going to Joppa to find work on a ship. That may be the only way we can convince the authorities of our reason for being here. We need to make definite plans to go there." Capt. Vitas stated.

"He's right!" Artemis interjected. "I've seen these soldiers at work before. They would just as soon throw us in prison or even put is to the blade if they thought we was lying to them. Remember, they're soldiers havin' to serve as if their life depended on it cause it really does. If they make one mistake—well, it will probably be their last."

"O.K. So it's agreed. We are all on our way to Joppa to find work on a ship for the summer. We'll make more definite plans when we stop tonight. Do any of you know much about Joppa or anything about the crews wintering there?" I asked.

"It's a busy place—goods comin' and goin'—people travelin' from all over the world. I've been there several times and have always been amazed at all that goes on there. I used to know some of the ship's captains, but that's been a few years back. I'd probably still know some of the deck hands." Ben replied.

"It's some city—that's for certain—a beautiful city in many ways. Of course, like so many seaports, it has it's dark side. If my memory serves me right, I should know three or four of the ships wintering there. I am a little concerned about our timing though—this weather has been milder than normal and some of the ships may have already set sail." Capt. Vitas added.

Conversation among the group seemed to wane after hearing about Joppa. We must have all been considering the things that had been said in the last moments. I know thoughts of sailing back to Athens strongly competed with my mind for thoughts of Jerusalem. I began to feel homesick for my family. I wandered how my mother was doing and if Marco's little brother, Stephan had made it home safely. I found myself nearly dreading the long ocean voyage back. I began to get angry at myself for not being enthused about getting to close to Jerusalem. We were very likely going to meet some of Jesus' followers—maybe even His disciples. Where has all the excitement gone?

The sun was setting behind hills in the west when we decided to stop to eat our evening meal. The thought of eating more hard biscuits and dried fish was hard to accept. For some reason, the taste of hot bean soup got im my mind to the point where I could actually smell it cooking. I asked Marco if we had any beans left and he thought we did. That was all the encouragement I needed.

"Let's find a good place to camp for the night and Marco and I will fix you all a hot meal." I suggested.

I short time later Alexus saw a small house off the road which a grove of evergreens just off the side of it. The place did look like a protected place to set up camp.

"I'll go ask the people who live here if they would mind us staying here for the night." Alexus said.

We watched him as he approached the house and saw the door open just a little before he got close enough to knock. We could only hear the sounds of their voices but couldn't understand anything they said. Suddenly the door opened wider and Alexus went in. The door stood open while he was inside. After a few minutes, we saw two people come out with Alexus. They waved to us as he walked back to our group.

"Well, what did you find out? " Cirro asked impatiently.

"We're welcome to camp for the night—even gave us some fresh meat and meal to put with our beans. I invited them to come over later and eat with us. Real nice folks. They even asked if we had heard about all that had went on with Jesus and the commotion that had been going on. I think they might join us to eat." Alexus replied.

"What did they have to say about Jesus? What kind of commotion? How much do they know?" Marco bombarded him with questions.

"I couldn't tell that they knew much for certain—mostly I think it was out of curiosity. I really can't say I learned anything new from them." Alexus answered.

"Anyway, lets get set up so we can get to fixin' a fine supper."

Everyone did their part to set up a shelter for the night and we gathered some wood for a fire. Marco took charge of preparing the food—it was just his nature to want to cook. It didn't take long before the air was filled with the wonderful aroma of beans cooking and meal cakes baking near the fire. The evergreens seemed to be holding the smoky fragrance around us so we could enjoy it a while longer.

Nobody said much as we waited for the food to be done. Alexus and Cirro talked softly to each other—not that they were trying to be secretive but they were just talking. I notice that Capt. Vitas was even quieter than usual. He appeared to be in deep thought about something. Ben and Artemis sat near the fire, poking at it with sticks. This began to irritate Marco as he tried to get the fire regulated to do his cooking correctly. I could see he was wanting to say something to them but held his tongue—and adjusted the old pot on the fire to compensate for their fidgeting. There was a tension building within our group that was becoming increasingly evident. I could find no reason to indicate that it was sprouting from any of us but it was most certainly establishing its presence with us, causing most of us to be distracted from our thoughts of Jerusalem. I was still in deep contemplation when I heard Marco asking for some help to set the hot kettle off the fire. This gave me the opportunity to speak with Marco to see if he noticed the uneasiness in our camp.

"Ya, I've felt it coming on. I can't tell you what it is, but I sure enough know something has come over us. What do you think it might be?" Marco said in response to my question.

"I don't know, but I'm determined not to let it come break down any of the ties we have established. After supper, we're going to get this plan worked out about Joppa and then I'm going to see if we can't get our attention back on Jerusalem. It's feels to me like there is a force that is wanting to keep us from getting there and finding more of what we have come all this way to find." I replied.

Marco called the others to come fill their plates as he stirred the beans and pulled the old tin plates and wooden spoons from the sack we carried them in. I was busy pulling the meal cakes away from the hot coals when I heard Capt. Vitas speak.

"Before we eat we need to give thanks for these provisions—if I may. Oh God, we ask your blessings on this food and we are indeed appreciative and grateful for all the provisions you have provided, for the protection you have given, for the guidance you have sent, for the care you have shown. Help us, Oh Lord, to always be thankful for all you do for us. Amen."

As the captain prayed, I was taken back to the evening we shared our camp with the Jewish family and how my new friend, Joel had prayed a blessing over the supper we had that night. To the best of my recollection, that time and now, this were the only times I can remember asking a blessing on our meal—especially asking God to bless it. I could feel a working in my spirit that convicted me of a shortcoming in life. I knew I needed to be more mindful to seek God's blessing and to be more appreciative of His provision.

The steam rose from each spoonful of beans and meal cake Marco dipped onto the plates. You could actually see mouths watering and tongues licking lips in anticipation of the goodness the plates of food offered. I noticed that the men were being drawn out of the sullen attitude that had fell over the group and were beginning to laugh and talk in a light-hearted manner that had long been absent. After the others had been given their plates, I filled one for Marco and another for myself. We then joined the others by the fire. With the very first bite I took, I could tell it tasted unusually good. I don't know if it was the seasoning of fresh meat or if it was due to the blessing Capt. Vitas had asked for that made it so delicious. Whatever the reason, I was truly thankful—thankful for the hot meal and even more thankful for the fellowship that was returning to our group.

We were all nearly done eating when Artemis asked. "Didn't you say our host would be joining us for supper, Alexus? I sure would like a chance to thank them for their part in making this a wonderful meal."

"Well, they sure acted like they would be coming. I'm surprised they're not here yet. I was wanting them to meet all of you." Alexus answered.

"If they don't get here soon there won't be much left." Cirro remarked as he returned to the pot to get another helping.

Conversation among us continued for quite a while and I remarked to Marco that maybe the situation had corrected itself. It was just good to chat with each other and not have anything so serious to contend with. Just as I was thinking that very thought, Capt. Vitas spoke again.

"Not that I desire to bring such a pleasant time to an early end, but I think it is necessary to conclude our plans for Joppa. We need to decide on some particulars so that we can all be in agreement should the need arise. Ben, do you or Artemis know any of the ships captains that might be wintering there? I know a couple but it might be better if we could refer to the men you were familiar with."

"Well, let's see. There would be Capt. Balthar or maybe Capt. Berek. Both of them normally spend the winter there. You know of them don't you Artemis?" Ben said.

"Sure I know of them. Both good men on the sea and off. There is also a captain by the name of Aristroph. He's pretty popular with some folks in these parts but, I know for a fact, most of his business in the last three or four years has been shippin slaves to the west. We'd best stay clear of him for sure. I want no part in such dealins'." Artemis answered.

We didn't get much further in our discussion before we heard footsteps on the hard-packed road. They were coming from the south, from Jerusalem more than likely. We could tell by the sound that it was not a small group. We were hoping if might be some of Jesus' followers but fear grew in our hearts that could also be those belonging to a Roman garrison. As they neared our camp we were able to hear a more pronounced clack—made by hard soled boots hitting the hard earth—boots worn by well equipped Roman soldiers.

"Quick, get busy cleaning up the plates and pots. Make small talk about anything but what we just discussed. Laugh and be at ease as much as you can. If they stop to question us, be very careful what you say. Remember! We headed to Joppa looking for Capt. uh, uh, Capt. Balthar. Got it?" Artemis spoke quickly and quietly.

We scurried to follow Artemis' instructions and began talking with one another about food, about the rain, about an early spring—in fact we found we had a lot to talk about without working hard to make something up. Our group was soon in high spirits and appeared not to have a care in the world when the troop came into view—there faces lit somewhat by the torches they carried. I was doing a good job of showing no concern on the outside but my heart was about to beat right out of my chest. I was hoping the clatter of their boots would keep the same tempo and that they would march right on down the road.

"Halt!" shouted the commander of the garrison.

My hopes were dashed to the ground and stomped on. I heard him call out to some of his men to follow him over to our camp. I heard the rasp of steel blades sliding from their place of rest in their scabbards as the men stepped off the road and headed our way. As they approached, the light of the torches revealed more of the features of their faces. I could see the firm, determined set of well definded jaw bones covered by bronze skin beneath the helmets of polished brass. When the commanded reached from beneath his cloak to take a torch from one of his men, he revealed an arm the size of a small tree. It too was contoured to display each of the taunt muscles that flexed beneath skins that was nearly as bronze as the armor he wore. I guessed him to weigh well over two-hundred and eighty pounds—and every bit of it muscle. I found myself wondering why he felt it necessary to bring any of the men with him, since he alone was intimidating enough, I'm not sure that our whole group together would have been able to overcome him—had we been foolish enough to try.

"What business do you have here?" he thundered.

"We are on our way to Joppa to find work on ship for the summer. We camped here for the night and will be on our way at daybreak." Artemis answered.

"Three of you are old. What work could you do to justify a wage?" he asked with such a sarcasm that we didn't bother to answer.

He looked us over for a few minutes—giving special attention to Marco and myself. We must have been quite a puzzlement to him as he started to look away and then, returned his gaze upon us. He began speaking to the others but kept his eyes fixed on Marco and me.

"Check through their bags. Look for anything unusual. Let me know what you find." he ordered his men.

"You have business in Jerusalem? There is no one you wish to see there? You can tell me—better yet! We can help you find them?"

"Sir, our plans are to pass through Jerusalem on our way to Joppa to find Capt. Balthar if he has not already set sail. What is it you want of us?" Capt. Vitas spoke, asking his own question in an effort to relieve some suspicion.

Just then I saw one of the soldiers pull my writing paper from my bag. I was now thankful that I hadn't had a chance to write anything yet. I could only imagine what would have happened if they had been filled with all that we had encountered.

"Who do these belong to? Which of you vagrants has enough brains to know how to write?" he bellowed.

"They're mine sir. They are for drawings I do." Marco answered before I could even think about saying anything.

"Drawings you say! Where are they then—these are all blank. Perhaps you would be so kind to draw something for me—as a gift for my kindness." the commander said as he ended with laughter that had the other soldiers with him laughing as well.

"DRAW!" he shouted as he slammed the paper down in front of Marco.

The laughter instantly stopped and it became deathly quiet in the camp. Marco looked up at him and then turned towards the fire, reaching down for a couple of sticks that had rolled away from the fire. He looked them over carefully and then selected one that had been burnt. He then looked at the commander for a moment of two and began to sketch. Soon he had the likeness of the commander captured on paper and handed it to him. We were able to see it briefly and we were amazed at Marco's talent. Each of us had to subdue our surprise and act like we knew of his ability. I then remembered that Marco had done quite a bit of sketching back in Athens.

"Not bad. Not bad at all!" he said with a chuckle as he let the sketch fall to the ground. "Pick up you stuff . You will be coming with us. Be quick about it."

The commander's face changed instantly as he turned to rejoin the garrison on the road. The other soldiers moved to make sure we gathered our stuff as fast as we cold. They wouldn't allow us time to take down the canvas we had stretched for a shelter. I hoped Marco would think to put the paper in his bag. I hadn't used it yet but I sure would be wanting to and it wouldn't be easy to replace.

"Get them out her now you bunch of idiots!" shouted the commander.

"He must be the most cold hearted person I've ever met." I thought to myself, but apparently not quietly enough that Marco didn't hear me think it.

"He just might be but be careful what you say. Right now, he is in control and it is in our best interest to give him as little reason to be upset as possible." Marco whispered.

I had just turned to look at Marco with no intention of replying when one of the soldiers shoved me from behind, trying to get us on the road quickly .

I could feel anger rising within me and resented being forced to comply with such men of little regard for dignity. What cause had we given to be treated this way? What crime had we committed? What right did they have to force us to leave? All these thoughts were racing through my head. I wanted to stop in my tracks and demand answers to these question but I knew such behavior would not be tolerated.

It would also mean that our whole group would pay the price for my actions. I decided, at least for now, that the best course of action was to go with this garrison, wherever it was they were taking us. As we neared to road I saw two people in front of the house where Alexus had asked for permission to camp. They watched as we were escorted from their property.

When we were all assembled with the commander and his troops, he turned to head south towards Jerusalem and ordered all to follow. Ben turned his head to speak to some of us behind him and was met with the blunt shaft of a spear across his jaw, harshly letting him know that we were not to talk. It must have hurt considerably but Ben held to his pride and tried not to let it show. Anger rose to a dangerous level and I was afraid Cirro was going to attempt to grab the spear from the soldier. Capt. Vitas gently reached over to place his hand on Cirro's arm and ever so slightly shook his head to indicate not to do anything.

We marched on without further incident for several hours. Without being able to talk to the others, my mind was occupied with a multitude of questions. Where were we being taken? What were they going to do to us? Were we going to be arrested? What part, if any, did the people who let us camp in the evergreens have to do with all this? How much further would we have to walk tonight? I was not able to find answers to any of these questions but I felt an unusual peace weaving its way through the situation. It was a peace that enabled me to believe that this would not be the end of our journey, perhaps a significant delay but not the end.

As we were escorted on for another hour or more, fatigue began to set in. I knew if I was getting tired, Capt. Vitas, Ben, and Artemis must be feeling the effects of the march much more than us younger ones. I grew more concerned for them when I saw them stumble. I hoped the soldiers would notice the need for them to rest for a short time, but that was not to be. The troops behind us kept up pace with the commander and did not allow us to slow our steps.

The sun was coming up when we first saw the outline of buildings in the distance. The city we had longed to see was now within sight. The first thing that I noticed about the city were the walls that enclosed it. We had seen walled cities before, but this one seemed dominated by the structure surrounding it. We could see that it indeed was a religious city, with many temples and mosques rising above the other buildings around them. As we neared the wall, we came to a wye in the road.

The commander took the one to the right and I thought for a while we would be going around the city, since we were passing by a walled section on our left. When we came upon a crossroad we saw some soldiers on a hill to the left setting heavy post in the ground. Others were letting down a man who was fastened to a cross arm on another post. I was beginning to realize what it was we were seeing when one of the soldiers behind us spoke.

"Better hope for someone to be in a good mood or we might be nailing you all to one of them logs." ending his remark with a muffled laughter.

Something was happening to me inside as we walked on past that dreadful hill. I knew in my heart that this was the place where they had hung Jesus. Tears flowed down my face. I felt that this city had a war going on within its walls. There was a force of goodness and mercy trying to overcome a barbaric culture that was being subsidized by those who were portrayed as being good. Where was justice?

How could people let this happen? How could people be so wicked?

As we marched on, I began feeling like nothing mattered; it didn't matter if they imprisoned us; it didn't matter if they killed us. Who would want to live in a society that tolerated such evil wickedness? Then I remembered what that old man had spoken to us way back on our journey—"*The One you seek can still be found*" Goodness had not been defeated. There was reason for hope. I felt ashamed to letting myself get so discouraged.

The garrison came to a stop when we were at a gate to the city. The commander left his men to watch us as he entered the gate. We could not see where he went and were left wondering what was to happen to us. He returned shortly and came directly to our group.

"You have been accused by the people whose property you used of belonging to the Followers of Jesus. Seeing no reason to doubt that charge, you are all sentenced to be held in prison here at Jerusalem until your fate be decided. You are now considered enemies of the state of Israel and prisoners of the Roman Empire.

Take them away." he ordered.

# CHAPTER TWELVE

# BEHIND BARS

The garrison then marched on with us in the middle and stopped a short distance up the road. We were grabbed by two soldiers, one of each side, and led to a cave like structure that sat off the road some distance. A huge iron-barred door was unlocked and we were shoved into the dark confines of our new home. The sound of the iron door slamming shut and then the lock clicking seemed to echo through the cave. It was such a final sound, not wanting to hear any appeal. The place was dark and it took our eyes a while to adjust to being able to see. The smell of urine was so strong that it made our noses sting. I was afraid to move for stepping in something I would rather not. Soon we could see other prisoners up against the walls. I guessed the room to be some 50 feet wide and maybe 80 feet deep. Some of the men were sleeping on straw if they could find it. Others were sitting with their backs to the cold wet walls. As we looked abound, it was evident that there was not room enough to find a place altogether. We started to separate and headed for a place to rest. My legs ached so much, I knew that Capt. Vitas and the others had to be in great discomfort.

"Come set over here." one of the prisoners said and he nudged a couple of men next to him so that they would move to make room.

We moved over against the wall and nearly fell to the floor. I didn't realize just how exhausted Capt. Vitas and Ben were. I wanted to give them water but there was none to be found.

"Mostly, we have to lick the stone to satisfy our thirst. They bring us food once a day with one bucket of water. Most of the time it is gone before half of us ever get to drink. Near the back of this cave is a tiny stream that trickles down. If you can find something to catch it you can have good water." the prisoner said.

They had made us leave our packs outside the gate to the prison. No use of wishing for a cup or pot. I felt for something in my pockets that I could use. When I ran my hand down the inner part of my jacket, I felt an old leather pouch that held some coins. I quickly removed it and took the coins out, trying not to jingle them so as not to advertise their presence. I made my way to the back and found the stream the old man had spoken of. It wasn't much of a stream but it had a steady flow. I let the pouch get about half full and them rinsed it best it could. It took a few minutes to let it fill again, but soon I had enough to take back to my friends.

As I gave the water to Capt. Vitas, Ben, and the others, I began to talk more with the man who had befriended us. "How long have you been in here?" I asked.

"Oh, not long—a month or more perhaps. You have a way of losing track of time in here. No one stays here long though, either your beaten with whips and let go or you die at the hands of the Romans. They are experts of death." he replied.

"Why are you in here?" I questioned.

"For simply being friends of Peter and John, disciples of Jesus. They are afraid to arrest them just yet for fear of a great revolt. Their tactic now is to cause fear in the people by putting the followers like me in prison. There are several of us in here. As a matter of fact, I don't think there is a real criminal among us." he answered.

"You're Jewish citizens, right?" I asked. "Why don't the authorities stop this cruel treatment?"

"The Romans are often acting on orders from the high priest. They are afraid of losing their power over the Jewish people. Who do you think the soldiers that brought you hear conferred with when they got to Jerusalem? It was more likely than not that Caiaphas was the one who ordered you placed in here." the old man said.

"You said you're friends of Peter and John—tell me about them. We have traveled here from Athens to find men like these. I would like to meet them, if possible." I asked, being careful to keep my voice down, not knowing who I could trust.

"You must be very careful. You are the kind of people that the Jewish authority fear the most. There are spies everywhere, even here I think. If we ever get out, then we will talk more." he answered.

I fell back to rest myself and pondered on all that had went on during this long, long night. I feared we would be in for a long stay in this prison. I must have fallen asleep for several hours. The sun was almost halfway down in the west by the way the shadows fell across the way. We hadn't been locked up for even a day yet and I was feeling like we had been imprisoned for weeks. I then recalled how I had a peace about this not being an end to the journey but a significant delay. Significant delay? How long might that be?

The rest of the day was spent with the men of our group. We talked about the things that had happened, about how the people back at the house must have sent for the soldiers to arrest us, about how unfair this all seemed. Our men seemed to have regained their strength and I was glad that the long march had not been too much for our older ones. It wasn't quite dark yet when a guard came to the door with our food.

"Everybody get back, Go on—back against the wall. One of you makes a move and you'll have some meat to put with this slop." he ordered as he dropped the buckets just inside the door and then backed out quickly.

There was a mad rush to the food bucket. The men reached in with their bare hands to scoop out a handful of what looked like gruel. There was a certain amount of shoving and struggle to get at the food. I guess we hadn't been in long enough yet to be that hungry. Soon a couple of men who could have been considered walking skeletons were taking turns scraping the bucket with their fingers and licking what they could to get a morsel of food to sustain them. It was a pitiful sight to see men brought such a level of existence. I determined in my heart that I would do what I could to make a difference in this world to stop this kind of treatment of humanity.

Things began to seem pretty hopeless for us. We had no one in authority we could go to for help. In fact, going to any authority around here would probably mean a swift end to our lives. The only shred of hope we had was to believe that Jesus was able to save us from this fate. As darkness once more overtook the cave, I quietly gathered the men of our group and we began to pray to be freed from this prison, we also prayed that the other men in here with us would be set free. We must have prayed for more than an hour. We were making enough noise that some of the others heard us and came to join in our petition. The old cave walls began to resonate with the low voices of men seeking help from God. I wondered what it sounded like from the outside and if there were any guards to hear us. Finally the prayers began to end and the men left the group to find their place to rest for the night. It was near mid-night, for we heard a temple bell ringing back in the city.

The men in our group also crawled over to find rest. My mind was debating over how the men who had prayed now felt. Did they have a renewed hope of rescue or were they back to giving in to disappointment? I wanted to stand up and shout loud enough for all to hear in the cave to have faith that we would be freed. *Just believe.*

I'm not sure how much later it was that we were all awoken but an intensity of light coming into the cave. It was so bright that we couldn't see anything and had to cover our eyes for protection. Suddenly we heard the old prison door fall from its hinges. Fear gripped al of us. We didn't know what to do. What if the guards heard all the commotion and were on their way to secure the cave? Where could we go once we were out? Why should we run if we were not guilty?

"Come on! All of you. Get out of here while you have a chance. If you have no place to go, come follow me. We must move quickly! Hurry!" the old man said.

As we left the cave we had to step over the old iron gate. I noticed it felt very warm and there were places near the hinges that still glowed as if they had been heated in a fire. No time to stop—just make sure to take mental note of it I thought to myself.

We ran along the bottom of a hill and stayed close to the cover of bushes and trees as much as we could. We hadn't gone too far down the way when the old man stopped. He motioned us to step into the brush where we weren't so easily seen. There were about 30 to 40 other prisoners who came along with us. The old man began to speak.

"You must now trust me to help you. I can take you to safety and some you can be back with your family by morning. I must have your trust. For some reason I can tell in my spirit that there are two among us who will betray us at the first opportunity. They have been promised a good reward for their efforts. What a pitiful price to put on a soul! I know not which of you are those two, but I know for certain you are here. There is one here who has four gold coins that amount to more than three times what you have been promised. If its greed that feeds your soul, then step forward to be paid now. Come while mercy it still extended. Wait and be struck down by the power of God where you stand.

One man started to come forward but was grabbed by another.

"Don't go. It's only a trick to reveal who we are. They will kill us once they find out!" the man pleaded.

"Very well, you have chosen!" the old man spoke as he raised his hand towards the heavens and commanded, "You have lived evil and now you die being evil! You shall no longer be an offense to God."

The two men fell dead instantly, one still clutching the other. Silence gripped the rest of us. I looked at Capt. Vitas and Ben to see if there was any sign of direction to come from them. Most of us were in a degree of shock.

"I can tell that you are having trouble trusting me. I have not much time to convince you. The only thing I can say it that if you want to seek God, to know more of Jesus, then you must follow me. If not then you are free to leave on your own. Stay in the brush and head southwest. We have but a few minutes to make a safe crossing on the road ahead. I will not wait any longer." the old man spoke.

Some of the men with us headed off into the cover of the growth that covered the hillside. Besides our group, there were about ten others who stayed with us. We moved ahead carefully, staying in the brush as much as we could. Soon the old man who was leading us stopped, turned to us and whispered that we must cross the road. This would put us in the open and we had to cross quickly. He told us to go in groups of five at a time, move very quickly, and dive into cover on the other side next to the city wall. We looked each way to see if any soldiers were on the road yet, and not seeing any, we sent the first group over—then the second. Before the rest of us were able to cross, a troop of soldiers came up to the cave entrance. They stood outside looking around to see if any prisoners were still hiding close to the cave. Some soldiers were sent into the cave with torches to see if any prisoners remained. A few of the soldiers began to move down our way, stepping into the shrubs and brush in hopes of finding us. I saw others going through bags just outside the cave. It was then I realized we had left all provisions we owned in our quick flight from the prison. These were the things we had relied on to help us sustain ourselves along the journey and now, they were gone for good. There was no hope of ever getting them back.

As the troops moved ever so slowly closer to our hiding place, we realized the need to act quickly. Our best hope seemed to be to make it across the road to the others. It was a dark night but the moon still lit the road enough that the soldiers could see us. My heart was pounding with my chest and I was afraid that the sound of it might give us away. To wait any longer would only make crossing more risky. Should we all try to go at once? It was just then that a cloud came crossing through the sky and covered the moon. It wasn't a large cloud but it would provide at least some protection.

"Get down low and get ready to move across as quickly as you can. Stay together so that we make only one form in the darkness. As soon as that cloud covers the moon, we move out. Try not to make any noise." I commanded.

It was just then that the old man on the other side of the road stepped out just enough for us to see him. He was motioning just up the road a piece, indicating we should go there. There was no time to discuss the matter, so when the moon was obscured, I led the way. We scurried out from the cover and moved diagonally to where the old man had pointed. We found he had directed us to small ditch that crossed the road. Some heavy planks formed a bridge and there was room for us to crawl through without being seen by the soldiers. We stayed in the bottom of the ditch until we reached the cover along the wall. The others met us there and then the old man motioned to follow him. It was only a couple hundred feet more that he stopped and motioned with his hands, indicating that we needs to crawl into a hole hidden behind some bushes. He then disappeared into the hole.

Sometimes it is not hard to be obedient when you know that there aren't any others choices. Each of us followed his leading. The hole turned into a narrow tunnel that I guessed must have been at least thirty feet in length. It was narrow enough that the only way to move through it was to use our elbows to pull ourselves through. I was not one who liked being confined to such tight places and there was a couple of moments that panic started to set in. It must have been Marco that was directly behind me, since I felt someone placing their hand on my foot and saying, 'Just keep moving'.

Finally the confines of the small tunnel gave way to an open area. I felt the bottom of the tunnel ended and was reaching around to find which way to move when firm hands took hold of mine and helped me to pull out of the tunnel and drop my feet to a dirt floor a few feet below. We were now standing in a dark room of some size. I don't know how large it was but I could reach out in all directions and not feel any walls. The ceiling was low enough to touch but we didn't have to crouch to be able to stand in it.

When the last of the group was pulled from the tunnel, the old man tried to gather us best he could and began speaking very softly.

"We are in secret tunnels beneath the city. Only a few people know of their existence and we should be safe here. We can move to several parts of the city and there are many places that will lead us outside the walls in nearly every direction. These tunnels have been here for many, many years. They were used by the priest and temple workers long ago. However, like so many things, they were forgotten by those entrusted with their care. They now offer great help to those of us who seek to follow the way of Christ. If you wish, I can get you back with your families, or if that is too dangerous for you; I can get you out of this city. Tell me what it is that you want of me." the old man said.

"Who are you? How do you know so much about all this?" Marco asked.

"My name is Demas. By some, I am considered a prophet; by others, a contentious man to be endured. Most would put me in the category of being a lunatic. But I myself, only claim to be a man who seeks God and then, tries to be obedient." he answered.

"What did you have to do with the prison door falling off its hinges?" Marco continued to question.

"Nothing more than what you had to do with it if you were praying with the rest of us. That door fell open by the power of God. I can't say He sent angles to do it, if He commanded it to fall, or just how it happened. The only thing I can say with certainty, is that God opened our prison." Demas replied.

"And the two men who were struck dead?" Marco went on.

"Those two had made choices in their hearts before they were ever placed in the cave with us. Right up to the very last moment, they chose not to change what was in their hearts. My part in their demise was this: I spoke to them what God gave me as a warning plea for them, revealing both His mercy and His wrath. Their actions revealed their hearts, therefore I petitioned God to administer His judgment. You were chosen as witness for the benefit of yourselves as well as for the benefit of those whom you will be ministering to in the future. We have a God who is loving beyond our ability to comprehend; however He is a God who has no tolerance for sin in the Kingdom. The Spirit of God lets me know this very moment that had those two men been allowed to walk the face of this earth another few moments, there would be many thousands of people who would not hear about Jesus Christ and His death for us. Many of you would be either be killed by now or you would soon be. Some of you have many people to speak with and to teach of the Way. Others of you will, by the change in your own life; a change that will be so evident, yes, you will offer a validity to a message being spread throughout this whole part of the earth. It grieves my heart that I had any part in ending the lives of those two men, but I am comforted in knowing I had a part in extending God's grace to countless others. You, therefore, must think what you want of me— judge me as harsh, as an eccentric. It really doesn't matter as long as God judges me as approved. My duty now is to get you to safety if you will trust me for that." Demas answered.

Demas' reply had a profound effect on all of us, even the men with us who we did not know. In one sense, he seemed to be the executor of justice; in another, one who had uncanny insight of the future. I don't think I was the only one who shared the opinion that he was different than anyone we had ever met. He would have been thought to be arrogant had he not been so sincere. In fact, I believe I was more intimidated of this frail old man than I was of the massive Roman commander.

And yet, there was a drawing to this person that I could not resist.

"Demas, you have our trust. Lead us as you think best." Capt. Vitas replied.

"Very well, then. How many of you wish to return to your homes here in Jerusalem? We shall assist you first." Demas stated.

Only three of the men thought it safe to return to their families. From there, they would go into hiding with their families. The others wanted to be led out of the city in whatever direction Demas thought best. We did not have any idea about where we should go. We placed ourselves into Demas' care.

We made our way very slowly through the tunnel, feeling our way as we went. Demas instructed us to attempt to keep one hand on the person in front of us as he led the way. Soon he had us moving along at an even step, indicating to us that he had spent much time down in these tunnels. We dared not use any light for fear of being detected. We were even careful to keep our voices to a faint whisper, not knowing when we were passing beneath an access shaft hidden somewhere above. After we had gone quite a long distance, Demas stopped to listen with his ear placed tightly against the tunnel wall.

"Wait here for a moment." he said as he went off into the pitch darkness of the passage.

"Just up ahead is a shaft that comes up in an old butcher shop. You three will know where you are when you climb out. If you're sure about leaving, then I wish you well. Be very careful and don't talk much to anyone. This city is full of people looking for an opportunity to endear themselves to the Romans and the priest and getting a few miserable coins in the process. May God be with you." said Demas.

We waited as the three made their way to the shaft and listened to hear them let us know they had made it out. We were getting lined up to continue on when I noticed something in my pocket. It was the coins I had taken out of my pouch in prison when I got the water. As I reached in to touch them, I felt four coins. Then I remember what Demas had said just after we left the prison.

"Demas!" I whispered. "I want to ask you something. Remember when you said someone had four coins to give the two spies before they fell dead after our escape? Well, how did you know who had them?" I asked.

"Oh, my son, I didn't know the individual. I only knew that someone had four coins worth more than what the spies had been promised and the owner of those coins would gladly give them away if it meant lives could be spared. I was correct in making that assumption, was I not?" he answered.

"Yes, sir. You were right." I whispered in reply.

We moved on through the tunnel in silence, each of us holding onto the shoulder of the man ahead of us. Sometimes we were stepping in standing water, sometimes in slick mud. Whenever one of us would stumble and fall, the whole group stopped and waited for the line to reform. We came to a shaft that led upward. Demas thought it might be near one of the temples and decided to send one of the men he knew up the shaft see what might be going on. Cirro and Alexus moved to help the man make his way up and then stood waiting with Demas to listen for any report. Soon the man came sliding back down and told us what he saw.

"We are right under the Caiaphas' house! There are soldiers checking all the streets—even banging on doors and wanting to know who is inside. I saw some of the Roman higher-ups talking with Caiaphas himself. They sure are stirred up about us. It's not safe to be around here!"

"There is one place we can stop before we reach the aqueduct. Some of the disciples use it as a meeting place. They can help us with some food." said another of the men.

"It might be too dangerous to go there tonight. If it's a place known by the authorities as meeting house for the disciples; I'd be mighty surprised if the Romans didn't have it covered." warned Demas.

"Can't we try to make it out of the city and be on our way to Joppa before daylight? I've seen enough of the holy place to make me think it ain't so hold." Cirro added.

"If you have told them that is where you are going, I can assure you they will have that road well covered. Your capture will go a long way in restoring the commander's good standing with the governor and with the Jewish priest. I am most certain that this last group of you who were arrested no more than a day ago are going to be blamed for the escape. The prison cave was a secure place that was known for its passive prisoners. Now, just when you seven men show up; the door falls off and the place is emptied. Yes, my friends, you have become very special to the authorities and I know they would thoroughly enjoy your presence at their next meeting." Demas said with a restrained laughter, letting us know that we would be in great danger if caught; but also letting us know he had confidence in getting us out from under their noses.

"All I can say is that the power of God is upon you men. I could feel it when you came into that cave." Demas said as he began to lead us on.

He led us on some distance and then stopped, told us to wait for him to return, and gave instructions to one of the other men with us as to what to do if he Shouldn't return. That all being done, he disappeared into the darkness. We sat quietly in the dark, waiting—and thinking. Thinking about what we were going to do. About where we cold go. We didn't even know where we were or which way was which. We had to trust this one old man—a man who had no doubt been ridiculed for his ways. He even made us wonder about his mental stability. There was one thing about him, however, that reduced all those doubts and uncertainty to naught—that being the undeniable fact that this old man knew God and God knew him.

I don't think we had waited an hour when we heard someone coming toward us. There was a rustling sound accompanying the approaching person. When Demas got close enough to talk softly to us, he began to tell us what he had been up to.

"I've got some fresh bread and water for you. Yes, I know it's prison food but you must be starving so you won't mind all that much. To finish off this fine meal, I also have some wine—it will help you get your strength back. When you are done eating, I will be taking our local men out to the hills and letting them be on their way. They will be able to find people to help them get away—besides they aren't the ones the authorities really want to catch right now. They, they will be safe, yes, I believe they will all get away safely. Then, I will return to take care of you, my friends—but now, eat and drink." Demas said with a soft chuckle.

There was such a light-heartedness about that old man. He seemed to be totally free of worry and almost seemed to enjoy the challenge of out-smarting the authorities. He had a way of saying things that came across as being childlike or naive—even insane. While all of this was draining our strength and wearing on our faith, Demas was being nourished by it. He was being filled with energy in his body and wisdom in his mind. As we listened to him whispering to us, we could tell he would in one place, and then, suddenly he was several feet away helping another. I had this mental picture of him hopping around life a grasshopper.

When we had finished eating the bread, he left with the local men—promising to return as soon as he could but not sure how long he might be gone.

"Stay where you are unless you are sure someone is coming. In that case, you are standing where three passages intersect. All three lead somewhere, none being dead ends. Take whichever way you feel led to go and I trust I will be able to find you when I return. For now, try to rest." he instructed.

It was a lonely sound hearing them leave. It was the first time our group had been alone since we were taken by the soldiers. We talked softly about what we could do and realized we were pretty helpless on our own. A few 'what ifs' were discussed but they always came back to the fact we were lost in a place where staying lost was our best hope for the moment.

"What is it that we want?" asked Capt. Vitas. "Do we want to try to get out of this land and to the safety of the sea? Do we want to find those who can teach us more about Jesus? Do we have some direction for Demas when he returns or do we want simply trust him to know what to do for us?"

"I ain't had much to say lately. Maybe some of you appreciate that." Ben said with a short chuckle. "But those hare hard questions, Capt. I don't know which way we should go. I do feel one thing for sure. Our journey is not yet done. We are not ready to go home just yet."

"Well, I kinda miss known what the weather is gonna be doin', Ben, but it has been sort of peaceful." Artemis replied, not wanting to miss an opportunity to tease Ben and lighten up the mood of our group. "It sound like we are gonna be in danger whichever way we go. I don't think we're finished yet either so maybe it'd be best to spend another week or so around here."

"What about you and Marco, Nic? What are your feeling?" Capt. Vitas asked.

I waited for Marco to answer first. I wanted him to let his thoughts be known before I said anything to influence his reply.

"There's a lot more to learn, that's for certain. My concern is that we can't be very trusting of the people around here." Marco answered.

I started to speak but felt held back by something inside. That was then followed by wanting to hear what Alexus and Cirro had to say so I asked them to let us know what they thought.

"I'd just as soon get outa here!" Cirro said. "We can do some learnin' somewhere else that is a little more friendly."

"I'm not used to having' to sneak around and always be lookin' behind you to see who might be after you. Never lived that way, ever. It wears on my nerves. As much as I'd like to be at sea again, I feel we ain't done here yet." Alexus added.

"That leaves only you, Nic. What's your opinion?" Capt. Vitas asked.

"I've been getting mighty homesick lately. My heart surely must be getting wore out from beating so hard—beating from fear and a stirring within my soul. I'd love to be home again to see my family but to see them without having the knowledge to change the way things are back there—going home would be rather empty. I don't know where to go from here. The only thing I can say for certain is that I want to be around people like Mary and Martha, like Demas. There are things to learn from them that can't be found in any book, taught in any class. Maybe if it's nothing more than the time spent with Demas leading us out of here—anywhere, than I want to soak up what's in him. If you think back on all the people we have met on our way here, it's been that connection that happens when were with them. It's like we can see inside them to understand what makes them the way they are. That's the one thing all these wonderful people have in common—a heart filled with love for people." I replied.

"I didn't feel much love comin' from that Roman commander!" Cirro responded.

"Exactly! That's because most people are just that way unless they have been changed on the inside. I believe there is hope even for someone like him to be changed." I quickly jumped in to reinforce my point.

"Seems like most of us see a need to stay long enough to see this finished. Cirro, we don't want you to feel out-voted—your opinion counts as much as anyone's. I suppose we'll have to wait until Demas returns to find out where we go then." Capt. Vitas said, drawing our conversations to a close.

## CHAPTER THIRTEEN

# WITHOUT
# A DOUBT

Some time later, Demas returned. It is very hard to have any sense of time when there is such darkness, with the exception that it seems to go on forever. That thought caused me to recall the times when I was younger and would wake up from a bad dream. The relief that the first light of morning would bring seemed to take forever to arrive. Darkness and light—in this world we have both. Some enjoy the darkness, it gives them cover and protection—hides their behavior. Others welcome the light as a power to overcome the forces of darkness—a beginning of hope with each ray of light that penetrates the darkness. Oh, yes darkness—I was so caught up in my thinking that I almost forgot that Demas had returned. We were not sure how long he had been gone or how soon it would be daylight. The old man still had considerable energy but the efforts he was putting into getting all of us to safety was beginning to wear him down. He took a few minutes to catch his breath and then gave us instructions.

"Somewhere close by you will find a bundle of clothes. I want you each to try to find a tunic and a sash to make a turban. Size won't matter much so don't Worry about which is which. When you all have what you think is right, we'll move on. As soon as daylight begins to penetrate these passages, we will stop and change clothes. I have with me a small bag of black sheep's wool for facial hair. It may take some work, but we are going to make Jewish men out of you yet." chuckled Demas.

We found the clothes and were soon on our way. We traveled a good distance through the tunnel until we finally saw a soft haze ahead of us. Daylight was finally dispersing the darkness of the long night. I found myself wondering why I hadn't been so appreciative of the morning light before. It seemed we must have been in the dark cave and now, the even darker tunnel, for days. I started to run to stand in the hazy light that was falling on the tunnel floor but was stopped by Demas.]

"Wait!" he whispered. "We must approach this opening with great caution. If my recollection is right, we are just south of the temple. Once we come up, we will step into a large crowd of people if we wait just a short while. When we climb up, we will be in the back room of a shop that sells articles used in offerings in the temple. I know some of the people who run the place—they will help us. Now, let's see what we can do to turn you into Jews. Aye, I have great task on my hands."

We tried to help Demas as he worked with us. He soon had Marco and myself looking very much like young Jewish men but he was having some difficulty with Artemis and Capt. Vitas. The sheep's wool looked very realistic and the captain's grey beard soon took on a new appearance with the black mixed in. Finally, he was satisfied he could not do much more with us and stepped back to see how we looked.

"Walk around just a bit." he said as he watched us carefully.

"Watch me!" he interrupted. "Reach out with step—lengthen your stride. Project some determination in your walk—seem anxious to get where you are going." he continued as he imitated what he wanted us to do.

"Now, your speech. Do you know any of our language?" he asked.

"Artemis and Ben know some words. Alexus knows a few. The rest of us might learn some." Marco answered.

"No, no! No time to learn now. Limit what you say to only what is absolutely necessary. Let Ben and Artemis speak for you if possible. Otherwise, just a nod or a smile. If you don't linger anywhere and keep moving, I think you will make it where we are going." Demas instructed.

"Where are we going?" Ben asked.

"We are going to join in with those leaving worship at the temple and then walk right through town as we head for Emmaus. It is important that we blend right in. Once we get to Emmaus, we will have friends willing to take us in. I will not be going with you, since I am well known and easily recognized by the authorities. I will make it there ahead of you, however and will be waiting there to lead you to safety." Demas explained.

"Demas, one other question. What did you use to stick these beards on with? —my face is itching terribly. How do we get them off?" Marco asked.

"Well, they won't exactly come off. I didn't want some soldier to be able to pull them off you if you got stopped. I'm afraid you will have to let them wear off, but the glue is not harmful—at least to most people. I'm sorry for the discomfort but it is for your own wellbeing.' he replied.

"I will leave one of my men with you to help you find the way. Remember, do not talk to anyone unless it is absolutely necessary. Keep moving and avoid eye contact as much as you can—wait! Listen! Hurry! Move over here into the darkness. Someone's coming!" Demas whispered as he pulled us away into the shadows.

We stood motionless and tried to keep our breathing shallow. We all listened but were unable to hear what Demas heard. After a moment or two, we finally began to hear the faint sound of sticky footsteps coming form down the tunnel where we had just been. I hadn't noticed our trip through the muddy section being that noisy. The sound of shoes pulling from the slimy tunnel floor then began to grow quieter but was replaced by the raspy sound of scuffing through dry dust that was on the tunnel floor around us. Gradually we were able to make out the figures of four or five people coming our way. They certainly weren't being as cautious as we had been and we were anxious to know who they were. I began to fear they might be soldiers sent down in search for us. They stopped just short of the lighted area across from us. We waited; being afraid to even breath and hoping our heartbeats were audible to them, to see what they would do next.

As they began to speak, Demas thought he recognized the voice of one or tow of them. He indicated to us by placing his hand on our chest and patting very gently that he was going to approach the newcomers standing in the dim light. Anxiety reigned and hearts pounded within us as we waited to see what would happen.

"Greeting my friends.: Demas called softly from behind them. "That is you standing there under that cloak, isn't it Thadaeus?"

Startled, the group quickly turned to face the voice that called to them. "Who is it?" they asked, almost too loud to maintain our safety.

"Yes, yes it is you. Demas here! It is good to see you again. It's been so long since we heard from any of you that we feared for your safety and well being." he answered as he stepped out to embrace them with a firm hug.

"What are you doing down here by yourself? We heard it is very dangerous to be out on the streets.." they continued to question.

"Oh, I'm far from being alone. In these last several days, I've felt the presence of God so powerfully with me that I can never say that I'm alone. Also I have some friends with me over there in the dark waiting. Come on out and meet some friends of mine and Jesus." Demas said as he motioned for us to come.

We stepped over beside Demas and greeted his friends with reserved handshakes. Our trusting ways had been diminished by the turn of event that led to our imprisonment and we were a bit slow to warm up to anyone now. We followed Demas mostly because he seemed to be our best hope of escaping and also because of his connection with God. Even with our skepticism being stirred, we could find integrity in Demas that allowed us to trust him. Now we were opening our trust to his friends based on his acceptance of them.

"Where are you going?" Demas asked them.

"We are trying to leave Jerusalem, at least for a while until it becomes safe to be here. Our plans is to go up new the rear of the temple area and walk right out of town with the other worshipers. I think this is the shaft that leads up there." Thadaeus answered.

"That too is our plan! It must be nearing the time for early worship to be ending. I will send someone up to see." Demas exclaimed

Several of us help lift the man up into the shaft and then watched him climb on up into the morning light. Crumbs of soil and dust fell in our faces as we watched for him to climb on out. Suddenly he stopped and retreated back down part of the way into the shaft. He carefully slide back down to us and motioned for us to be very still as he led us back away from the shaft area.

"It will not be possible to climb out of this opening without being noticed. They have extra guards posted all around the temple. We would definitely be spotted if we were to attempt it." he reported, his eyes darting back and forth as he spoke—relaying to us the danger encountered just by raising his head above the ground.

"Very well then, there is one other place we need to try. In fact, it is the last opening on this side of Jerusalem. If I recall correctly, it comes up in an old stable just outside of town. It is well hidden and we can leave from there a few at a time. Thadaeus, will you be going up into the hill country when you leave?" Demas inquired.

"Yes, we will go straight up to the hills and then separate. We will be harder to find that way. Perhaps in a week or so tensions will calm down here in Jerusalem and it won't be so dangerous to return to our families." Thadaeus answered.

The rest of the journey through the tunnels didn't seem to take long and we were soon standing under the opening Demas had remembered. It was somewhat larger than the others we saw. As if all at the same time, we noticed an unusual silence. Not a sound was to be heard above us. At first, it seemed to be a good thing, but the longer we listened for any kind of movement or noise, the more concerned we became that it might be a trap—that soldiers were hiding to watch for someone to come out of the hole behind the stable.

"We'll never find out much down here. Boost me up a little!" Demas quipped as he moved to get in place to reach up into the shaft. Since it was larger, he had to use his feet to press his back against the wall and work his way up. Dirt clods fell and enough dust come down to look like smoke in the sunlight that was filtering down. He soon came scampering down.

"Right where we want to be and not a soul in sight! Quickly now, everyone—let's get up and out of here. Alexus and Cirro, you are strong men. Let's get you up first and you can reach down to pull the rest of us up." he ordered.

The desire to be out of the tunnel must have been strong among all of us but we also appreciated the safety it had offered us. One by one, the men climbed out. Capt. Vitas, Ben, Artemis, Marco and myself were waiting to let the others go ahead of us. Suddenly Cirro spoke as loud as he dared telling us to step back and stay quiet. Someone was coming toward the stable. He was gone in a flash and before the last dirt fell to the floor, we heard people talking. They didn't sound to be Romans and that was somewhat a relief, but only a short relief. From the sounds we could tell they must have went into the stable. As best we could tell, there were three of them and they seemed to be drinking. In fact they sounded like they had been at that task for more than a little while.

Demas had already made it out and there was only one of Thadaeus' men left with us. After waiting for several minutes, we decided we would have to wait them out and so slumped to the tunnel floor with our back against the wall. I must have been especially nervous about waiting because I was startled to hear Capt. Vitas speak to me.

"All of this time and you have yet to develop patience, Nic? You have learned so much but in this, I'm a little disappointed. Just as fine food is made to taste better with salt, so wisdom is multiplied when seasoned with patience. Master this and you will have a key to much of life." he instructed me.

I wasn't aware I had been so obvious in wanting to get on with our journey. My first response to hearing Capt. Vitas's words was to be offended and embarrassed that he had pointed out my faults in front of my friends. But I knew Capt. Vitas and knew he intended his words to be of encouragement and teaching— not hurtful in the least. Deep in my heart I knew he spoke rightly. I sat silently-feeling that chunk of pride sticking in my throat as I tried to swallow it.

"I'll try if you will give me some time." I said with a tone indicating I had heard his instruction and couldn't wait to try to live it. It took a minute or so before my fellow travelers caught on to what I had just said. Then we all laughed at my lack of patience and my eagerness to hurry up a learn it.

Not long afterwards we noticed the talking from above us had ceased. We weren't sure if they had moved on or if they had finally passed out from their drinking. Marco was the first up and headed toward the shaft.

"Come on Nic, help me up. I will see what's going on." he spoke to me softly.

I cupped my hands so he could step in them and then on to my shoulders. He was soon up and out, disappearing from view. It must not have been more than a couple of minutes until he was back—laying at the top of the shaft, reaching down for us.

"Come on! Hurry! Those men are sleeping for now but I don't know how for how long. We've got to get out now while we can." he said.

As I was getting ready to send Ben up, Alexus and Cirro appeared next to Marco, reaching down as far as they could to help get us out. They soon had Ben out and were trying to reach Capt. Vitas when we heard someone telling them to move out of the way. It was Ben and he had found a ladder that he was lowering into the shaft. Leave it to Ben to find a way. It sure made our task much easier, not to mention being less stressful on Artemis and the captain.

As I stood on fresh green grass and inhaled clean air filled with the smell of spring blossoms, I was deeply appreciative of welcome change. It seemed that the burning in my nostrils from the urine smell of the cave and the musty odor of the tunnel would remain for quiet some time. I was now pleased to find that it was quickly being replaced with the sweet smell of spring. We were all walking away form the shaft when we heard Ben call out...

"Artemis, give me a hand here. I don't want to leave this ladder here to advertise about the tunnel and besides—I've got a plan for it. Grab the other end." he ordered.

Artemis got hold of the ladder and followed Ben into the stable. We couldn't see just what they were doing, but they soon came out with big grins on their faces.

"I'd like to wait for those guys to come around now. I bet they never will be able to figure out just how they got tangled up in that ladder. Might even be enough to make 'em give up drinkin' so much." Ben chuckled.

# CHAPTER FOURTEEN

# THE ROAD TO EMMAUS

To be outside, feeling the warmth of the sun driving off the morning chill— what a wonderful feeling. It seemed to put energy in our step and hope in our soul. We had been walking along the road for nearly an hour without seeing any other people. Demas had left us back at the tunnel and Thadaeus and his men were off into the hills. Now we saw a small group of men coming down the road toward us. I tried to remember all that Demas had told us and reminded the others.

"Reach out with your step. Show determination! Come on!" I encouraged as I tried to lead by example as well. Amazingly I felt a confidence in my walk and I tried it. It was almost like taking possession of the ground I stepped on with each stride. I wasn't sure that I altogether liked that feeling, but; non the less, it was there. I found myself wondering how large an estate I might accumulate if I walked far enough. What could

I do with a very long, very narrow piece of property? Now, wait! Let me get back to the reality of the moment.

Purposely trying to walk in a way that projected Jewish characteristics was working. I felt Jewish. My friends were able to master that determined walk as well. It was working and now the strangers coming near us would have no reason to notice us, let alone, be suspicious of us. Demas sure knew how to help.

We made good time on the road that morning. Our new style of walking even helped us cover more distance. We didn't seem to tire as easily but then again, we didn't have to pack anything with us. I suspect a person can find something good in just about anything if you set your mind to it.

Emmaus was a short day's walk west of Jerusalem. By mid-morning we were far enough away from the holy city that we began to feel more at ease about being caught by the authorities. Most of the attention of the Romans and the Jewish officials was focused on Jerusalem even though we were able to learn that they had set up check points on roads leading up into Galilee. A little before noon we began to become aware that we were growing hungry and we had absolutely nothing to eat with us. If we had any food with us, we didn't have a way of cooking anything or preparing a meal. I had even forgotten about the blankets and old canvas sails we had used so often for shelter. Lost too, was the few precious sheets of parchment that I had hoped to use to record this tremendous journey on. I don't recall having seen any paper available for purchase since we left Athens.

As we continued walking, a plan formed in my mind that before we each departed to our own ways, it was crucial that we all worked together to help remember all the events of our trip. Most likely the best time for that would be on the ship headed back to Greece. I reminded Marco to help me be watching for something to write on during the rest of our journey.

The sun was past the mid-day mark and headed towards the western sky when we stopped to rest. No one mentioned our lack of food or the fact that our stomachs were growling. It seemed like we just started talking together in much the same way we had many times earlier. Our group was more at ease than we had been for several days. We had learned much during our short stay in Jerusalem, had met several people who had helped us have understanding about much of Jesus and His ministry. It wasn't a time without cost but precious things usually come with a cost. I suppose the most precious knowledge we learned was knowing that Jesus died to give us the most precious gift of all time. In my heart I had definite knowledge that this was foundational to the purpose of our whole journey. It was something beyond our ability to fully understand at present but held great promise to provide significant hope to all men. I cannot say how I knew this, but I can assure you with all certainty that I'm in possession of this knowledge. It is embedded in my soul in such a way that it cannot be denied, rejected, or stolen. It is beginning to burn within—wanting to be given out—but never to be depleted.

I started to tell the others about what was going on in me, however, I didn't need to tell much before I realized that they too were familiar with this knowledge. I can't say if they felt it as deeply as I—who knows? Maybe even more than me.

That wasn't what was important. Soon after I began sharing my heart with them, there was not one man who wasn't weeping at the appreciation of knowing what we had been privileged to learn. We sat quietly far a while longer and then Ben got up and started down the road. The rest of us followed—walking in silence but not in sadness.

By mid afternoon we came upon the small village of Emmaus. It was a town noticeably more at rest that the one we had just came from. The people would look as us and not jut pass by with their heads down to avoid eye contact. Now, we didn't know if it was because they were more friendly or because we now looked like their kinfolk. For whatever reason, it was a pleasant experience to have strangers smile at us as we walked by them.

We hadn't went far into the town when someone reached out from behind a building and pulled Marco around the corner. Before we could rush to his rescue, Demas swung out from the place where Marco had just disappeared and motioned for us to come with him. We were all startled and had to collect ourselves before we could follow him. That old man must have ran at least half the distance to be there ahead of us; except he didn't show the least indication of being winded. He led us to what seemed to be a residential part of the town and had us to gather around a well that must have supplied most of the homes in that area.

"I believe we will all be safe here. From what I have been able to learn, the only soldiers around here are ones just passing through and those have been few. I take it you had no problems on your way here?" Demas asked.

"No, no problems at all. In fact, we had a wonderful time." Capt. Vitas answered. "I trust yours was a safe one as well?"

"Oh, yes, yes—usually is." he said in a quick way which indicated he had other things on his mind and didn't want to spend time talking about anything else. "I want to take you to some folks here in Emmaus who have helped several of my friends in the past. They will have a place for you to rest where you will be safe. I cannot guarantee they will have any food—if they do you will be welcome to it. They ask nothing in return for their kindness but that you return kindness to others. If you have to give, they will gladly accept it. It does not change the way they treat you. They are very special people. But before you meet them we need to get these beards off. Come quickly with me." Demas ordered as he led us by the arm to a small shed nearby.

"Take these cloths and soak your faces with this goat's milk. It should dissolve the glue. Hurry, hurry! We must get going!" He instructed.

When we put the clothes up to our faces, we could smell the goat's milk and it must have been aging for a while. I wasn't sure if I wanted to trade the itchy glue and wool for the odor of soured goat milk but he was still insisting we get it done. I was surprised at how easily the glue was released and the milk actually felt soothing to my face, even if it did stink.

"Here, now wipe your faces clean with this water and towel. These people are waiting for us—Come now, come!" Demas chattered as he darted around taking care of us.

From everything I knew of my short acquaintance with Demas, his haste to get us to these people caused me the believe that he had more in mind than just finding food and shelter for us. It wasn't anything I feared but a growing anticipation of what it might be and, by the way Demas was hustling to get us going, I wouldn't have long to wait. He soon had us on our way down a narrow street. We didn't walk very far when he told us to stop and wait outside a neatly kept home. Demas went to the door and was soon taken inside. It was only a moment or two before he came back out and stood motioning for us to come in with him.

When we entered the home, we saw a modest but well-cared for room and three or four people greeted us. Demas ushered us in quickly and told the people that we would need a place to rest for day or perhaps, two. He also told them we hadn't ate much for the last three days and would appreciate any food they could spare.

"Don't go to any trouble to accommodate us. We need only a place to sleep tonight. We do not want to burden you more than that." Capt. Vitas said.

"You all are not a burden to us. You see, we have dedicated this home to helping fellow believers. It is yours to sleep in tonight, even for the next few nights if needed. Tonight, we have enough food to satisfy your hunger. Sometimes, there isn't food for ourselves when we have no guest; but when the Lord sends His people, He has not failed to provide food. It is something we don't always understand, but we accept it to be the way the Lord works. Now, come and eat with us. Let us be found to be willing servants." said one of the men who must have lived in the home.

No one was willing to argue with that kind of explanation so we followed them into a dining area that was small but adequate. The aroma of hot food made me even more hungry. The pots and kettles on the hearth looked rather small and I looked over the rest of the room but saw no other cooking equipment. I guessed there might be enough food to feed about four people, maybe five if it was served sparingly. I decided that I would be the last one in line to eat and let the older ones go first.

It was then that a man with two children entered the room from the back part of the house. Now this really complicated the situation. I was beginning to feel really awkward and like we were imposing on people who didn't have much to give and, now, we were taking what little they had. There was also something about the man and his children that intrigued me. Alas, we were inside where there was some warmth and a safe place to sleep and it even smelled clean. I was determined to be grateful for that.

The lady of the house set worn plates along with some spoons on the old table and called for someone to bring in fresh water. She then retrieved the pots from above the glowing coals and placed them at the end of the table and looked to her husband to indicate her part was ready.

"Let us pray." he said. "Lord once more you have favored us with fellowship of new believers. You have allowed us to be a part of your work here on earth and for that we are eternally grateful. Now, Lord, we ask your blessing on this food and pray that there will be enough. You know how many you have brought to us tonight and how hungry they must be. Lord, even these small children here can understand that there is not enough now in these kettles to meet our needs; therefore we will all know that when everyone has been fed, it is because of your provision. You have generously helped us before and now, we ask again. We thank you for you great care for us. Amen."

Our host took his place at the head of the table and began to ladle out nice portions of food onto the plates. By all common sense reasoning, there would only be enough to serve three plates at the most. I found myself wondering when the Lord was going to work His multiplying powers. Would the kettle suddenly begin to overflow? Would there be other kettles I hadn't seen? By now our host was putting food onto the fourth plate and he wasn't having to scrape to get it. I wasn't doubting that God would help, but I certainly was curious as to exactly how He would do it. My hope of getting something to eat was growing as I watched those ahead of me continue to be supplied. I was just behind Marco as he was getting his helping when we heard someone coming in. I turned to see and it was a young lady carrying a pail of water. I assumed she was the couple's daughter since she had a strong likeness of the mother. I started to return my attention to getting my food but I found my attention becoming focused on the young lady. As I looked at her again, I was taken by her beauty. As she moved closer to the candlelight, I could tell she had a radiance on her face that outshone any flower I had ever seen. She kept a smile on here face as she filled the cups with fresh cool water. By now I was almost totally unaware of the food that was being dished onto my plate. In fact, our host had to take hold of my plate to keep me from letting it fall to the floor.

"God is good to provide for our needs but we shouldn't try His patience by wasting any." said the host with a light-hearted tone.

I felt embarrassed once more, this time at being caught staring at his daughter. I was left without words to say to recover. I could only raise my eyes to his and grin slightly. His eyes showed that he could understand my behavior and for that, I was glad. It was at that moment that I saw into the kettle that he had been serving from. It must have been just about at much left in it as had been when he started serving. Once more, I just about dropped my plate.

"I'm sorry, sir. I didn't mean t.. .It's just as.. ..you've already fed nine people from that small kettle and there is still enough for more!" I stammered.

"You act surprised? Is this your first miracle, my friend?" he asked.

'Oh, No sir. Not the first for sure! It just so amazing—" I continued.

By now I realized everyone was watching me and embarrassment flooded over me once more. I felt so childish, and now, especially in front of this young lady. Then I realized something else. Here was a pot of proof. We had just joined together in a prayer asking for provision for enough and here it was. I reached for a cloth to take hold of the hot kettle and tipped it for all to see.

"Would this kettle hold what was put on your plates if you were to dump it back in? I THINK NOT! We all know what was there to begin with and we can clearly see what is left here now. As for me, I think that is something to get excited about. PRAISE GOD!" I shouted as I moved around the table taking hold of my friends and hugging them as I made the round. I ended up back at the end of the table and was going to take my plate and find a seat. The young lady was finishing with the water and was right next to me. She almost immediately recaptured my attention.

"Take this plate! I'll get another." I blurted out without really thinking what I was saying. She refused my offer and accepted the one her father held out to her. I made my way to a empty chair at the other end of the room, hoping I hadn't offended her by offering my food to her. Sometimes I can really put my foot in my mouth.

I found it hard not to keep looking at this young lady even though I was hearing some interesting talk about the man with the two children. I wanted to know everything that was being said concerning the man but I was feeling a drawing to this young woman that was different than anything I had ever felt before. I was attracted to her with a longing to be with her—to get to know her. Even though she was very beautiful, there was a much more powerful attraction pulling at me. I was experiencing feelings that I never had before. I had heard from other young men back in Athens about the physical attractions they had for girls but his was new and different. I can't say that I understood what was happening in my heart but I can say there was a new beat to it.

The young lady left the room with her mother, taking their food to eat away from the rest of us. The father served himself and then sat down to join us, asking many questions and wanting to learn all we had to tell. It was a long evening since there was so much to tell about. We had just about completed our story of Mary and Martha when our host interrupted us.

"You know them?!" he shouted. "You actually talked to them! This is incredible! You have heard from their own mouths about Jesus and His suffering? Do you know who this is?" he cried, tears coming down his face and he held his hand toward the man with the two children.

"This man is Simon. He and his children, Alexander and Rufas here were in Jerusalem to observe the Passover when he was taken by Roman soldiers and made to carry the very cross Jesus was carrying. They had beaten and whipped Jesus so severely that He had no strength left to drag that huge wooden beam. They made Simon here help Him carry it!" he said, having some difficulty telling us while he was weeping at the thought.

"You were that close to Jesus?" Ben asked, looking at Simon.

"Yes, I was very close—face to face in fact. It was such a horrible time. We had to watch Him being tortured and kicked. By the time I was made to help pick up that heavy beam, He hardly had enough strength left to breath with. Blood was pouring down His face and His back was torn beyond belief. His blood was dripping on me and it had soaked much of the beam He was holding. I was soon covered in many places by His blood—on my clothes and my skin. As I took hold of the cross, He turned to look directly into my eyes. I have never seen such compassion coming from another human. His eyes were able to communicate so much." Simon said.

"You'd think He wouldn't have much compassion for those who were beating Him. I would have been dealin' with feelings of hatred." Alexus spoke.

"Most of us would have." Simon replied, "But that is just it. He held fast to the very end of His life on earth to the things He taught. He showed us how to love each other. If He had given in to those feelings of hatred, then all would have been lost. As much as I despised being made to drag that cross, it was a great privilege to get that close to Jesus during those last hours—not only close in body but close in spirit. I cannot tell you all that transpired during that walk with Him. It is beyond the ability of words to describe."

We were all greatly moved by what Simon had told us. Demas was weeping almost uncontrollably and our host was sitting by him, also weeping and trying to comfort him. It was very quiet in the room except for the sounds of crying and heartache. It was during this time that I noticed Simon's two children. They were left at the table to hear all we had talked about. No doubt, they had witnessed the beating of Jesus and watched as their father was made to carry that cross. I felt such deep sorrow for them. They appeared to be almost numb to all that was going on, but I knew in my heart that they were experiencing this grief as we all were. They needed someone to help them let it out—someone to hold them and to let them know someone understood how they felt. I wanted to go to them myself, but I didn't know what to say. I watched them a bit longer until I knew I had to go to them. While I hadn't had experience with children or with counseling, I would have to give them what was inside my heart and try my best to let them know I cared.

At first, they were reluctant to let me get close to them. This caused me to retreat from my efforts. I wished their mother could have been there for them and then realized Simon hadn't mentioned anything about their mother. They may not have had one. This thought refortified my determination to reach out to these children and so I tried once more. This time they allowed me to hug them both at the same time and began to listen as I spoke to them.

"It's alright to feel sad and it's alright to cry. You saw some very bad things happen to a very good man. Your father was made to do something he didn't want to be a part of but he had to. Actually what he did must have really helped make it better for Jesus. He knew He wasn't suffering alone—there was someone there to help. I want to be here to help you." I told them quietly.

Whatever I said must have reached into their hearts because they both began to cry and turned to hug me from either side. I just held them tightly and let them get it out. I hadn't even thought about the others in the room. The first one I even noticed was Simon. He had stopped weeping long enough to notice his children and started to come to them, but stopped when he realized they needed to finish their time of grieving. I could tell in my heart that I had been given spiritual direction in going to these little children. I had been obedient and because of that, they were helped. That is what this journey was all about—seeking the truth, finding it, and then living it. It wasn't a complicated doctrine to be learned or a complex set of instructions to be memorized. It was finding Jesus and then loving others the way He loves them. Pretty simple and not all that hard to do, if you will just do it. The love that I felt pouring into those little boys under my arms was something that I didn't know I had in me. I was being helped as much as they were. I am finding that is usually what happens when you do things for God.

We sat quietly for a short while longer just letting our emotions and thoughts have some time to process all that had happened in that room. It took some time for the weeping to end. In most cultures, if would have been perceived as a weakness for men to weep as these men had. Unfortunately, most cultures have failed to discover the foundational knowledge we had encountered. None of the world's ways seem to matter to us this evening. There was a spirit drawing us together in this room tonight that was powerful but yet amazingly gentle. The world would not have understood or appreciated the significance of it. It is ironic that the ultimate purpose of all that we were coming to understand was for the benefit of people all over the world; people who were working hard to prevent the spread of such understanding and knowledge. I have absolutely no doubt that each person in this room was divinely appointed to be here to experience perhaps the most intimate and insightful accounts of the crucifixion of Christ. Something in my heart led me to believe that we may not get to meet Jesus on this journey, but it didn't cause great disappointment. We had been greatly blessed to have met so many people who were able to transfer to us the character of Jesus as He had shared it with them. Now, it seems, it was our privilege and duty to share the same with others we would meet. Simon, in particular, had been able to convey so may aspects of that agonizing walk that morning—the torture, pain, and suffering; but he also conveyed the unrestrained love, even for those who had beaten Him, the forgiveness, and most of all, the hope.

I did not want to move a muscle for fear of disturbing the precious work that was being done among us. I did not want to release my hold on these two little children and I did not want to cause any of my friends there with me to miss anything that was yet to come for them. I felt a welling up in me to begin to praise God for all that had happened and started to softly and quietly. Soon Ben and Marco were joining me and then a couple of the others. We were not loud but it was audible to all in the room. Suddenly, there was a voice that sounded like it said, "Blessed are you Simon!"

It caused us to stop to listen. We didn't hear anything else and although we looked at each other, none of us wanted to ask if anyone else heard what we thought we did. Soon Demas and our host got up and most of the others followed their lead. Cirro and Marco helped clear the table. I spoke a little more to the children and tried to show my care and love for them as I released them from our precious time together. Simon was standing by us with a radiance on his face. He reached down for the children and then reached out to me. I started to give him my hand but he bypassed that and reached behind me to hug me close to the three of them. Not a word was spoken but much was said in that embrace. The moment was broken when Demas announced the arrangements for sleeping for the night.

"Since there are so many of us tonight, some will sleep in the next room and some in here. There are some blankets, but not enough for all of us. Keep in my those who might need them most." Demas instructed.

"Please forgive our manners, Demas, but we have not introduced ourselves to our host and his family. I would like the honor of knowing the name of our most gracious provider for the evening." Capt. Vitas inquired.

"Oh, I'm sorry as well. I should have done that when we first arrived but I was so excited about all that I knew." Demas replied.

He then asked our host to come to him and told us his name was Levi and his wife was Serirah. It seemed really strange to have to be introduced because it was like we had know them for a long time. We thanked them for their hospitality and began to make our way to the best place to sleep for the night. I passed close to Levi on my way and hesitated for a moment. He must have sensed my desire to ask him something because he asked me.

"What is it you have on you mind, Nic?" he asked.

He remember my name! I felt both impressed and honored. I then felt somewhat embarrassed but reached down deep for the courage to ask him the name of his daughter. He had taken hold of my hand and before answering looked into my face for a time. I'm sure my hand was getting moist with perspiration as I waited for him to speak.

"My daughter is most precious to me. She is a young lady filled with compassion and dreams. I am very proud of her and try my best to protect her from those who might be drawn by her beauty. Most young men who wish to become acquainted with her do not have her best interest at heart and I have insisted they look elsewhere. But you, Nic, seem to be a young man I can trust. Perhaps tomorrow the two of you might get together for a short while. Her name, by the way is Keturah." Levi answered.

I wasn't sure if I had been given a stern warning or received a compliment from Levi. It was certain that he was very protective of his daughter and would have no hesitation in defending her from anyone he perceived in doing wrong by her. It was then that I realized I still had hold of his hand. He must have thought I was completely void of manners. Having released his hand, I told him I understood his concerns for his daughter and I would do my best to honor his trust in me. We then said our goodnights to each other and headed for our place to sleep. I spent a good bit of time thinking about Keturah and the precious events of the evening but weariness soon overtook my thoughts and sleep came at last. I was laying on a wood floor with not much more than a small rug for a pillow, but I was thankful for that. It was much better than the ground, especially the filthy cave floor, and I found it to be quite comfortable.

A stirring sound awoke me and then a wonderful aroma of warm food. I had to strain my mind to recall where we were and replay all that had happened just hours ago. Suddenly my thoughts stopped racing through my mind when it came to Keturah. This was going to be the day I got to be with her. I was excited about it, even to the point of not wanting any of the wonderful food that was being prepared in the fireplace at the end of the room. Then I began to wonder how Keturah might feel about me. Was she wanting to spend time with me? Was it going to be only because her father had said she would? Did she even like me? I had just about talked myself out of getting to be with her before I had even gotten up off the floor. Then I thought about that radiant glow about her and determined that I wasn't going to let this opportunity pass without giving my best effort. I wanted to know her better—even if she didn't like me—yet!

It didn't take long for the smell of warm food to awaken everyone and our group assembled outside by the well to freshen up and take care of other business of nature. The morning air still had quite a chill about it so we were glad to get back inside and feel the warmth of the fire. Serirah and Keturah helped Levi prepare the table for us once more. Levi lifted an iron pot from the fireplace and carried it around the table as Serirah ladled out steaming porridge into bowls for us. Keturah followed with a large pitcher of milk and filled a glass for each bowl. I certainly enjoyed the aroma of warm food and I could almost taste the cold milk, but I could not stop thinking about Keturah. She seemed to move about her work with no attention to any of us. I was wondering how she was feeling about spending time with me and was just about to convince myself that she wanted no part of any of us—me in particular, when she turned to look at me with a definite smile as she walked past. She set my heart to racing and suddenly food lost its appeal. I was so encouraged. She must like me, at least enough to want to get to know me a little better. I was so happy inside I was concerned what I looked like on the outside, then I decided I really didn't care all that much.

I can't say that I can recall how the food tasted that morning except for the fact that the milk was so refreshing. We hadn't had any milk in weeks. It seemed like breakfast lasted for hours when in fact it was more like 20 or 30 minutes. I was so anxious to go somewhere with Keturah but it was beyond me to know what to do next. I decided it might be best to wait for either Levi or Keturah to ask if we might go. As I waited, I began to think about what to say to her. There was so much I wanted to tell her about and so many questions I wanted to ask her. I didn't know how much time we would have. I was beginning to get all tied up in knots and worried about making a fool of myself. Then I remembered thinking about the divine appointment of those gathered in this place. If we were together by divine appointment, what did I have to be worried about? Just when I got this all figured out, Keturah came and asked if I would go with her while she went about her morning chores and, of course, I gladly agreed.

## CHAPTER FIFFTEEN

# I GIVE YOU MY HEART

The morning air had warmed considerably and the sun was bright on a beautiful spring day. We began talking about the things each of us liked and about our families. Keturah had some amazing stories to tell about some of the guest they had and I could really tell a lot about her heart as she told them. I found there was a lot to like about this young lady. Suddenly she stopped and turned to face me and said I had heard enough about her and wanted to know more about what I was doing in Israel and all about me.

We talked for what must have been quite a long while. Everything we learned of each other seemed to bond us together in a strange way—at least in a way I had never felt before. One thing that really impressed me was that she was not concerned about getting her hands dirty as she went about her work. She was able to do things that some of the men back in Athens would think of doing. None of the women back there would even stoop to doing physical labor. This kind of work might have made her strong but she still had the build of a very nice looking young lady.

"Why are you doing so much of this work yourself? I mean, most of the women I've seen in this country have been working in the home—you have not stopped doing things since we left you home way back there." I asked her.

"Sometimes it's hard to think of it as work. Papa has always wanted to be able to help others and we don't have a lot to do with. It just seems the only thing to do is to do what I can to help. That makes me happy because it helps Papa and others all at the same time. I really don't mind and it's something I can do." she replied.

I can't say how far we had walked since we had been so involved in talking, but Keturah said we would be heading back as she lifted a bag of potatoes to her shoulder that she had traded for. I reached over to take them from her and touched her in the process. I felt something in that touch that stirred my heart—something that processed in my soul and resulted in a knowing that *this is it.*

I wanted our walk to last all day if it could. There were things I wanted to tell her but I didn't want to overwhelm her with the deep things that were on my heart. I didn't know how long we would be staying in Emmaus or even if we would ever be back that way again. Would it be unfair of me to let her know of the feelings I had if we were going to be leaving. I wrestled with this for a while and she must have sensed something was wrong.

"What's on you mind? You have suddenly stopped talking to me. Have I said something to offend you?" she asked.

"Oh, no. Not at all. It just I was wondering how long we would be here. I don't want our time to be over so soon. I wish we could have the whole day. I have enjoyed being with you. There is much I would like to say but I—" I started to speak but couldn't finish because I didn't know what I should say.

"You are bothered about something. Are you sure it isn't me? Please tell me so." she insisted but I stopped her before she went on.

"It is you but not in the way you think. I'm almost scared to say what's in me right now. You will think I'm forward or maybe even crazy but I'm not—or at least I don't mean to be." I answered.

"Why don't you tell me and let me decide for myself what I think about it?"

We had now stopped walking and had sat down on a fallen tree just off the pathway. I was glad she had felt led to stop as it allowed me to have her full attention. I was also thankful for the extra time this gave us. I started to speak but found myself just looking at her beautiful face. We had looked at each other during our walk but this time was different. We were really looking at each other and I could see her beauty was not just on her face but was coming from within. My staring at her must have made her a little uneasy as she once more asked.

"Are you going to tell me or not?"

"I'm sorry. I didn't mean to stare. Keturah, something has been going on in me ever since I first saw you. It is a feeling I have never felt before. I find myself attracted to you and the more I talk with you the greater the attraction becomes. I have very deep feelings for you and we only met last night. I don't understand how a person could develop such strong feelings so quickly but I can tell you for certain that it has happened and that these feelings are real. Just a while back when I took those potatoes from you, I accidentally touched you and there was something in that touch that got in my heart. It was, *this is it.* I know this is probably enough to scare the daylights out of you but it's what's in me right now. I suppose the only way to fully describe it is to say that I love you." I finally managed to say with a voice that was cracking.

Keturah sat looking into my eyes as tears rolled down her soft cheeks. It took her a minute or two to speak. I reached out to hold her hands as I waited for her to answer. She started to speak a couple of times but her voice could only quiver, making several attempts to express the feelings that we rising up within her.

"Nic, I don't think you are crazy at all. I can believe you with all certainty because the very same workings have been stirring in my heart since I first set eyes on you. I know it's only been-." she spoke in barely more than a whisper before I interrupted her.

"Keturah, I was so afraid of freighting you with these forward thoughts but I was even more afraid of loosing you forever if I didn't at least try. You have made me so happy. My heart is overflowing with gladness and now to know you share those feelings! It's more than I could have ever expected." I said softly as I put my arm around her and pulled her gently against my side. "

Tears were rolling down my face as freely as hers were. She rested her head against my shoulder and my tears fell into her soft, brown hair. We sat like that, quietly without a word for a good bit. It was then that I placed both hands on her shoulders to slowly push her back far enough to be able to look into her eyes once more—I wanted to enjoy looking into those beautiful eyes that were windows to the most wonderful heart I had ever known.

"Oh, I'm so sorry! I interrupted you. What were you saying?" I asked, hoping she would fortify what I thought she had just said.

"I was trying to say that as strange as it is to have only met you last night, that there could be such an attraction to you is nearly beyond belief. At first, I thought that you were indeed quite handsome and seemed to have a decent manners. That was only the physical part. Before the meal was finished last night that was drawing towards you that I can only describe as a kindred spirit bond. It was as if I could feel what was in you before you spoke or acted to reveal it. And now, during this short time it seems we have revealed nearly mirror images of each other." she explained with an occasional tear making its way down her face.

"Yes, I know. I'd be lying if I was to say that I didn't find you to be about the most beautiful young woman I ever saw, but there was a radiance to that beauty that was fed from within. You seemed almost out of reach for me and I was afraid you didn't notice me or just thought I was another person just passing through. You father wants so much to see that you have only what's best for you and I know this will surely be difficult for him to understand. What am I saying? I don't even understand it all!" I said.

We sat silently looking at each other, glancing away occasionally to enjoy the beautiful spring scenery. At one point we both turned back toward each other and found faces to be only and inch or so apart. I hesitated at first and then found the confidence to place a gentle kiss upon her lips. It wasn't a long kiss but it was one that seemed to seal our affection for each other. I felt my love for her deepen and she must have as well. To this point my motives and desires for her had been pure and honorable. There was the briefest of time that I began to experience another kind of attraction. I knew I had to stop right then to make a determination to commit myself to maintaining that purity and honor. The precious gift I had found was much too valuable to be spoiled with anything that might only have momentary rewards. I had a definite sense I was getting spiritual help during this time.

I rose to my feet and Keturah followed my lead. We slowly gathered our goods and began making our way back to her house. It was a walk that I did not want to end but it was one that we knew we had to make.

"I don't understand all that in going on and how such strong feelings could happen so quickly, but I can say they surely have. I don't know when we will be leaving or, for that matter, where we will be going. It's hard to even think of going on without you now." I said, mostly thinking out loud.

"It's amazing to me as well. I know in my heart that I have come to love you deeply since last night. I wasn't expecting it to happen—I had not given it much thought for that matter. It's here now and it's so real, but I can't tell you not to go if you must. I think part of why I have fallen in love with you is because you are driven by the very things that stir my heart. I cannot ask you to abandon what you have set out to do." she said.

"If only there was a little more time—time to know what to do—time to think. It's so hard to think right now because I'm so excited over you. Oh my! Your father! What am I going to say or how am I ever going to explain all this to him? He's so concerned for you." I continued to think aloud.

"Don't be so convinced that my father will be angry about this. He is a fair man even though he is very protective of me. He is a respecter of honesty. Should you decide to talk to him, just tell him what's in your heart. You might be surprised." Keturah admonished.

"Maybe so. I want to find out how long we will be in Emmaus before I do or say anything. When we first started out it was just me and Marco. Now, our decisions are usually made by the whole group. If I can get some sort of idea as to how quick we will be leaving, then I might know about us. I don't want to leave you, not just yet." I answered.

"I know. I want you to stay too. How did things get to complicated so quickly. Life yesterday was not without its problems and adventure, but today I feel like the doors to my heart have been flung open to let you in and me pour myself out to you. What I am experiencing in me is more than emotions and feelings. It is a definite awareness that something very real and wonderful is happening in my life that is only the beginning of a relationship that is meant for a lifetime..." Keturah was saying when I interrupted her.

"Yes! That's exactly it! Just how I feel. This is so wonderful. It has to be the truest kind of love—a man for a woman. Another great truth revealed without even knowing it was being sought. Back in Athens, this would be so rare— probably very few ever find it. I'm so lost in the awe of it." I rambled.

I had reached out to take Keturah by the hand as we were walking and talking. Just as we were both telling each other what was going on within our hearts, I stopped, placed my hand on her shoulder as to have her face me and just looked at her. He face had such a radiance about it and her eyes sparkled in the early morning sunlight. Tears once more streamed down my face. Words seemed to be lodged in my throat. My heart was spilling over—with joy, with abundance of love for this young woman, with gratitude for being given this most precious gift, and with an awesome wander of what to do about it. I wanted to hold her close to me—so close that we would just meld together. I was reminded of my commitment to keep purity and honor in this and knew it would be easier to keep that commitment if I did not allow opportunity for temptation to enter in. I also felt that Keturah deserved to be respected and honored before her family. We finished our walk in silence and attempted to wipe away the tears before we returned to the others. This had been the walk of a lifetime—one that would always be fresh in my memory—one that I would cherish forever.

We turned up the path to Keturah's house and were met by Capt. Vitas, Ben, Artemis, and Levi. I could tell Ben was working hard to think up some remark to tease me with but he must have felt the need to contain himself on account of Levi. I looked the group over, hoping to find help in knowing what to do next. I was so full of joy inside I knew it must be showing on the outside. Yet, I didn't feel it was the right time to share this with anyone until I had talked with Levi, Keturah's father. Before I talked to him I knew I needed to know when we would be leaving Emmaus.

"You two must have enjoyed your walk on this fine morning. It must have refreshed you, Nic. You looked quite rested." Capt. Vitas said, sensing a bit of uneasiness in the air.

"Yes, yes we did. It is so fresh this time of year. I enjoyed talking with Keturah." I answered as I watched her go on to the rear of the house with the potatoes.

"She is a fine young lady—a great help to Serirah and me. She's is always willing to do her part and then some." Levi said, taking the opportunity to praise his daughter.

"That she is, Sir—that she is." I replied with a smile.

Demas came out followed by Alexus, Marco, and Cirro. I waited for a few minutes to see if there was any talk of our plans to move on. When it was apparent that the weather, the beautiful spring, and just a little politics was going to be the extent of the conversation, I felt it necessary to just get to the big question.

"Has anyone decided when we will be leaving and where we're headed?" I asked bluntly.

It was silent for a good while and then Marco spoke up.

"I can only speak for myself but I think what I'm about to say pretty well sums up how most of us feel. The very focus of what we have been searching for has been found here—with Demas in the tunnels and now here in this home. I know we all wanted to meet Jesus and have time to talk with Him, but last night, last night He was here with us—His spirit. It was so real, wasn't it?" he spoke as he turned as if to seek our agreement with him on this. "Our search could be over, ended successfully—right here on this spot. I don't think any of us are anxious to move on. We want to soak up what is happening here—in that room last night! There is such a peace here while only a few miles away people are being put in prison and killed for the very thing we are doing. These people—they have opened their home and gave to us..." his voice breaking as he was being overcome with all that he had mentioned.

"That pretty much says the way I feel about it. Fine folks and a night of a lifetime." Artemis agreed.

While Marco was speaking, Simon and his boys had come out to join us. He listened intently to Marco and Artemis speak. After waiting for a bit, he began to speak himself.

"Each of you has been greatly blessed with an understanding that few know about. The connection I felt with Jesus—that cheek to cheek, eye to eye contact— that definite sense of touching of hearts,—you now know the reality of that. You can continue your search to find Jesus but you will not find Him closer than He was in your hearts last night. You can nourish that closeness by following Him now that you have found Him." he said.

"That is right, ever so right!" Demas added.

"Of all the times we have opened our house, I can never remember a time when the presence of God was so strong. His anointing was and still is on this place. You are welcome to stay. I could not ask you to leave what is going on here. We'll trust that He will provide our needs of the body as he provides for the needs of our souls." Levi stated.

"That is most kind of you, Levi, however we must be careful not to take advantage of your hospitality. You may have others who come for help." Capt. Vitas replied.

"It is strange you should mention that. I have been deeply affected by your desire for Christ. I'm not sure what that is going to do with our work here of providing shelter for other believers. It is something I have been in much thought and prayer about since last night. I need to speak with Serirah and Keturah to see if they have any leading. Perhaps, I need to do so now if you'll excuse me." Levi said as he got up to go back into the house.

I wanted to go with Levi to tell him what had happened with Keturah and I this morning, but knew I should allow him have time with his wife and daughter first. I then began to consider the thought that he might even be thinking about bringing his family on the journey with us. That would almost be too much to hope for. I found myself in a whirlwind of situations—everything seemed to be spinning so fast. Then I remembered what Marco had just said to us. I was so amazed at him and how he has grown right along with the rest of us. It was truly incredible to hear him reveal his heart to us.

My next thoughts returned to Keturah. She had only been away in the house for less than an hour and I was missing her already. I was head over heals in love with this girl and was having a really hard time allowing any thought to not being with her. I didn't know if I was to stay here of if she was to go with us. Neither option made any sense—one being foolish and the other didn't seem to be in the proper way of things. It was then I remember what Levi had just said about being in prayer during the night. He was trying to find what God wanted him to do. That is what I needed to do as well. After all, He had worked to get us to this place and His hand had been on us since we left Athens. It was obvious in so many ways. He had also brought Keturah into my life. It should have been easy to trust Him for direction now, but I had never been so overwhelmed with such strong feelings in my life before. I knew I was going to have to work at letting Him have His way.

Simon moved to stand before our group and had his sons beside him with a hand on each of them.

"We must be leaving now and make our way back home. Meeting all of you has given me the affirmation that Jesus' work didn't end. It has just began for many of us. It has been a blessing to spend this time with you. Please, keep doing your best to follow Him. You can help change this world if you do." Simon said.

As he was speaking to us, both of his boys came to me and gave me the most loving hug I believe I ever had. It seemed like people were coming into our lives, becoming dear to us and then, leaving or we had to go on. It was not easy for me to accept this. I had always valued true friendship and wanted relationships like these to last. I was now learning that I had to hold these people with open hands— being willing to let them go. The very thought of letting Keturah go really frightened me. The place in my heart for her was not like what I felt for others. After saying good bye to Simon, Rufas, and Alexander, I made my way to a quiet spot to be alone and began to pray like I never had before. I'm not sure if I even knew how to pray like I was now—desperately seeking His direction. Every time I tried to ask help for something, I was reminded in spirit of how thankful I was for being given all that had been poured out on us over the last weeks. I was soon spending more time thanking Him than I was in asking for help. By the time I finished, I was praising God with all my heart and I didn't seem to have needs that mattered any more.

How much time had passed, I did not know. It must have been past noon when I returned to our group who were gathered under a tree near the well. By now many people were coming to get water at the well and Demas was making conversation with nearly all who came. We did not learn of any news that amounted to much. The soldiers were still searching Jerusalem for those they considered a threat and the Jewish officials were beginning to calm down, thinking that they had succeeded in regaining control. Many people were still leaving the city for their safety.

Capt. Vitas asked where I had been when I joined them and I told him I needed some time to think things out and had been praying.

"You're taken by this young lady, are you not?" he asked.

"Well, yes I am, but how did you know? Has someone told you something?" I asked hurriedly, hoping to see if Keturah had mentioned anything.

"No, nobody has said anything, at least to us. It seems pretty evident though, just by watching you. I can tell your thinking on something pretty serious and you had a gleam in your eyes this morning that comes from a young man being smitten." Capt. Vitas answered.

"You really are serious about this aren't you?" Marco asked in a tone of disbelief.

"Ya. Serious is probably a good way to describe it. Serious about my feelings for her and serious about what to do now. I sure wasn't expecting this to happen." I replied.

"What do you mean? You thinkin about stayin here to be with her? Ben asked.

"No! Well, I don't know. I don't even know what our plans are about leaving Emmaus and where we are going from here. It seems no one wants to take the lead this time. It's hard for me to know what to even think about when we haven't decided where and when we are going." I explained.

"You must have deeper feelings for this girl than I thought, Nic. I didn't intend to make fun of you by asking about this, but now I can tell you are very serious about her. Please forgive me if you will. As for our plans, well, I haven't felt any certain direction yet. Marco seems to think we have already found what we were searching for and I'm inclined to agree with him. Do any of the rest of you have a suggestion?" Capt. Vitas asked.

"If knowledge were cargo, I'd say we've got a boat load already. My question to all you now is, what do we do with what we have learned, what we have had revealed to us? Ben and I and the captain are gettin on in years. I thought I knew a lot about people, but come to find out; I didn't know about such things that matters most. Simon said before he left that we could change our world if we would follow Jesus. I want to spend what time I have left doin just that. I'm just waitin now to know if that's to be done here or somewhere else." Artemis said.

"That's pretty much the way I feel about it. Just needin to know where and when." Ben added

"Cirro and I have not ever been much of a leader. Mostly we have trusted the rest of you to set the coarse and helped you get there. You've done a good job so far. Guess we best not make much change now. Right, Cirro?" Alexus said.

"Nic, have you said anything to Keturah's father about how you feel about her? I know he seems to be protective when it comes to her." Marco asked.

"No, Not yet. That is the next thing I want to do. I can't expect him to let her go with us. That just wouldn't be right. I'm not sure what he will have to say. Just have to see." I replied.

"What was Levi meaning about being affected by our journey? It almost sounded like he wanted to go with us. Did any of the rest of you take that to be what he was getting at?" Ben questioned.

"That's what I took it to mean, but I can't imagine him quitting this work here. He seems so dedicated to helping people around here." Capt. Vitas commented.

"I need to find Keturah and her father. After I know how he feels about me, then maybe I will know what to plan on." I said as I got up to head to the house.

I was feeling a mixture of being nervous and anxious. I wasn't fearful of her father, but I had a healthy respect for his protection of her. I knew what she meant to him. I also knew that I had to make my feeling for her known to him and hoped he could understand how two people could fall in love so quickly. My main purpose in meeting with him now was to convey to him the sincerity of my love for his daughter. From my brief acquaintance of him, I believed he would understand, after all; he had raised this young lady.

I knocked on the doorway before stepping into the kitchen and found Keturah still talking with her parents. She had been crying, at least some. Her mother turned away and tried to go about her work, not wanting me to see her face. I could not tell if she had crying as well, but I suspected so.

Levi sat quietly looking at me for a minute or two. I felt like it must have been much longer.

I started to speak but he chose to go first.

"Keturah tells me you two had a very interesting morning. She says you have become very fond of her and she likewise of you. You will have to agree that such deep feelings usually don't develop so quickly won't you?" he asked with his eyebrows raised—seeming to suggest he doubted what he had heard.

"No, not usually. But there has been nothing usual about anything that has happened since we arrived here. I know it must sound strange to you but I can tell you without the slightest doubt, Keturah is the one I want to spend the rest of my life with. I don't know when or where we can be together, but I am willing to wait for her. She is the-" I answered but was cut off by his next question.

"She also tells me you showed proper respect and honor to her. Is that simply because I suggested that it would not be wise to take advantage of her?" he asked.

"That 'suggestion' came to mind as I was with her but, no; there was a much greater reason to respect her—that being she deserved it and also it was the right thing to do." I said.

"I believe you, Nic. Keturah has always be truthful to me and I have no reason to doubt her. You have shown me that I can trust you with her. I will not oppose your commitment to her but I do ask that you consider her best interest before asking her to be placed in a dangerous or possibly compromising situation." Levi replied.

"I understand completely. I do not wish to put her at risk in any way. I do not want to take her away from you and her mother until she knows in her heart that is what she wants. Now, with your consent, sir; I can begin to plan for our life together but I'm not sure how soon these plans will come about." I assured him.

"Her mother and I knew this day would come, but neither of us expected it to be this soon and without some idea it was happening. It is not going to be easy for us to let her go and thus, your patience and understanding will be of great help." Levi said as he got up to go place his arm around his wife, trying to comfort her. "What have your friends decided about moving on?"

"Nothing definite has been settled yet. It seems to be that most of us feel we have found the truths we sought and are ready to return to Greece. It seems we are waiting for someone to just say, 'It's time to go.' Demas hasn't said what he thinks we should do yet." I answered.

"Glad you mentioned him! Sarirah and I have also discussed another matter. We are thinking about going to Greece with you or perhaps coming over sometime later. Our hearts have been stirred so as we have spent time with your group. What do you plan to do when you get back to your home? Will you remain together as the group you have now? Will you be returning to Israel?" Levi asked so many questions without giving me time to attempt to answer.

His questions sent my mind whirling. Not only did I not know how to answer him; I hadn't even thought about these things myself. We had functioned as a group of men so well that I hadn't even considered what we would do when we ended our journey. The only things I was sure of was that I wanted to tell others about what I had learned of Jesus and that I had found the one person I wanted to spend the rest of my life with.

"Levi, I really don't know how to answer your questions except to say that on this journey we have found that we have been led almost step by step. You have asked some good questions that we need to consider. I don't know what the others plan to do when we get back to Athens, or for that matter, how many of us will even go that far. Why were you glad I mentioned Demas?" I said.

"Well, he also shares your enthusiasm for Christ and I feel he might be one to assume our work here in Emmaus should Serirah and I leave. This work here is yet needed but I'm sure others could do it as well as we." he replied.

"If you were to leave with us, I suppose that would mean Keturah would be coming as well. That would certainly make me happy but I think we need to see what the others have in mind first. Let's go talk to them. Maybe Demas is back from the well by now." I suggested.

The men were still gathered near the front of the house and Demas was telling the latest news he had heard. He had learned that renewed efforts to drive disciples of Jesus out of the area. There was even rumors of persecution and killing of those who insisted on teaching what Jesus had started. Even Roman authorities who had been at odds with each other were now working together to help the Jewish leaders make life miserable for anyone who opposed them. I listened to what the others had to say for a little while and could tell that all of our group was ready to head for Greece. Ben and Artemis allowed that they would be just as happy there as in any other place just as long as it had the scent of sea air blowing in off the waters. I helped Levi share his thoughts with the others and no one seemed to mind if they were to come along. Demas was a little taken back at the thought of running the shelter home, saying he had no means to purchase the home from Levi. He was assured that the home was his to use as long as he would offer it as a shelter for those in need and with an outside chance that someday Levi and his wife might return.

To say that I was excited would have been quite an understatement. Now, it seemed like Keturah would be coming with me as I went home. I would not have to leave her, not even for a short time. I was hoping she would come out of the house so she cold hear what was being planned but she remained inside with her mother. As the men were talking over their plans, Marco came to me, took me by the arm and led me off away from the others.

"Have you thought this through, Nic? You are talking pretty serious about Keturah and things are moving fast with the two of you. Have you thought about how your parents are going to respond to this? How are you going to support her and will this hamper your efforts to teach people about what we have learned?" he questioned.

"No, Marco, I haven't! But we haven't thought about a lot of things on this trip have we? I'm sure that I will have things figured out when we get there." I answered him somewhat shortly, thinking to myself that he sounded a little jealous and was trying to dampen my happiness.

"Look, I'm sorry! I know you have deep feelings for her—there's no doubt about that. I'm just concerned about the timing, that's all. When you get so busy in your mind with thinking about love and personal matters, it's hard to keep on track with the others parts of your life. You've been my best friend a long time and I care about what happens to you. Can't fault me for that can ya?" he countered, sensing my aggravation with him.

"I guess I could but I shouldn't. I really love this girl, Marco. I know it in my heart. I appreciate your concern and all but just trust me to know the timing. I've been praying a lot about it. Who knows—it may be a while before we even get married. I just know it's meant to be and I'm committed to doing my part in it. I want you to know that you will always be my best friend and that Keturah won't be a danger to that." I tried to explain.

"I'll hold ya to it!" he said as he hit me on the upper arm and smiled. "Thanks for caring." I told him as we made our way back to the others.

The discussion continued for a while longer in the front yard. By now some of the people of the town had stopped in to join in on the conversation. Demas was in his glory, being able to hear the latest news and then sharing it with others who had not heard it. Some folks might consider him to be a gossip but he wasn't that way at all. He would only tell words of encouragement or warn people of impending danger. His purpose in life seemed to be able to help people around him get closer to Christ and he was determined to do his best at it. After a while, Levi went to find Serirah and Keturah to further discuss the possibility of leaving with us for Greece. I found a place beside Marco and spent most of the rest of the afternoon just listening to all that was being said. It was interesting conversation, but nothing really captured my attention.

As evening came and the sun was sinking into the western horizon, Levi came to the door and called for us to come in. There were still some folks from the town there with us and I felt a little uncomfortable in not knowing what to do-should we go in and leave them in the yard or ask them to join us. This wasn't my house and I didn't know how much food there would be. I decided the best course of action was to just wait a few moments to see what the others would do. I was keenly aware that the amount of food really wouldn't matter if God led for more to join us. I was also aware of how God was working with those of us who had been gathered there just the night before. I felt pulled in several directions—wanting to show proper manners by responding to Levi's call to the table, not wanting to be selfish in excluding the new people, and hoping God would once more anoint our time together; meaning it for those of us who experience it last night.

It was beginning to be a little aggravating—not knowing how to respond or what to plan for. Just as I was embracing my right to be aggravated, I sensed I was being given an opportunity to learn some foundational lessons on walking with God in an everyday, step by step, way of life. All of the thoughts I had there in the yard were good and honorable.

I wanted to respect Levi's efforts to feed us by being prompt, I didn't want to leave the others in the yard and only think of my own need for food, and I wanted more of the wonderful time of God's anointing. It wasn't a choice of good over bad, but what was God wanting to do at that moment? What plans did He have for us in the next few minutes? Who did He want to involve? How can I know when I obeying what He wants me to do?

All of these thoughts and questions were racing through my mind in less than seconds. Thoughts that were deep and profound. Ones that normally would have taken hours to meditate upon to discover answers to. Next in mind, I recalled how unsure I was about the future with Keturah and what to do about leaving Emmaus.

I wanted desperately to be in God's time and will but I wasn't sure of how to be.

It was then I was certain I heard a voice every to softly and quietly say to me, *"You didn't get up when you heard me tell you to wait and you have opened your heart to being taught. Now, be careful to keep your ears open and your heart quiet and I will speak to you often. Your part is to trust and then obey. You are mine and I love you!"*

The only thing I can tell you of what happened next is that I started to stand and fell forward, face down on the ground. When the others came to see about me, they said I was praising God and saying some things they couldn't understand. Cirro was quite concerned for me and tried his best to comfort and help me, thinking I had fainted or became sick. He had a cloth dipped in cool water he used to wipe my face and forehead with. His care for me endeared him to my heart even more than he had been.

"It's alright, Cirro. I'm fine. It's not anything wrong with me, just Jesus working. Thanks for helping though. I wish you could have —well, I know you are not far away." I told him and could see he still thought I was somewhat incoherent. I just smiled at him and trusted he would soon discover for himself what I was trying to tell him about.

After things settled down a bit, we started making our way into the house. My thoughts didn't return to who was staying and who was leaving, we just went in and were glad to have food to eat and a place to stay for another night. As it turned out, three of the people who had been visiting with us outside came in to eat with us—a man and two women. The room was full and, this time, there was only enough food for each of us to have a small portion. It was tasty and nourishing, so good that I would have liked to had more.

*"Different times—different ways, just trust and obey!"* I thought I heard. Or was it just in my mind to think that way? Not trusting myself to know, I decided that I would trust and obey as best I knew how. I found a greater appreciation for the abundance of food last night and a thankfulness for the amount we had this night. I learned not to expect God to repeat his blessings simply because He had done it that way before.

My next thoughts were about sharing what I had learned with the others. I sensed a need to be very careful not to present myself as being more gifted or knowledgeable concerning the things of God. I wanted the others to know what I knew but I felt it was not for me to tell them; at least not yet. It was a that moment that Keturah entered the room. I immediately felt almost guilty for not thinking about her during the last hour or so. Her presents caused me to return my focus to our relationship. It was amazing to me that my heart had the capacity to hold so much love; love for Jesus, love for her, and for my companions. No sooner had I pondered this miracle than one of the women who joined us spoke up to say something that got in my heart. I'm not sure even what it was but now she had become another person who shared a place in my already full heart. Of course she didn't hold the place that I shared with Keturah or Jesus, but she found a place in it sure enough. I found myself caring about her, wondering about if she had family or if she had need of help. I was glad she had shared in the food but sensed there were much deeper needs in her life and I wanted to try to help her somehow. Most of the things I thought about helping her with would only last a while and then be gone. But Jesus, yes, knowing Him would be help that would last through eternity. I knew right at that moment that she must not leave this evening without having been given the opportunity to know Him if she didn't already. As soon as I had finished thinking that, I knew in my heart that I needed to accept that responsibility myself and not expect someone else to do it.

Through all of this, I was beginning to get a better understanding of what Jesus had in mind for us—well, at least for my part. I had an undeniable sense that He had given me an understanding of His way, and His teaching that was to be shared with others—people I would meet here and then, wherever I traveled. I was perplexed to know how this woman had gotten into my heart that I should have such concern for her. I had never seen her before, had no knowledge of who she was or even her name. I had not been a people person and could only recall a few people back in Athens that I really cared anything for. Now, there was a burning desire to get to as many people back home and tell about all that had happened to me, to us, on this journey. It was exciting to just think about it, however I knew also that there would be many who did not share my beliefs.

The whirlwind of thoughts came to a halt when Levi stood up to speak to us. Nearly everyone had finished eating and conversation had began to fill the room. Keturah came over to sit beside me. I sensed she knew what her father was going to say, nonetheless, I was anxious to hear.

"I have discussed the possibility of joining you on this journey. Serirah and Keturah have both agreed that it would an adventure but they are leaving the decision up to me. I have been in prayer nearly the whole day and believe Jesus to be leading us to join you, that is, if you will allow us. Our work here is important but there are those who can continue to carry it on. What I would ask of you is to permit us to have one day to take care of a few things here in Emmaus and sell a few things so as to have a little finance to help us on the trip. We would be ready to leave with you early on the next day. My family and I will now leave so you may have the freedom to discuss this among yourselves and trust God to help us find His will." Levi spoke.

They left the room and went outside into the evening air. Keturah had been holding my hand and, as she rose to leave with her parents, it was not easy to left her fingers slip through mine. I wanted so much to be with her, not just at the present moment, but in the days and weeks to come. But I had a deep sense that I had to rein in my wants and be more submitted to what God wanted from me and from the others as a whole. I knew in my heart that His timing was critical in this matter and that I needed to be careful not to let my personal feelings get in the way. As the others began discussing our options, I felt it best to remain quite and let them come to a conclusion without my input, feeling I could possibly lead them to biased decision.

"One thing that bothers me is that it has been a long standing tradition that it can bring calamity to a cargo vessel to have women on board. I've seen it happen a few times myself." Cirro said.

"That is a concern of mine as well." Alexus agreed

"I'm aware of that tradition but in the instances I can recall, the calamity had nothing to do with anything but a lack of attention to duty on the part of the crew. They simply failed to carry out their duties and turned their attention to being distracted by the women. It is apparent to me that it has absolutely nothing to do with bad luck or superstition, but with poor judgment. That is where we must use wisdom in making our decisions here. Can we keep ourselves focused on our responsibilities as we continue this trip, and not be distracted from them by these ladies or by anything else; including superstitions.? Having considered all this, we then need to determine how it lines up with what God wants of us. I'm afraid it might be a delicate balance and not an easy decision to make." Capt. Vitas spoke.

"Even if we decide to take them with us and commit ourselves to staying focused, we may have a hard time finding a ship that will take us on board with the ladies with us. Some of them captains put a lot of stock into superstition." Ben commented.

"I think we might be missing something here. You've been thinking about how people might respond to having women on board ship, but we haven't talked about including them in our efforts to learn all about Jesus. It seems that since we have been with this family, we have come to understand a whole lot about what Jesus wants us to be. We have experienced some mighty workings of His spirit since we have been in this house and I believe it has been their willingness to help people that has allowed us to be a part of that." Marco spoke up.

"I think you're right, Marco. We need to look at what's in these people's hearts first and then figure out how we can get them back with us." Artemis added.

"You have been quiet about all this, Nic. How do you feel about taking them with us?" Marco asked.

"Yes, I've been trying to stay out of the discussion until you have had your say. I don't want to influence your decision just because of what you think I might want, but now that you have asked—Of course I don't want to leave Keturah here, even if I know I am going to come back for her some day. I do have some concerns about being able to keep them safe on our journey back and I don't know what to do with them when we get to Athens. I'm not sure what would be best." I answered.

"We understand your heart, Nic and you have answered with considerable wisdom. Might I suggest that we ask ourselves what we plan to do when we go back to our homes? There seems to be a common desire among most of us to tell other people about all that we have learned. If that is true, then our new friends here in Emmaus probably have as much or more to tell than we do. Also, once we get back to Tyre and get my ship, I think we will be able to take good care of them. Until then, we will just have to take extra care to keep them safe with us. I say let's welcome them to our crew." Capt. Vitas spoke.

"Anyone feel differently about what the captain just said? If so, then speak up—if not then let's tell Levi so he can get done what needs done." Marco said with a tone of determination that let us know it was time to get on with our journey.

Nothing else was said in response to Marco's question although I certainly felt there were some reservations on Cirro's mind. There was a silence in the room that was only interrupted by the scuffling of shoes on the old wood floor. It was beginning to get a little uneasy until Artemis got up and said he was going out to tell Levi that we had agreed on taking them with us.

"Now that we have settled that matter, we need to see what we have among us in order to get us back up to Tyre. I doubt if we will have enough to but let's find out what we do have." Capt. Vitas suggested.

We each emptied our pockets out on the table and, although there was more than what I had expected, a quick glance was enough to know that we didn't have nearly enough for passage to Tyre. Then I remember the four coins I had hidden away when we were locked up in the cave. With them added to the collection, we might be able to work out something with a ship's captain. Marco and I were still pretty good as cooking. We would just have to trust for a way to be made.

Artemis came back into the room with Levi following him. His face revealed the joy and exuberance in his heart as he shook our hands in appreciation for accepting his family into our journey. I could see that going with us was so important to him that I began to feel guilty about even entertaining the thought of not letting them go because of the women being on a ship. His enthusiasm was so great that I was perplexed at how he could be that excited about leaving his ministry here in Emmaus, a work that was touching so many lives almost on a daily basis. What did he know about going with us that was feeding his excitement? I know I envied his commitment to the work his family was doing and would have like to have experienced the blessing they must have felt over the months they care for people. The things I didn't know seemed to be overwhelming so I decided to take stock of what I did know. First of all, we were getting ready to head back home; secondly, Keturah was going to be going with me; thirdly, none of us knew for sure what we would do when we got back; and fourthly; Levi was a man who knew God. If he was that excited, then he must have had good reason. I knew I could trust him to follow what God was leading him to do—giving it his best effort. What more did I need than all that?

# CHAPTER SIXTEEN

# HEADING HOME

The sun had not been up long before nearly everyone was ready to begin the day. Levi was the first one out the door, wanting to take care as much of his business as possible. The men in our group decided we might as well explore the town of Emmaus to see if there was anything that we could trade for or work for to equip us for the journey home. Capt. Vitas and Artemis decided to stay at Levi's house to rest up for the journey ahead and the rest of us felt it would be safe enough to walk around the town by ourselves, considering the things we had heard. Even though we had little money to buy anything, it was in our hearts to see if we could do some work in exchange to a few items we needed. As always, food was one of the necessary items we sought.

We had been walking through the town for not quite an hour when we came upon a shop that looked like it was used to make sails for ships or maybe even tents. We thought it would be a good place to look for work so we went in. We were quite surprise to find Levi there talking with a young man. He had a good sized bundle of canvas under his arm and a small bag in the other hand. When he turned to see who had came in, he had a look of astonishment on his face. It bothered me considerable at first, since he acted like he was keeping something from us.

Marco was the first one to speak to him, explaining we were going to see if we could trade work for supplies. He then turned to the young man to ask if there was anything we could do at which the young man referred Marco back to Levi.

"No, no! It's not my store any more. It's all yours now. Alright, alright! Let me confess. This man was my partner for several years now. He has run this shop for me pretty much by himself. I was here as much as I could be but he has done most of the work. The money I earned from this has helped us to be able to buy food for the people God has sent to us. Now, this morning, I have sold my part out so we can have some finance to help with our journey. Not many knew I owned part of this shop and I did not want you to know where this money came from. Now, please, let me do my part to help. I should have known better than to try to keep such things from God's people. They always seem to have a way of knowing." Levi confessed.

"Since this is now my shop, what is it you have need of?" the young man asked us.

"Well, we could use some extra money if you have some work we could help you with. Several of us have had experience with mending sails. Whatever you might have for us to do would be of great help." Marco answered.

"I do have quite a bit of work to get done that has needs to be finished. The only problem is that I have used almost all of my money to pay for the shop. I might be able to trade some work for some food if your would be interested. My father brings me more than I can use from his crops and animals. What do you think? Eh?" the young man asked.

"Sound just like what we were hopin' to find. Where do you want us to start?" Ben jumped in.

We spent all morning and into the afternoon helping our new friend get his work done. Levi had left not long after we came into the shop. We had quite a long conversation about what he had done to make provision for the trip we were going to be making. We knew he would rather have kept his methods to himself but it was really a testimony to his character to know how committed he was. Even though we talked most of the time we worked, we soon had all the mending caught up.

"You have done a fine job and finished much sooner than I thought. Come with me now to the back room where I live. We will see what we can find in the way of food for your journey." he said.

We were amazed at all we saw. There were fresh vegetables, several kinds of grains, nuts, cheese blocks, and some cured meat. He had it all stored away neatly on shelves behind a canvas. I hadn't seen that much food since we left Athens.

"Please, take whatever you need. You have earned it. Your work will bring satisfaction to my customers. I only wish you could come back to help more often. Here, put some food in these sacks." he offered as he began to fill them himself, knowing we would be reluctant to take as much as he wanted us to have.

"It's alright! My father has been blessed with good land and he knows how to produce abundant crops. There is usually enough here to help Levi feed the people he brings into his house. I cannot possibly use all that my father brings—I think he knows that I give it to others. That is his way—wanting to be of help to others but not wanting them to know where it comes from. Much like Levi in that way." the young man chatted as he continued filling the sacks.

We stood in amazement as we watched him fill the two sacks with all kind of food that would keep until we were on board Capt. Vitas's ship. It was beyond our ability to comprehend how we could be given that much food without having to buy it—when we had very little money to buy anything. Now, we were being given some very good food that would serve us well on our voyage back. I say given because our friend had long passed the point to putting enough in the sacks to compensate us for the work we had done. He was pouring out on us just as he had been poured upon. It was renewing to the spirit to see how people who loved God were willing to love others.

After thanking our generous provider, we decided to take the food back to Levi's house and then continue to try to find other necessary supplies, including some clothes—since the ones we had on were all we had left and they we in great need of being replaced. For the rest of the afternoon and into the early evening, we covered much of the town and were able to buy most of the clothes we needed, along with some cooking equipment. I still had two of the coins left and thought we had done quite well considering we had come to town with only what we had on and a little money hidden away.

It was a little late when we returned to Levi's house. Demas was there helping to make some soup from milk and potatoes. The house smelled so good as we came in. I had forgotten we hadn't eaten all day and hadn't noticed being hungry until the aroma of the soup woke up our hunger. Conversation during supper was about how we had been able to get so much food and then new clothes. We would have liked to told how much Levi was helping with the money he raised from selling his part of the canvas shop but most of us felt that we would respect his wishes for privacy in the matter. He never said a word concerning his business of the day except to say that God had been a wonderful provider this day.

Most everyone was lighthearted and relaxed during the evening. As the hour grew late, Artemis and Capt. Vitas suggested that we try to make the trip to Joppa in one day. They figured it was a trip of around twenty five miles or so. It would be a full days effort to make it but they wanted to have the next night to scout out some of the taverns where the ship's crews would be gathered. It had always been a good way to find a decent ship to take and this time they wanted to be extra careful about getting a ship that had trustworthy crew.

"I probably know some of them fellers. There's some that we can do alright with and then there are a few that would do you in about your first day out to sea just so they could have whatever you carried on board. I tell ya it is givin bein a seaman a bad name all over the place." Ben added.

"We'll just have to listen close and also hope you will know which one we can trust, Ben. I guess we need to work a little harder at being a decent and honest crew to help restore the reputation of seamen. I mean that in the most sincere way—I care about my profession and I want it to be something to be proud of." Capt. Vitas replied.

We could tell he was trying to restore the conversation to being more positive and at the same time help Ben understand his concerns were worth being heard. The captain seemed to have a renewed strength—his voice even seemed to be stronger. Since he and Artemis were probably the oldest ones of our group, we felt more at rest about making the last part of our journey in a day's time; assuming they wouldn't have suggested it if they weren't up to it.

Demas was spending a good part of the evening talking to Levi. He must have been apprehensive about taking over the ministry Levi and his family had been doing since we was asking a lot of questions about where to get supplies of food and how to know which people would be safe to take in. It was a new experience to see Demas at a loss to know what to do.

Levi smiled and said, "You just have to keep your heart tuned to what God wants you to do. Although there are places we get food regularly, many times I do not know until our shelves are bare where to go. As far as people go, Demas, you have spent much of your own life knowing people. That part will not be new to you. I have every confidence in you, otherwise I would not have asked you to carry on the work here."

Keturah was in and out of the room several times and each time she came in I wanted to pull her close to sit by me. I knew in my heart that if she were going to be going with us, I needed to be careful in showing my affection for her in the presence of the others. To me, it seemed respectful to all concerned if we would refrain from being too forward in embracing each other, and certainly not to kiss in their presence. This kind of thinking might sound strange to other men, and perhaps to other women—it was not strange to me. I sensed a clear leading in this matter. I had found a young lady to love and she loved me. She was not some prize I won to be shown like a trophy. She was something of great value to be protected and honored. The best way I could do that was to watch from a distance to make sure she remained safe—keeping a watchful eye on those around her. It was strange in that way; until now, it had been her father's duty to protect her and, now, it was growing in my heart that his duty was being shifted to me, hour by hour and day by day. Beside all that, I knew there was a time coming not to far off when it would be right and proper for Keturah and I to be together. That would be in God's time. To do so now, even though there would be opportunities with her sailing back with us; would dishonor both God and her.

Most of the rest of the evening was spent in making final preparation to leave early the next morning. There was a growing excitement in the house about being on our way home. Cirro and Alexus were talking with Marco, Ben, Demas and Capt. Vitas. I needed to get some fresh air so I went out to the front yard to have some quiet time. I was looking up at the star-filled sky, taken in by its beauty when I felt someone take my arm. I turned and there was Keturah, standing at my side. She rested her head on my shoulder and asked what I was thinking about.

"Those stars, they seem so far away. How long have they been there? How can someone make such vast expanses and yet put us together? How big is life?" I answered her, simply speaking to make my thoughts audible.

"What do you mean—putting us together? You mean you and I finding each other and being in love?" she asked.

"Yes, that too. But just to think that God created you and me, knew us before we were ever formed, wants us to know Him personally. That is just about more than I can comprehend." I said.

"How do you know that? How can you know He knew us before we were born?" she asked with a tone that indicated she wanted to know more about the matter than she was doubting what I had said.

"It is just something I know in my heart. I don' know if someone ever told me about such things or if I ever read them, but this I know—He cares so much for each person who ever walked this earth. That's what Jesus came to teach us and why he died for us. I can tell inside that I am telling you right." I answered with tears streaming down my face. It was another one of those wonderful times when I knew God was with me and helping me speak what He wanted others to hear. I knew it was the beginning of my calling.

We didn't stay outside much longer and when we went in several of the others were already asleep. Our good night to each other consisted of slowly releasing our hands, hooking the fingers slightly enough to help the hold last for a few more seconds, and looking deeply into each others eyes. I truly did love this fine young lady. Sleep came quickly as I finally laid down for the night.

# CHAPTER SEVENTEEN

# THE LAST MILES OF ISRAEL

T he moon had not given over its authority of the night when we began to get up. Someone was already preparing food when I finally work up and others were stuffing their possessions in whatever bags or sacks they could find. Levi was anxious to get started so he made a little more noise with the pots while he cooked up the food. Breakfast was soon over and we were gathering outside just as the sun came up. It was still pretty chilly for a early spring morning and I missed the warmth of the hearth inside. Keturah came out with a small blanket that she had warmed near the fire. She placed part of it over me and the rest over her as she stood close to me. It sure helped to chase the chill away and she warmed my heart from the inside too.

Levi came out with quite a stir and was saying goodbye to Demas and looked longingly at his home that he was about to leave. As he stood there, people began to come from around the town, wanting to say their goodbyes as well. It was quite a testimony to the life he had led before these people. Wanting to get on with the walk and hoping not to become overwhelmed with emotion, Levi led us off.

"Come on! Let's get moving before the sun gets too high in the sky." he shouted as he marched up the front yard to the road, turning occasionally to wave us on.

And so another difficult moment taken care of. It seems that sometimes you just have to dive in and get about what needs to be done and not spend too much time dwelling on things. That's when I need a lot of help. Most of the time, I'm too emotional or sentimental when it comes to things like these. In fact, I'm probably more surprised than anyone that I had the guts to leave Athens. Nonetheless, we were on our way to the coast. After a couple of miles walking down the road, it was noticeable that the older men were taking the lead among us. They all seemed to have a youthful spring in their step that kept us moving at a good pace. Before the sun reached its noonday mark, we could smell the sea air coming in from the coast. That must have inspired Ben and Capt. Vitas even more as they picked up the pace a little more.

"No one's hungry yet are they?" Ben called back to us, sounding like he was hoping we wouldn't be and probably wouldn't have stopped if we had said yes.

It must have been going on 2 o'clock when we noticed some clouds building in the west. It had started out as a beautiful day but now it looked as if we were bound to get soaked if we didn't find some shelter in a hurry. As the sky grew darker we began to watch for somewhere we could find shelter. We must have walked almost two mile before we saw some people coming down the road toward us. They were also hurrying along, trying to avoid the bad weather that was nearly upon us. As best as we could, we tried to communicate with them. Most likely, because of the excitement of the approaching storm, they did not wish to waste time trying to figure out what we were saying. One of the older ladies who was with them took Levi's wife by the arm and pulled her along as she made her way off the road to a hillside, motioning for the rest of us to follow them.

At first, we were terrified that Serirah was being taken captive but soon realized we were probably being led to safety. Without further hesitation, we all followed. The old lady entered a thicket that was nearly dark because of the storm and trees. Staying close to them, she led us through the thicket and came out on the other side into a sheep pen. There was an old shed built up against a couple of large boulders that formed two walls of the shelter. We all huddled in the back corner as close as we could get as the rain began to come down. Almost immediately, the wind came up making it impossible to stay dry. Even though the rain was blowing in on us we were not getting the soaking that we would have without a roof over us. Then the lightning began to strike around us. It was then that the old shed was really appreciated.

The rain didn't last very long but the wind and the lightning continued. It was striking nearby and with not enough time between strikes to get settled down from the previous one. Just then shelter was filled with a blinding flash and an earsplitting crack. As soon as our eyes readjusted from the flash, we saw Cirro fall to the ground. Marco jumped to his side and was going to take hold of him to see if he was still alive but Capt. Vitas shouted, "Don't touch him! He might still have lightning in him!" he warned.

As we watched, steam was rising from his shoulder and right arm. He began to move slightly and Ben took a stick he found and touched him with it. Then he pulled him onto his back and we saw that Cirro's face was blackened on his right side. Ben carefully took hold of him and Marco and I helped pull him up and drug him to the back wall where we leaned him against it. Ben had hold of his arm and noticed it was almost hot. We began to fear he was going to die from being struck. He could slowly turn his head just a little and he was still breathing.

"What are we going to do now! Is he going to be alright?" Alexus shouted.

"Don't know, Alexus. He's been hit pretty hard. I'm surprised he's still alive. I just don't know what to do for him." Ben replied.

"There's not much we can do I'm afraid—I imagine most of the damage to his shoulder and arm are deep injuries that we can't help much. Let's let him rest here for the rest of the evening and then see." Capt. Vitas was saying when I felt I just had to interrupt.

"Well, we can pray for him. I'm all for letting him rest but we need to get to praying with all the faith we have for his recovery. I can tell I'm telling you right cause I feel it in my heart right now." I blurted out.

"Ya, he's right!" Levi agreed.

The others of our group didn't wait for direction but knelt before Cirro and began to pray for him in ways that came from their hearts. They didn't need to ask how to pray or what they should be praying for—they just began to cry out to God to heal their friend. The old shed soon came to life with a reviving spirit that I must have spread throughout the countryside. It wasn't long before I began to feel something coming upon me. It was similar to how that warm blanket felt on my shoulders and back—the warmth being put on me and then penetrating my body. This was very much the same sensation except that whatever was penetrating my body this time was much greater and more help than that warm blanket. It seemed to be like the hand of God Himself being placed on my back and His radiance going right to my soul. I happened to look at Marco and Keturah and could tell that they too were experiencing the same thing I was. It was spreading all over the old shed. The only ones who were not yet being touched by this wonderful help were the old lady and her companions—they just stood in awe and new something of great spiritual power was going on right before them.

Our praying went on for a good while. The spirit that was so thick in that shed stayed even after our praying subsided. Cirro was able to move his arm a little. He still had a lot of pain in it but was making progress. I was thankful that he was getting better but I hated for him to have so be suffering with what must have been excruciating pain.

The lightning was still striking around us but not as close and frequent as it had been. Levi came to me and pull me aside.

"I believe God has chosen you for great works. I have seen many things in you that help me to believe this. Now, I want you to try something that requires great faith, a faith not of yourself but in the One you believe in. Get Keturah, since she is to be your life partner, and place your hands on Cirro's shoulder. Pray then, reaching to the very bottom of your soul to muster all the faith you two have in you for his complete restoration. I do not think God wants him to suffer and He can use the two of you to show

Himself strong. It is in my heart that this is what you have been called to do with your lives. Go! Believe! Do not doubt." Levi instructed us privately.

He had motioned for Keturah to join us and she heard his instructions for us. I turned to look at her for a moment before we were to go to Cirro. As I looked upon her face I could tell that she had submitted herself to obey. She had long been obedient to her father and to God and now that obedience was being transferred to me. Something stirred in my heart about this—a deep stirring that helped me to know that I was gaining a helpmate that would last into eternity. As I took her hand to move towards Cirro, I could feel a power being increased in me and it must have done the same in her from the glow on her face. This was an extremely special moment for the two of us. I don't know if any of the others could see or sense what was happening in us—it didn't really matter if they did or didn't. We both knew God was working in us to prepare us for a work hand in hand together.

We both knelt next to Cirro and very carefully placed our hands on his shoulder, being careful not to cause him more pain and to make sure our hands were touching each other. I don't know why I felt that it was important that they touched, but knew it was. At first, we prayed quietly and softly to ourselves, but not for long. I was soon loudly crying out to God to help Cirro and Keturah was backing me up almost as loudly. I felt a freedom not to hold back because of what anyone might be thinking. We prayed for a good while and suddenly Cirro got a strange look on his face and he turned a little pale. Some of the others must have thought he was in trouble but we just kept on.

"It gone! It's gone! Look! I can raise it way up. It doesn't hurt hardly at all." Cirro shouted as he rose to his feet.

He put his big arms around both Keturah and me and began to thank us. He has so happy to be free from the pain and to be alive.

"Don't thank us, Cirro. All we did was to ask God to help you. Give Him all the praise and thanks—not us." I said.

All this time the old woman and her family were watching with great curiosity. They might have been more than a little frightened by what they saw and heard, but they remained with us. Serirah went to them and tried her best to communicate to them what had just happened in the sheep shelter. Sometimes it is not easy to explain God to people when He has demonstrated Himself to be so great and powerful. She must have been able to help them understand as least some of what went on. By the time we were ready to leave the shed, she had told them to find Demas when they got to Emmaus and he would help them some more. It was almost more than I could comprehend and I probably knew more about what was happening than anyone else in the shed. It would take more than just a few minutes to come to understand the greatness of God.

After giving Cirro a little more time to rest and making sure the storm was over, we made our way out of the shed and thicket back to the road. We still had a few hours of daylight left and wanted to make the most of them. We would reach Joppa before darkness set in and we wanted to find a safe place to stay for the night.

The remainder of our trip to Joppa was less eventful. The temperature had dropped after the storm went through and the air was getting a bit nippy. It must have caused us to quicken our pace since we were soon within sight of the city of Joppa.

"Lets find a place to make camp on this side of town. We should be safe here. Once we get situated, I'll take Artemis and Capt. Vitas with me to see what we can find out. The rest of you will need to guard the camp." Ben directed.

"Yes sir, Admiral Ben!" Alexus abruptly replied as he stood to attention with a salute.

"I'm sorry! I didn't mean to be giving orders—it was just that I was thinking it would be best for us older ones to be the one to go into the town. We have a better chance of recognizing some of the crews and besides that, we will be less likely to be taken as forced labor." Ben apologized.

"Oh, you don't have to be sorry, Ben. I was just trying to give you a hard time since we haven't had much of a chance to lately. Your advice sounds really good to me. Anyway, if something should happen to you, I sure they would soon be returning you before you talked their ears off." Alexus replied laughing as he finished.

"I'll be lookin for a crew of heathens just so I can have them take you with them. Maybe you'll learn to appreciated good company then." Ben answered.

We soon found a grassy area that was protected from the northwest wind that was blowing in an effort to recapture the winter weather that had given way to spring buds and flowers. We unfolded one of the canvases that Levi had brought and soon had a nice shelter built. I had acquired a flint stone back at Emmaus before we left and soon had a small fire going. Marco came with enough wood to keep us warm well into the night. It was good to be enjoying the evening with our group sitting around the campfire, even though our group had now grown somewhat.

After we had eaten a light supper, the three older men left to make their rounds of the taverns and pubs. There was some small talk for a while after they left but several of us were getting pretty tired form the day's journey. I made my way to sit beside Keturah and Marco came to sit next to me.

"Do you two think you will be staying in Athens when we get back?" he asked.

"Maybe for a little while, but I doubt we will make it our permanent home. Actually, I just don't know what we are going to be doing yet. I want to see my family for a few days and give them a chance to get to know Keturah and her parents. After that, well, we just might be headed on another journey—Who knows?" I answered.

"How about you, Keturah? Is that what you want to do?" Marco asked her.

"What we do or I do really isn't that important to me right now. I just want to be with Nic and try to do what God has called us to do." Keturah replied.

"That sounds fine while love is still young but what about later when it's time for a family of your own. Life can get hard sometimes and it takes more that love to make it." Marco continued.

"Such a worrier! Almost sounds like you don't think we can make it. Let me—" I started to answer but was stopped in the middle of it.

"It's not that at all, Nic. It's just that I don't know what I would do if I were in your place. That is a lot of responsibility to take on." he interrupted.

"We are going to have to trust God to lead the way. I know in my heart that He has called the both of us to reach out to people for Him. I could not deny that if I really wanted to. There is really no choice to be made here. To reject that call would only lead to misery and disaster." I said.

"I know. Yes, I know. It is such a noble and gallant thing you do. What are you parents going to do when they get to Athens, Keturah?" Marco asked.

"I haven't heard my father say anything for certain but I can tell you that he will most definitely be doing something to care for people. That is what he has been doing for as long as I can remember. I just know in my heart that they will be able to make it, wherever they end up." Keturah answered.

"Marco, why are you asking so many questions? You are giving me the impression that you think we are making a big mistake or something. You have been with us on this trip enough to have witness the power of God and what He can do. Where is you faith my friend?" I asked him.

"Maybe that is just it, Nic. I have been your friend for a long time now. We did a lot of things together and you have come to mean a lot to me. Now, well now, I don't see much need of me to be in your life—at least the way we were before—." he started to reply but stopped short of finishing what he wanted to say.

"You mean before I met Keturah?" I finished for him.

"Yes, I guess that's what I mean. I'm sorry Keturah. It's not anything at all about you—It's just that I feel so left out and alone—like loosing my best friend!" Marco said with tears streaming down his face.

His comments ripped at my heart. Even though I knew my feelings and commitments to him had not diminished in any way, I understood what he was saying. I reached out to hug him closely and held him for some time, trying my best to reassure him that he was still my best friend and that he would always have a place in my heart. We were all three shedding tears as we made our way though these touching moments and knew it was good to get these feelings brought out into the open. After I tried to convince him of our undying friendship, I just held him for a while longer. Then the Lord began to give me help in knowing what to tell him next.

"Marco, God has helped me to understand much about the human heart on this journey. It seems our hearts have an enormous capacity to love, especially when we have Him dwelling in them. The amazing part of it is that when we think they are filled to overflowing with love for someone in particular, there is room for that same kind of love to develop for another. Now here is the part that He has just helped me to know beyond any doubt or debate! As that new love grows in our heart, it does not take away from the love that was already there. I know it defies common sense and logical reason, but I'm telling you right in this. Let me offer you some degree of proof to this—when you father and mother were married, they must have loved each other—with a heart full of love, right? Then when you were born, they loved you with all their heart, right? Then when your brother, Stephan was born, they didn't have to take any of their love for you away in order to love him did they? The ability of our hearts to love is limited only by our willingness to do so. Now God has set some limitations on how we are to express that love so that is stay honorable to Him and to those we love—It is something He has put in us and designed according to His purposes. Now, here's where we get into problems. While the love of our hearts has so much capacity, our time is under definite limitations. There is only so much time that each of us has. We can not do anything to create more, only make adjustments to use what we have more efficiently." I expounded on the matter with such confidence that I amazed myself more that I did Marco.

It seemed to me that I had just crammed years worth of philosophy and humanism into a nugget the size of a walnut shell and done so without the intellectual authority to do so. Marco was looking at me in a way that showed two definite things were going on in him. The first was that he knew in his heart that I still held him as close as a dear friend as I ever had, possibly even closer. The second expression showed that he was left in awe of what he had just heard—not in unbelief, but in amazement of such concise teaching being condensed into a brief moment of consolation and comfort.

"I know you have spoken from your heart, Nic. I'm sorry for being jealous of our friendship. I can tell God helped you just now." he said as he grabbed my hand to squeeze it tightly.

"It's O.K! I understand and I will try my best to share some of my time with you—as for my love for you—that is something that doesn't have to be shared. It is a love of its own that doesn't diminish as it is given to others. Who knows, maybe you will be with us wherever we end up?" I said, trying to lighten up the conversation.

"You don't have a sister we haven't met yet do you Keturah? I might not feel so lonely then." he asked jokingly.

Levi, Serriah, and the others had already went to sleep while we had been talking. I was getting tried and wanted to get some sleep myself but felt it best to stay up until our investigators returned. I was getting anxious for them to get back, partly because I wanted to hear what they had learned, and also because they had been gone for quite a while. I wondered if Marco and I should try to go and find them but knew that probably wouldn't be wise since we didn't have any idea of the where we were going. My nervousness must have become noticeable since Alexus spoke up form his bed on the ground.

"They'll be back soon enough. It takes time to get around to these places and find out what you need to know. You just can't hurry and start askin questions or you won't get anywhere. You got to spend time listen and talkin with them before you go askin. Just rest a while—they'll be fine. Ole Ben knows his way around them folks." he spoke.

"You young ones need rest too. Relax now and trust God to return our friends to us. Keturah, come now. Get some sleep while you can." Levi encourage us.

Keturah left to go lay down near her parents and Marco found a place to lay down by Alexus. I wrapped a blanket around myself and leaned against at tree that was close enough to the fire to feel its warmth. I wanted to stand guard while the others rested and felt an inner stirring that it was of some importance to do so. I don't know why if thought it necessary but I did. I began to think about what to do if someone came along. The only thing I could find to use as a weapon was one of the big sticks that was burning in the fire. I knew my stature and size would not be intimidating to hardly anyone but something kept troubling me that I needed to stay alert. As I looked around our little camp I saw people who I had come to care much about. I was determined in my mind that I was going to do my best to protect them from whatever might come at us.

The night went on and I was growing more and more sleepy. I was dozing off and waking myself up on a regular basis now. It was during one of those times I was waking back up that I thought I heard something in the brush beyond our camp. It sounded close enough that I didn't want to speak to wake any of the others. I very carefully moved over to the fire as if to mend it and found the strongest stick I could. As I held it in my hand, I listened for more movement in the darkness. Out of the corner of my eye, I saw two figures crouching as they moved toward Levi and his family. I waited until they came just a little closer and saw they had knives raised, ready to pounce on their victims. I tightened my grip on the stick in my hand and grabbed a smaller on with the other hand. All in one motion, I sprang to my feet, slung the small stick which was on fire toward the two, and charged at them with the bigger stick pulled back, ready to swing with all my might at the both of them. As I lunged at them I yelled with an animal like growl that woke those in the camp. My aim must have been good since the lead man was hit near his face with the burning stick I threw. He was distracted from his attack and was tearing at his clothes in order to get the burning coals out of them. I wasn't sure but I thought I saw him drop his knife as his attention turned to his burns.

That left me facing the other man. He still had his knife and was ready to take me on. I knew that he had to act quickly, even to get away. My yell had brought the others out of their beds. Marco was already pounding on the man who had caught the wrath of my fire stick and Cirro was going to help him. Alexus and Levi were coming to back me up.

"Back off or I'll throw this right between her eyes!" the man yelled at me, aiming the knife right at Keturah.

I would have been willing to let him turn and run off until he threatened my new found partner. In an instant, my mind had made a decision that he would have to answer for his action and he was going to answer to me. There was a brief struggle going on in me about what was right and not right. The struggle ended with a determination that the rightness of it would be discussed later. For now, that thief was going to pay the price for his wickedness.

I stepped more between him and Keturah so as to defend her and block him from hitting her—having to hit me first. We were now face to face, only a few feet apart. Desperation showed on his face. He was by himself now, his partner being held captive by Marco and Cirro. His only hope was to give up or try to slow us down so he could escape. It was apparent that giving up was not a option for him as I saw his hand go back, ready to throw the knife. I saw the blade gleaming in the light of the fire on my stick. It was on its way toward me, heading right for my chest. Almost without thinking, I brought the stick down from above my shoulder so that it was across my chest. I heard the knife make a thud as it landed.

The only pain I felt was from a few sparks that landed on my face as the knife landed. As I glanced down to see where I was hit, I saw the knife had embedded in the stick I was holding. My anger flared even more now and I threw the stick down and charged, in slow motion at the man. He had turned to run and was being pursued by three men now who had good reason to do him great harm, me being the one who was the most intent. I was close enough now to lunge out and grab for his legs. My arms went around one leg and then found the other. With all my strength I pulled them together and caused him to fall forward. I was now in the process of reaching up to grab hold of his arms when I felt Alexus dive across his upper body. Levi was soon there taking hold of his arms and holding him to the ground. I was wanting to beat this man, to cause him pain, when it occurred to me that it was now time to deal with the issue of rightness that I had just seconds before dismissed until a better time. My fist was pulled back, ready to place a blow to his face, probably repeated blows.

"You can't do this!' I heard someone say. "It is no longer in you!"

I knew this voice was not one of those in the camp. I had heard it before and knew who it belonged to. I found myself suddenly dealing with a strong feelings of hatred and anger for this man and his partner, feelings I knew I had to curtail. I moved away from him as Alexus and Levi restrained him with some rope along with the other man. As much as I wanted to hurt him I knew that I couldn't. To do so would have destroyed so much of what God was wanting to build in me. I was mad, though. This man had just threatened the one I loved. He intended to harm all of us and take what little we had.

"We'll hold these two til morin and see what the Capt. and others want to do with them. You alright, Nic? Did he hit you with that knife?" Alexus asked.

"Ya, I'm fine. The knife is stuck in that stick. I'm just upset more than anything. Thanks for your help." I answered.

"Well, thank you for being awake and alert. If you hadn't been, who knows how many of us would be lyin there stabbed. Them was some mean ones, let me tell ya." Cirro added.

"For some reason I just felt I had to stay up and watch. And it wasn't just luck that I pulled that stick in front of me to stop that knife. But what's more incredible is that I heard a voice telling me not to hit them for what they were doing. It was as clear as anything. Not only have we

DRIVEN HEARTS

been protected but we have been stopped from becoming like these men. God was at work here if you haven't already figured that out." I replied.

We heard someone coming up the road from the town and soon could make out that it was Capt. Vitas, Ben, and Artemis. They had made it back from Joppa but we were surprised to seem then return this late at night. We thought they would have stayed in Joppa instead of risking walking back here in the darkness.

"Why are you all still up? Doesn't anyone sleep around here? Who are those two guys and what are they all bound up for?" Ben asked without giving time for answers.

"We got ourselves a couple of thieves who were set on doin us all in. If it weren't for Nic, we would have some of us been killed." Alexus answered.

"Did they harm anyone here? Everybody alright?" Capt. Vitas asked.

"We're fine, Just a little shook up." Marco said.

"What are you goin to do with these two heathens?" Ben asked.

"Don't know yet. Figured we'd wait til morning and see what you all thought." Alexus replied.

"You all get some rest and I'll watch them for a while. They had better not move or I'll whomp them aside the head. I'll hollar out if I need help." Cirro offered.

"Good! We all could use some rest for certain." Artemis spoke.

"What did you learn in Joppa tonight?" Marco asked.

"Better wait until morning to tell you. Best not take a chance of our plans being made known around here." Capt. Vitas answered.

Most of us made our way back to our beds. I was heading to make a place to lay by the warmth of the fire when I felt someone take hold of my arm. It was Levi.

"I saw you place your life before my daughter's tonight. As her father, I want to thank you but more than that, I want to tell you how touched I am by your love for her. Not that I doubted it before, but your willingness to protect her was proof of the genuine love you have for her. I am most proud of you my son." Levi spoke.

I did not offer a reply, only looked him straight in the eye, swallowed hard, and then nodded my head. After that, I went on to attempt to get some rest for the night. It had been a long day and now, the evening had drained what little energy was left. I wanted so badly to sleep but as I tried to lay still enough, I kept wondering about someone else coming along. What if those two had any friends who would be looking for them? What if they were able to get untied? What made that noise out in the darkness?

I just couldn't get to sleep and soon found myself thinking about what made those men try to attack us. What would happen to them if we turned them over to the authorities? Was there a chance that they would try to convince the authorities that we had attacked them and then we would find ourselves behind bars once again. At last I glanced over to where Keturah was laying with her parents and soon had more pleasant thoughts passing through my mind and sleep came quickly.

I was one of the last to wake when morning came. I heard Capt. Vitas questioning our attackers. Even though I was interested to know what they were saying, I thought it best to let him finish before I went over to them. Before I reached them, Capt. Vitas got up and walked over to meet me.

"These two claim they were only trying to defend themselves and only intended to ask us for some food. I know that isn't the way our men say all this happened. Since you and Keturah were the one's whose lives were threatened by them, I want to ask what you want to be done to them. I am also going to ask Levi since Keturah is still his daughter. After seeing that knife they threw at you, I would not be opposed to having them imprisoned. It would have surely killed you had it not been stopped by that stick." he explained.

"Did they tell you why they tried to attack us?" I asked.

"They said they only wanted to ask for food to take back to their wives and children if you can believe them." he answered.

"It seems that God helped me to know to be alerted to them coming and I know He helped me to place that stick where it could stop the knife. Since He was so aware of all that was going on last night, I know He must be aware of what they will be doing again. He stopped me from becoming like them when I was so filled with anger. It probably would feel pretty good to hit them hard with my fist a time or two but that would be just for the moment, so here's what I think we should do—-untie them, keep that knife, give them some food and send them down the road.

Now so as not to seem to soft on them, let's have Cirro and Alexus make sure they get started by grabbing them by the shirt and seat of their pants and sending them off with a swift kick. I don't think prison would help change them but maybe kindness would. Well, that's my thoughts—see what Levi thinks." I replied.

"No need to ask. You have spoken wisely and well. I have only one request to make. Before we send them off, I want to say something to them." Levi spoke up.

"Fine! Better go to tellin them then cause were ready to get em out of here." Ben said.

Levi walked over to where Alexus was taking the ropes off the two and got right up near their faces as he pulled the two of them together.

"If either of you ever even think about harming my daughter or my new son again, I can promise you that I will not be so kind to you next time. You are going to be let go now and you can thank God Almighty for your freedom. While you are thanking Him, you might want to get to know Him better because He's going to be taking notice of you—I'm sure of that." he told them as he held them tightly by their shirts.

He held them that way for what seemed like several minutes. His eyes were as cold as steel and yet had a gleam of compassion shining through. He was as serious as death itself and they knew it. I could tell in my heart that he was telling them right about God's attention being on them. The amazing part of it was that I found myself wanting to encourage them to hurry up and get their hearts right with God—only hours after being ready to nearly kill them.

Soon Alexus had them by their shirt collars and was taking them to the road. Neither he nor Cirro were know for their outward compassion, especially to those who threatened them, and they were a little rough in sending the two on their way. I suppose a person could have said they demonstrated tough love if you had a healthy imagination. We watched them hurry on down the road but noticed they were looking in their sacks to see what food they contained. Maybe, just maybe, they were actually hungry. I was praying to myself for seed to be planted in them when I heard Ben say,

"Finally, we can get about business!"

"Yes, we must decide quickly. Time is becoming short if we are to make ship. Gather around now and listen closely." Capt. Vitas instructed. "Basically, we have three ships to choose from and all three will be leaving today. Two of them are reputable but the third might be too risky. Ben knows the captains of all three and I will let him tell you what he thinks."

"They're all men of their word but a couple of them have a hard time keepin their crew in line. With the women with us, I think it best to consider only two, and the safest of them would be the ship, Whitecross under Capt. Minert. They want a pretty good fare to take us on and expect us to help considerable. That would be my thinking." Ben said.

"Do we have enough for the fare?" Marco asked.

"Yes, but it will use up a good bit of what we have." the captain answered.

"Seein how you all handled those to thieves last night makes me wonder if you couldn't hold your own with even that other crew, but no sense in borrowing trouble. We'd best sail on the Whitecross." Artemis added.

"We'd best be on our way then. Hurry up and gather your things. We have to be on the other side of the city before noon, since our ship will be sailing shortly thereafter. We have a few things we must get done before we board ship.

I would like to do some more trading and the rest of you should get something to help you get your sea legs back." the captain spoke with a sense of frustration in having to be rushed for time.

"How many days will it take us to reach Tyre?" Levi asked.

"I'm figurin it might take most of three days if the wind is helping— but not more than four at the most." Ben answered.

"I assume you will be taking your ship out to sea when we get to Tyre?" Levi said with a questioning tone.

"I hope they have made the necessary repairs and she will be ready to sail. I would like to get her back to Greece. From there—who knows?" Capt. Vitas answered, seeming to be lost in thoughts about what the future had in store for him.

"Can you think of anything else we might need before we leave?" Marco asked, looking to the three older men who had worked out our plans.

"It would be good to find a couple of seamen who could help us get back home from Tyre. I know you men have good experience but we could use a couple more hands when the water gets rough and I'm pretty certain it will." Capt. Vitas replied.

After hurriedly gathering our belongings, we quickly made our way into the city of Joppa. It was a much different city than we had been in for quite some time, being clearly evident that life there was heavily dependent on sea trade. Most of the city was contained within great walls and the buildings often told of the age—some must have been quite ancient. It was different than the city of Tyre in that there wasn't such a strong distinction between the social levels. There seemed to be something that had an influence on life that contributed to this difference. It wasn't necessarily something that had only been recent in its influence, but must have affected society for quite a long time. It was evident in the buildings, at least to me; the architectural style carried throughout the city. I began to sense that there were godly people living here that had help to shape the social makeup of the city. It stirred me in my soul to even ponder the fact.

The air we breathed began to become more permeated with the smells of the sea that stretched our on the western side. I could tell that Ben and Capt. Vitas were being refreshed just to be able to inhale it into their lungs. The sun had risen to shine brightly on the walls of the buildings and they seemed to be gleaming white. It was an awesome sight to behold. I must have been so preoccupied by what I saw that I was oblivious to where I was walking, as I crashed right into a push cart that on old man was rolling down the street. Keturah had grabbed my arm to pull me out of the way but it was too late. As I hit the cart, fruits and vegetables spilled onto the ground and the cart tipped on its end. I felt like such a fool and quickly tried to gather up all that had spilled. The old man was chattering away something I couldn't understand but I could tell he wasn't thrilled at my hindrance to his morning. With the help of Keturah and Marco, we soon had his cart reloaded and back in order. Even with him still carrying on, I reached out to take his hand, gently but firmly took it to shake, and place my other hand on his shoulder—trying to apologize as best I could by looking him right in the eyes and attempting to love him in spite of his complaining. It seemed to work. I had connected. What I could not say with words, I was able to communicate with my eyes. He immediately stopped talking and returned the biggest smile I had seen in a long while. He even reached for some fruit to offer me, and knowing bridges were being built, I accepted it. Just a brief moment in time—nothing significant in the mechanics of the accident—an outburst of emotion, him upset;

me feeling embarrassed,—potential conflict—spirit led response—God honoring conclusion— another friend made.

I don't know if the rest of our group understood what had just happened but I knew I had to share it with Keturah. As I began to tell her she simply said,

"Yes, I could see it all!" smiling as much with here eyes as with her lips.

"Fascinatin place ain't it? Been here many times but I never get tired of seein her again." Ben said, indicating my thoughts were being easily read.

"It certainly is! This place must have a rich history." I replied.

"That it does! That it does. It's been here for centuries. It was the only natural seaport for a long ways, especially to the south. You had to go way down to Egypt to the next one. Jerusalem relied heavily on gettin what they needed from this port. Why, even the cedar logs that were used in the temple long ago were delivered here and hauled inland—right through this very street most likely. That must have been somethin to have seen— massive logs full of color—by the thousands they say." Ben explained.

"It's so different from Tyre. The people here are different. I wonder why."

I asked almost absent mindedly.

"Could be that God fearin folks from Jerusalem and the surrounding area made their way here and have had more of an influence on the city. Sometimes a few people tryin to do what is right and godly can really make a difference. Maybe that is what you are feelin." Ben suggested.

"I believe you're right, Ben. Something has. I can sure feel it!" I answered.

Most of the rest of the walk through the city was done without much more conversation. There were beautiful sights to behold and a lot to take in. There was merchandise that we had never seen before. Capt. Vitas, Ben and Artemis walked with a determination to get to the seashore. For older men, it was hard to keep up with them. Their fast pace quickly had us coming into the western section of the city and we were soon to behold a glorious sight of the sea stretching out way into the distance. A few ships, all seeming so tiny against the vastness of the sea, dotted the seascape. The city, at least the main part of it was setting high up on natural walls, well above the seaport. It gave us a panoramic view of all that was going on in the docks below. It seemed we could see for miles—the view was breathtaking.

Almost reluctantly, we made our way down the winding streets to the docks and found the captain of the Whitecross. He was pacing from one place to another, calling out instructions and often yelling orders flavored heavily with the foul language of seasoned sailors. When he saw Capt. Vitas and the rest of us, he started to greet us in a tone of agitation at our not already being on board the ship. He softened his words and demeanor quite a bit when he notice the ladies with us. I felt an uneasiness about the change in his attitude. I couldn't decide if he changed out of respect for the women or if he was hoping to charm them into some devious scheme. I was quickly coming to regret the decision to set sail on this ship.

Levi must have been feeling the same concerns as I was as he pulled Capt. Vitas over to the side and began to talk privately with him.

"Do you really think we can trust this man and his crew out on the sea?" he asked.

"I think we will get to Tyre safely. I've known this captain for many years and even though he has a crude and often vulgar manner of speaking, he has never been known to committed any offenses that would cause me to feel we would be in danger. Remember, we only have to contend with this crew for maybe four days at the most; and, if things start to get out of hand, we do have some pretty strong men to stand up for us. Just try to keep the women with some of us and watch to prevent opportunity from happening. We can make it—just trust and have faith." the captain replied, looking at both Levi and me.

## CHAPTER EIGHTEEN

# BACK ON THE WATER

We boarded the ship and stowed our belongings, then turned our energies to helping the crew finish loading. Soon the Whitecross was ready to raise sail and be on her way north. I had to overcome feelings of anger and resentment several times that afternoon as many of the crewmen would look at Keturah and mumble something I tried not to hear as they would walk past. She must have been aware of their attention, since she asked me where she could stay that would give her more privacy. I wanted her near to help protect her but I did not like those men looking at her. I thought for a moment and decided it would be best to send her below to stay with Ben and Artemis for a while. As we were headed for the galley stairs, one of the men who had been watching her attempted to stop us. He was beginning to reach out to take her by the arm when the wooden beam of one of the sails swung around in the wind and caught him on the back of his head. He fell immediately to the deck and others came running. The blow had knocked him out and left a good size gash on his head.

Keturah started to move to help him but I stopped her at the same time the other crewmen stepped in to prevent her from touching the man.

"Leave him alone! You have done this to him! Isn't that enough for you or do you want to finish him off with one of your spells? Get away from us now. Stay away!" they commanded her.

Having not even been on the water for a hour or more and we already have problems. By just trying to get away from men with self gratifying intentions, Keturah had now become thought of as a woman with evil powers and spells. At first, it angered me and I wanted to defend her honor, but then I realized that at least they might leave her alone. I kept my mouth shut and decided to wait to see how this would play out. Keeping her safe was more important than restoring her honor, at least for now. It was a necessary compromise and maybe time would permit the matter to be corrected later.

We had not done very well in establishing friendly relations with the new crew. This incident was not going to improve the captains attitude. I knew we could tolerate their dislike for us but that wasn't what was really bothering me. It was now our purpose to attempt to love others as Jesus has loved us. While that was our purpose, we certainly had met our share of people who were not so lovable. For most of the rest of the afternoon and evening, I gave a lot of thought to how we might tear down the barriers that had been set between our group and the crew. The only way that seemed to have any merit was to use Marco and his cooking once more. I knew we had to try because I, for one, was not going to be content to write this crew off. We just had to help them come to know the love of God.

The Whitecross made good time that afternoon and since we were in familiar waters, the crew kept her sailing through the night. I had nearly forgotten just how beautiful the night sky looked from out on the open sea. Keturah had came up on deck with Levi. I went over to place my hand around her and we gazed at the heavens together. It was a special time—the star studded sky and the sound of gentle waves coming against the hull of the ship. There was such a peacefulness in my heart at that moment—maybe because Keturah was beside me or maybe it was even something greater—that being a definite sense of obedience to what God was calling us to. I found it rather odd that I could feel such peace when in the last twenty-four hours, Keturah and I had been directly involved in two specific incidents where someone intended to do us harm. Even though they were stopped from bringing their intentions to completion, it should have had a more unnerving effect on us.

The rest of the night went smoothly and Marco was up early trying to do his best to fix some food to win over the crew. He had captured their attention with the aroma coming from the galley. I can't say that I even remembered his best meals on our way over to Israel ever being that enticing. After breakfast was finished, we notice the crew seemed a little more accepting of us. Even the man who had been knocked out with the sail beam was showing us some respect—from underneath the bandage around his head. I have never ceased to be amazed at what Marco could do when he sets his mind to it.

Our voyage went on without further incident and we heard the captain say that we should reach port in Tyre early to next morning if we sailed through the night once more. He had heard that there were pirates already operating around some of the larger shipping areas and that it might be safer to lower sail and drop anchor for the night, since the area had several inlets and bays that could hide smaller ships.

"It isn't for me to agree or disagree with your command of this ship my good captain, but have you considered that it might be more difficult to notice a ship sliding quietly through the water under cover of darkness than one trying to make the home stretch in broad daylight. Also the longer we set out here the better chance there is that we will be noticed. My experiences of knowing their behavior leads me to believe they are usually too inebriated to function well until just before daylight. Now, please forgive me for expressing my opinion and continue the fine job you have been doing of sailing this ship to our destination." Capt. Vitas said with unusual eloquence.

The captain of the Whitecross looked at Capt. Vitas for a moment—I was unable to tell if he was furious or it he was attempting to decide how to implement his suggestions without loosing face. He soon turned and walked swiftly to the helm of the ship and called out,

"Head her out 10 degrees and let her run at half mast. In three quarters of an hour bring her back straight. We're runnin through the night. Keep a sharp watch for any other ships. I want to know about them at first sighting."

My thoughts returned to Capt. Vitas' old catapult and how it had been so useful in taking care of the pirates who attacked us. It would have made me feel a little better to have had it on board with us and then I began to wonder what plan the crew had to fight off an attack. There was nothing visible on deck. Curiosity was driving me to ask about what plan they might have, but knowing that the captain was working at being comfortable with Capt. Vitas' advice caused me to hold my tongue. The one thing that was beginning to make life a little easier was that we were all learning to operate on trust and faith. Even though we made plans and preparations and tried our best not to do anything foolish—each of us had made great progress at not worrying. We were learning to trust God to help us get to where He was sending us and to provide the way of getting there. It was something that we were each learning on an individual basis and there wasn't a lot of conversation about it. Collectively, we were practicing what God was helping us with privately. It was being more easily recognized each day as we continued our journey home. It was also making life quite a bit easier.

The night passed without incident and it was not long after sunrise that we caught sight of Tyre in the distance. Fog rolled in from time to time, but we were able to see clearly enough between times to know we would soon be docking. Capt. Vitas grew somewhat anxious to catch sight of his old ship. He was pacing back and forth on deck, quietly looking over the water hoping to find her. He hadn't said much about the ship since we left her in Tyre but it was plainly evident now that he still had a fondness for her. He had only made brief mention of selling her and I knew now that it would not be an easy choice for him should he decide to. However, I wouldn't be completely surprised by it since all of us had been changed in our thinking about material things. While there were things of great value in our lives and things we depended on for a living, they seemed to have lost their place of priority in our lives. For that matter, there were many changes among those of us who had made this journey—changes that would bear witness in eternity.

I was surprised at not being overjoyed to docking at Tyre and making ready to sail back to Athens with Capt. Vitas. I felt a sense of melancholy sweeping over me. I found myself reflecting on all that had occurred on our trek through this holy land we had just left. I remembered all those wonderful people we met along the way, the old shepherds, Mary and Martha, so many others. There was a longing within me to see them once more. Even though we had faced real danger and even the possibility of being killed, our journey had allowed us to be a part of so much. I was looking past the city of Tyre to the distant hillsides of Israel when Keturah came up to stand by me. I turned to look at her and smiled briefly before returning my thoughts to the land of God's people. She must have been able to read my thoughts as she spoke,

"It isn't so much that we are leaving this land as it is that we are taking a good piece of it with us."

Those words she spoke right at that moment got so strong in my heart that I knew she had spoken wisely and rightly. Instantly, she had spoken and it made sense to me. She was able to put into a few words all that had been stirring in me since we had set out to sea again. I was giving her a hug of appreciation for her help and understanding when I heard a voice saying,

*"Your journey has only just had its beginnings. Walk now with me into new hearts in new lands. Hold unto me and I will help you."*\

This voice startled me a little but this time it was more familiar. It only took to a few seconds to recognize it was the same voice who had spoken to me before-one that I could only assume was that of the Lord.

"Yes! I know." I answered out loud.

"You know what?" Keturah asked.

"Oh, I'll have to explain it to you later. There isn't time to tell it all to you before we dock and I don't want you to miss any part of what I have just found out." I answered her.

"I hope you don't make a habit of doing this to me. Making me wait to hear about something that has really solidified in your heart. I can see by looking in your eyes right now that your soul is being stirred anew." she said with a tone of resignation to the fact that it was indeed something she would need to get used to..

As the Whitecross docked and we left the crew to finish securing the moorings, it was not hard to see a noticeable difference in the crew's character. A few of them even treated Seirrah and Keturah with respect as they departed. I found myself wondering if we had anything to do with the change in them. Whatever the reason, I was convinced that we were to treat people with kindness, respect, and understanding—even if they were less than pleasant to us. There simply wasn't any other option for us. It was the way we had learned on our journey and it was to be the pattern of the rest of our lives.

# CHAPTER NINETEEN

# AN OLD SHIP SETS WAITING

C apt. Vitas didn't take long to find his old ship and his face brightened at the sight of her. There was little doubt that we would be taking her on the trip back to Athens, that is, if she was still seaworthy. Artemis, Alexus, Cirro, and Capt. Vitas went to find the man who he had left the ship with and we made our way up to the shops and inns just up from the waterfront. Having Keturah and her mother with us, we decided it best to avoid the taverns. We stopped at a small place with outdoor seating that let the morning sun warm us while we were able to enjoy the fresh air and take in the view of the city. It was a busy place, cartloads of goods going and coming to and from the docks. People were scurrying everywhere, going about business, looking for people—it seemed to be their life's purpose. I began to feel out of place since we were content to sit and wait for Capt. Vitas and the others join us with the latest word on our plans. As we enjoyed some fresh fruit, I began to feel an ache in my heart for those people. I wondered if they ever found time to give thought to matters of life other than their work. What was family life for them? Small children were pulling with all their might at heavy carts loaded with merchandise to be delivered. Most of the children's bodies bore evidence of hard labor. There feet and hands were covered with skin as tough as leather. It most likely had been several days since they had bothered to clean themselves or their clothes.

I nearly startled myself back to an awareness of the others in my group as I was deep in thought. I found myself doing a lot of analyzing of people and situations. I was noticing the details of life and seeing the character of people in a whole different way. I wasn't even sure that I liked being that way, but none the less, it was definitely the way I had become. I was afraid I was being too judgmental. My thoughts must have been such that they showed on my face since Keturah ask me what I was thinking about. When I told her she responded with another amazing but very practical suggestion.

"It could be that you are seeing life through eyes that are now spiritually focused. If your heart has been changed, then it is only logical that your mind, eyes and body were also changed. What you are describing does not surprise me in the least, as a matter of fact, I would be more surprised if you weren't seeing with a new perspective." she offered.

My heart started to dance within me as I once again come to appreciate the gift God had given me in this young woman. She was such a strength to draw upon, a helpmate to carry the load, an encourager, yet a soft and gentle comforter. I knew she was far more than I ever deserved but I was deeply grateful to have her in my life. I vowed to myself and to God that I would do my best to love, honor, and protect her for the rest of our lives. I attempted to seal that vow by taking her hand and holding it gently but firmly as I looked deep into her beautiful eyes and let my heart speak to hers. Somehow I could see that her heart was getting the information from mine and two small tears began their way down her lovely face. I had to swallow hard and try to keep my own tears back as my eyes filled to near overflowing. It was a quiet and private moment we were able to share in the midst of hundreds of people.

"What're you all settin' around for when we got to get a crew together? I guess it's up to us ole folks to get things done if we want em done. Now come on! We got lots to do—let's get movin'." Ben said with growl in his voice.

"Didn't take you long to climb back up in rank. A feller gets his lungs filled with sea air and it just plain goes to his head. I guess we had better get about our business before we get sentenced to work in that dingy ole galley trying to cook up something them picky old men can actually chew." Marco answered with a mocking tone that caused us all to laugh hard before we made our way to finish our business.

We spent the rest of the morning walking thru the city and buying a little here and there. We had most of what we needed in the way of food and supplies stashed away down at the docks. It was a light-hearted time of just looking at things we didn't need at all but to hold them and think about how far away they may have come from. For just an hour or so we were able to be carefree and frivolous. It was fun. We began to mix right in with the people around us. Several people were buying items that we saw simply no useful purpose in and they were quite happy about it. Not more than an hour or so of this casual use of time and I began to realize a great tragedy that lie hidden just beneath the surface.

These people we were shopping with knew little else about life. For them, this was the cream—the best to be had. It was suddenly evident nearly everywhere I looked. Those who had any money to spend were quite willing to part with it on things that would have short term benefit or they were spending their earnings on things that could only bring heartache and disaster. As we walked a few more blocks down the streets the shops became less appealing and there were rooms with women selling themselves to any man with money in his pocket.

What had started out as a joyous and light-hearted time had now became filled with sorrow and heaviness. I was thinking I might have been the only one in our group who was seeing any of these things, but the look on the faces of Levi, Serriah, and even Keturah told me that I was not alone in this. In the hustle and bustle of being a center of trade for that part of the world, Tyre had became a city more of things than of people. As I looked at people, there was a lack of integrity, of being genuine in their hearts, a lack of care for one another. They were friendly enough. They made us feel welcome. However it was evident that they were not the least bit troubled at selling anything they had to sell, including themselves. There was something lacking in that city and it took me a while to figure it out but at last, it came to me. I began to suspect that there were no standards set for anyone to live by. The only deterrent to doing wrong was hoping someone bigger or stronger wouldn't do wrong back to you.

Had I changed that much? Had I become so morally and spiritually minded that the world around me was so repulsive? Had this city always been like this or was it that I was seeing it differently now? I could not reach a verdict on these questions as we turned to make our way back toward the docks, but I certainly was feeling the crushing weight of a burden for the people there. As we walked along I found myself wandering about Athens and how the people there would seem to me. By the time we neared the docks, I was thinking that maybe I had become arrogant and thought that I was better than all those people who had been so carefree about their lives.

Before we had reached the docks, we met Capt. Vitas and the others coming to toward us.

"The old ship has been worked over some, if fact she probably in better shape than she been in for quite some time. They still want to put some new rope in her sails but, other than that, she's ready to set out to see. We can more than likely set sail by mid-afternoon if you all think we ready to go by then." he reported to us.

"Would it be possible for us to stay the night on board the ship and set out at first light? I have something strongly on my heart for this afternoon or evening but I would like to talk it over with Keturah before I tell any more about it. Will that be a problem with anyone? We should be safe on the ship tonight, right?" I asked, mostly speaking to Capt. Vitas but also to the others as well.

"Sure, if it's that important to you, we can wait. Probably be safer to get a full days distance out anyway. For my part, I will be more than willing to oblige you; but I an curious to know what you have in mind." the Captain answered.

"Let me talk this over with Keturah and then I will tell you what I have in mind.." I said as I led Keturah off to the side to speak privately with her.

"Keturah, I've had such a heaviness for those people we saw this morning that I want to do something before we leave here. I've been thinking and it seems that it would be worth trying to tell them about Jesus. We have learned so much and to leave them without sharing what we know would not be right. I saw you and your family as we passed though that part of town. You all had the same burden that I have—it was evident on your faces. Tell me now if you think I'm right in this." I asked her.

"That seems to be what we have been called to do isn't it. Yes, you are right about not leaving them without telling them but how do we go about it? What are we going to say to them? There were so many people back there who have no idea of who God is or what we want for them. It is just so big!" she answered.

"Yes, I know, but here's my plan. I've been thinking on it ever since I saw those young women selling themselves just to make a living. We need to get about five or six of them to come out into the street to listen to what I want to tell them. Hopefully others will hear and stop to see what is going on. It's all I know to do. We'll just have to trust to have the right words and rely on God's help. I definitely need your parents, you and Marco to help me. What do you think?" I asked.

"Sounds like a plan! Now let's get back up to that street. I'll get your help! You just keep asking God for the right things to say. We need to reach a few of these people who will be seed to others. Mother and I will bring the ladies to you. I'm sure we can get six or eight to listen. I'll take some food to encourage them. Let's hurry!" Keturah hurriedly spoke with a growing enthusiasm.

"I'm so glad we are making our first mission effort right here in Israel before we leave. It seems so fitting." she continued.

"Well, there is one other thing I would like to do before we leave this land. It has been on my heart for a few days now but I haven't said anything." I said, letting my words trail off without really ending my thoughts.

"Are you going to tell me or do you want me to try to read your mind?" Keturah asked with a hint of expectation in her voice.

"I would like for us to be married standing on the soil of this holy nation, where we met, where we have come to know Jesus, while all our friends are around us." I told her with tears streaming down my face and my voice failing as I thought about what I was saying to her.

Keturah did not answer in words but she jumped into my arms and embraced me so tightly that I nearly had the wind knocked out of me. Here actions captured the attention of our group and they were now demanding to know what we were planning.

"Let's get our work done on the street first then we can see about your other plan." she said as she smiled at me then turned her focus on getting the others lined out for their jobs.

Only Capt. Vitas, Ben, and Artemis stayed with the ship and the rest of us briskly made our way back up the way to the busy streets of Tyre. Seirrah and Keturah ran ahead of us when we reached the business district and began to talk to the women on the streets. They would pull them along to the next shop or house and get more to join the group as they did their best to explain about a meeting that was about to start just a way up the street by the open market stands. It was amazing to watch the two of them work so swiftly to assemble a rather sizable group of women. They were even able to get some men to come along with them. I noticed that they had not even used any of the gifts to entice them to come. It was only by the enthusiastic and sincere words that the people were following them.

Now it was quickly becoming apparent that my part was at hand. The crowd was much bigger than I had envisioned and their faces showed they had eager expectation for help. It was more than likely that many of them didn't even know what help they needed but it was evident that they recognized a chance to better their lives. My heart was pounding within my chest to the extent that I thought my arteries were going to explode from the pressure. I felt a cold sweat coming over me and began to get nauseous. It was then that I remembered Keturah's instructions for me to be seeking God's help, and I had been; but now, the only strength I had left was to simply say in a verily audible voice, "God, Help me!" Immediately my body felt weaker and my legs began to buckle, but just as quickly, my strength returned and my posture seemed to stand straighter and taller than I even had. There was confidence and determination sweeping over me with such exuberance that I now found it hard to wait to get up onto an empty cart to begin speaking to the people.

"Friends and people of Tyre. Hear what I have for you. Your life! Are you happy and content in it? What are you living for? Is there something else for you? We are here to tell you about the very One who created you. The One who knows all about you. He wants to be a part of your life here today so you can be whole and complete with Him some day. Many of you are trading your bodies and your strength for money or things that only last a day, if even that long. Some of you have children who have to work harder than most adults just to have something to eat. This is not what was intended for you or them. There is a better way. The One we speak of is the God of the universe. His Son and spirit want to live in you. He may not take away all your problems and struggles, but He will give you hope. My heart has been broken ever since we passed though here earlier today because your faces and your spirit showed that you have no real hope. We are here this afternoon because we want you to have this hope that we know to be true and real. It is very difficult for me to try to explain something so great and of such tremendous value in such a short time. What we are asking you to do is so simple that it may seem that it is too simple. I cannot tell you enough in the time we have with you to help you fully understand what we believe with all our hearts; but our God can. Each one of us here has felt led to come back here to talk with you because we believe that is what He has given us to do. Our God, the only true God, can help you know what we are saying is true and right. He can do a work in you that will give you hope, give you a reason for your life, and give you the understanding of the value He has for you life. Trust in what I am telling you. Trust in God and in His Son Jesus Christ. Let Him work with your hearts." I said without hardly stopping to catch my breath.

I hadn't noticed but I must have been speaking fairly loud as people a block or two down the streets in most directions were stopping to listen and then they would move in closer to hear more. Levi was doing his best to translate for me but there was a spirit working to help the language barrier to be lessened considerably. I was amazed when I saw how many people had gathered to listen, but I was awe stricken to see how they were being touched by the words and by the mighty presence of God's power.

"Now that we have their attention and they seem willing, what do we do with them?" Marco asked.

His question wasn't meant to be aimed at manipulating them but he was serious about what our part was to be now that their hearts were open. I did not know myself but Levi made a wise suggestion.

"Pass among the people and touch them as the Lord leads you. There is an anointing on you that they will be able to feel. Let God work through you. Marco, you should help him—the same anointing is spilling on you as well. I will get Seirrah and Keturah to sing with them as you go through the people. You will be looking to find those who will be able to continue the work that has begun here."

Levi spoke with a gentle authority that let me know he was seeing through spiritual insight of the situation.

We did as he instructed and the power of God flowed mightily through the crowd. I was right in the midst of all of it and even I did not understand the greatness of what was happening to the people. Some of the people were weeping so profusely that it was most evident that their hearts were open and made tender. I could sense that many of them were receiving help and letting God into their hearts—some just seemed to the opening themselves in hopes of having something better than they had come to them. As we walked through the crowd, I would feel led to place my hand on the forehead of certain ones. Almost without exception, everyone one we touched would fall to their knees or even face down on the streets. There was a supernatural power entering into them that that was changing them before our eyes. I was stirred to my very core by what I was in the middle of but I was also determined not to let my amazement hinder the work that was given me to do. By the time Marco and I had walked through most of the crowd there must have been nearly twenty people who we had touched.

Levi came to join the two of us as Seirrah and her mother continued to sing. We watched as the ones we had placed our hands on were beginning to draw others to them and we could hear them explaining the great love of God to these people—a God who they had just met themselves.

"It can only be the power of God that can plant so many seeds and then have them sprout so quickly and begin to produce fruit in only a few moments of time. It is something that would not be believable had we not seen it ourselves. Nic, you and Marco had just had an experience that very few men ever encounter. God truly has His hand on the two of you." Levi spoke so softly that he was hard to hear.

"I have never felt such power! It was not a power of my own, but a power flowing through me. I feel so unworthy to have my body as a host to such a holy anointing—to know what to say, who to make eye contact with—who to lay my hand upon! It is more than." I tried to say when Marco spoke up.

"I truly is a most precious time. It is a confirming time for me as well. I must admit that there have been times when I followed you, Nic, just out of friendship or because I believed in you. Now, after this! There is no need to follow in your faith since I am now filled with a faith of my own. I am thankful to be allowed to be used by such a magnificent God to reach a people I don't even know."

"These people—they now have been given a hope, a reason to live. We have done what we were to do and they have ones who can nourish them. Perhaps I can write to Demas and have him come here to see how they are growing in their hearts and minds. Their knowledge is more secure and stable than if we had been able to teach them for a year or more. What God has given them cannot be taken away by any man. Let us slip quietly away and get back to the ship." Levi said as he waved to his wife and daughter to join us.

As we walked back to the docks, we frequently turned to look back at the people we had just spoken to. There were still more people coming to hear what was going on and those who had been given the divine knowledge of Jesus were busy telling all who would listen. We were tempted to stay and watch, just for a little while, but realized it would be best not to hinder the work going on. We certainly did not want to cause them to turn their attention on us.

The others were filled with joy to hear what had happened and wanted to know all the details. As we began to explain what we knew, it was apparent that they had difficulty accepting all that we told them—not they thought we were making it up but that it just did not seem possible. It took several minutes before our friends fully understood what we were telling them. What followed was a time of quiet reflection on the immeasurable power of our God and His Son, the Lord Jesus Christ. Just as the lives of the people of Tyre were being changed, so were the souls in our group—it was a maturing and growing unity that knitted bonds of love and compassion for each other and with God himself.

As evening approached, our group was still rather quite. It would have been expected of us to be jubilant and full of praise for what had happened earlier but our celebration was clothed in a deep reverence for the Holiness of the power that flowed through us. Our hearts were quietly being filled with the assurance of being obedient servants and they were pouring out gratitude for being found worthy of being given a part in God's great kingdom.

It was nearly dark when Ben asked Keturah what she and I had been so excited about before we left earlier in the afternoon.

"Oh, Yes!" How could I forget such a thing? You should ask Nic about it though, since it was his idea." She answered.

The abruptness of the question somewhat startled me. I somehow felt a little uncomfortable in telling the whole group what I had asked Keturah in private—but they were my friends—family even, so I proceeded.

"I has been on my heart to ask Keturah to marry me while we are still in the land of Israel. That would mean either tonight or tomorrow before we set sail. She seemed to like my suggestion but I haven't actually received her answer in actual words. I am also aware there are some other obstacles in the way such as not having an ordained minister or a wedding party, not to mention a beautiful gown for such a beautiful bride. In fact, I am so close to this whole idea that I don't trust myself to know what is best. Now I don't mean about loving Keturah and wanting to marry her, but if this is to be the right time. I would really appreciate knowing your thoughts on this. It is just so in my heart about not leaving Israel before we are married."

"Our opinions hold little value in comparison to Keturahs. What would you like to do?" Aretmis asked her.

"Oh, I love him so much, I would marry him right now. My only concern is that he does not have his family here to share this time with him. This land, Israel has been a blessed land—a place where I have grown to know much about God and He has been most generous in caring for me with wonderful parents and friends— now with a special person to share the rest of my life with. I would like to be married in this land, but I only want what is best for us as God sees it." Keturah replied.

"You've answered wisely my daughter. It is you who have been a blessing to us and whatever you decide, you will have our blessing. As for the minister to perform the ceremony, I don't think there would be a better qualified man than and one of these men sitting right here. Yes, I know you don't carry the credentials that some find so important, but there is not a one of you who God would use to unite these two fine young people in holy matrimony. Why, just so you can be certain that its done right, He might use the whole bunch of you!" Levi said with a hint of laughter in his voice but the expression in his eyes showed that he wasn't speaking lightly about the matter.

"Keturah and Nikos—two finer young people I dare not hope to meet again in this life. You love is genuine and your hearts pure. My only hesitation in telling you that this is the right time concern Nic's parents. They have no choice in this because they do not know anything about it. They can neither accept or reject the marriage; and not being given that opportunity, it is likely that they might reject Keturah simply because they didn't get the chance to accept her. I can only offer you my thoughts on this because this decision is to be made by the two of you and hopefully you will know God's will and timing in it." spoke Capt. Vitas.

It became very quite for a few minutes. Capt. Vitas had spoken from his heart and given us cause to think. His comments made us examine our motives and desires for wanting to get married so quickly. It was evident that the others were searching their souls to know what to say.

"Well, Nic. It seems to me that you two should wait. Til morning that is. I've got a few things to do and I just can't take time out right now to sit and watch you two get married. Now, do you know what you're going to do or not. Just tell us so we can get on with getting ready to set sail. Sometimes you act like the whole world sets its time by what you do. So what's you answer?" Marco ranted, acting like he was upset at Nic.

"Morning it is then! Sunrise sound good to you Keturah?" Nic answered, with a smugness that showed he knew Marco was up to something.

"Sunrise it isn't !" shouted Seirrah. "Not a minute before nine o'clock!"

"Great! Nine sharp then!" Marco snapped as he sprang up to leave and made his way to the ship, carefully motioning Seirrah to join him when she could.

Keturah got up from her resting spot on a keg and gave Nic several hugs and a few kisses. The others began to talk about the wedding and wondered why Marco had been in such a big hurry to leave. Levi and Seirrah went over to stand by Keturah and Nic, two parents quietly grieving the loss of a daughter but being comforted by the gain of a son. Soon we could hear the banging of pots in the galley and knew Marco was a work. Seirrah said she was going to help get the galley organized and would see the rest of us later.

I was a little suspicious of Marco and knew he was planning something. I thought it would be best to let him carry out whatever he had in mind and wait to see what it was. My mind turned quickly to Keturah's parents. I could tell on their faces that it was not an easy thing to give up a daughter, especially one like Keturah. She was such a part of what they were and how they spent their lives giving to others. Without her, what would happen to their way of life. I felt somewhat guilty for taking her from them, even though I knew that was a normal plan for most families—to leave their parents to be united with someone to begin a new family for themselves. Normal plan or not, it was still painful, both for me and for them.

Seirrah joined Marco on board the ship and the two of them could be heard working on something. Even though we could hear the sound of pots and pans banging, there was too much silence between the banging. Soon Marco came up and went to the dock where our belonging were waiting to be taken onto the ship. He dug through a few bags until he found what he seemed to be looking for and quickly folded it under his arm as he dashed back to the ship, nearly diving into the galley. Seirrah was the next one up and she carefully went through a bag that contained some of the items the man in the canvas shop had given us. Near the bottom of the sack, tucked in between the jars of fruit, was a piece of white material with lacey overlays on it. She unfolded it just enough to give it a careful inspection; then taking it close to her chest, she went back to the galley. Lamp light streamed up the galley stairs and there was no longer any pretense of banging pots and pans. We only heard a soft voice now and then, with an occasional exclamation of excitement. The rest of our group went about loading the rest of our belongings onto the ship and lit a few lamps on deck. It had been a long day and some of us were getting quite tired. The older men headed for the bunks below not long after coming on board and Cirro and Alexus sat with Keturah and me for a while. Not a lot was said with the exception of how much had happened on this journey. A word or two of reminder would set our minds whirling with recollection of all that had occurred.

My curiosity began to grow and I wanted to go see what Marco was doing, but Keturah grabbed my arm to prevent me. She seemed to know what was going on and knew it was better to let them finish. She tried to get my thoughts on other things like the great move of God that afternoon there in Tyre. It indeed was a marvelous time and the way God was using us was something that would stay with me for the rest of my life; but I was going to be married to this wonderful young lady sitting beside me in just a few hours. As great as God had been that afternoon, it was hard not to be thankful for the greatness of Him bringing Keturah into my life.

"What is our wedding going to be like, Keturah?" I asked. "Who do you think will do the officiating? Where will it be? Such a wonderful event should be celebrated, don't you think?"

"I don't know for sure about all the details. I do think it would be in order for Capt. Vitas, Ben, Artemis and my father to perform the ceremony, since they represent the wisdom and maturity of our group. Each of them has the heart of Jesus and I would be honored for any one of them to marry us but it might be better if each of them has a part—they have each been so much a part of us." she answered.

"That seems good! What do you think about us standing on the docks as we are married and then boarding ship to complete the ceremony. My only regret though, is that I wanted you to have a grand celebration to follow the ceremony." I commented.

"Don't you worry about that part. Alexus and me know how to put on a party. You'll see." Cirro chimed in.

I had almost forgotten that they were still setting there. I had just got so caught up in talking with Keturah. Alexus added his assurance to what Cirro had said and then told him it was time to find a place to sleep for the night, wanting to give us some privacy to continue our wedding plans.

# CHAPTER TWENTY

# THE WEDDING

It was in the stillness of dusk that my thoughts once again returned to marrying Keturah before we set out to sea.

"Our wedding. Do you want to get married now or wait until sometime later? Tell me what's in your heart."

"I think it is a wonderful idea to get married here. I know our love is so strong that we could wait until later, but it seems so fitting to make our vows here in this land. God seems to be so close to everything we have done here. It doesn't need to be fancy."

We announced our plans to the others. There were several words of encouragement. The smiles on their faces told most of their feelings. Now, with that said, what needed to be done to plan a wedding?

"Well, Nik. It seems to me that you two should wait. 'Til morning that is. I've got a few things to do, and I just can't take time out right now to sit and watch you two get married. Now, do you know what you're going to do or not? Just tell us so we can get on with getting ready to set sail.

Sometimes you act like the whole world sets its time by what you do. So what's your answer?" Marco ranted, acting like he was upset.

"Morning it is, then! Sunrise sound good to you, Keturah?" I answered with a smugness that showed I knew Marco was up to something.

"Sunrise it isn't!" shouted Sirerah. "Not a minute before nine o'clock!"

"Great! Nine sharp, then!" Marco snapped as he sprang up to leave and made his way to the ship, carefully motioning Sirerah to join him when she could.

Keturah got up from her resting spot on a keg and gave me several hugs and a few kisses. The others began to talk about the wedding and wondered why Marco had been in such a big hurry to leave. Levi and Sirerah went over to stand by Keturah and me, two parents quietly grieving the loss of a daughter but being comforted by the gain of a son. Soon, we could hear the banging of pots in the galley and knew Marco was at work. Sirerah said she was going to help get the galley organized and would see the rest of us later.

I was a little suspicious of Marco and knew he was planning something. I thought it would be best to let him carry out whatever he had in mind and wait to see what it was. My mind turned quickly to Keturah's parents. I could tell on their faces that it was not an easy thing to give up a daughter, especially one like Keturah. She was such a part of what they were and how they spent their lives giving to others. Without her, what would happen to their way of life? I felt somewhat guilty for taking her from them, even though I knew that was a normal plan for most girls, to leave their parents to be united with someone to begin a new family for themselves. Normal plan or not, it was still painful both for me and for them.

My curiosity began to grow, and I wanted to see what Marco was doing; but Keturah grabbed my arm to prevent me. She seemed to know what was going on and knew it was better to let them finish. She tried to get my thoughts on other things like the great move of God that afternoon there in Tyre. It indeed was a marvelous time, and the way God was using us was something that would stay with me for the rest of my life; but I was going to be married to this wonderful young lady sitting beside me in just a few hours. As great as God had been that afternoon, it was hard not to be thankful for the greatness of Him bringing Keturah into my life.

Keturah and I continued to discuss just how to go about the ceremony and finally agreed that ten o'clock in the morning would be a better time. This would allow some extra time to make preparation in the daylight. It would also give our dear friends a little time to carry out their plans to help us celebrate. What had come to life as a last-minute plan was now coming into reality. A precious and memorable event was starting to unfold right before the two of us.

Marco came up from the galley and scolded us for not already being turned in for the night with such a big day ahead of us. I was so tired that I normally I could have fallen asleep just sitting down on the bunk, but tonight, my thoughts would not allow me to find rest. I could hear Marco and Sirerah in the galley, and now Alexus and Cirro had joined them. Pots were once more clanging, but this time I could tell that they were actually using them to cook with. I finally went off to sleep to the aroma of fresh meat being roasted in Marco's oven. My sleep that night was broken with several short dreams, some which were brief visions of what the wedding might hold. Others were more disturbing ones, ones that portrayed angry parents demanding that the foolishness of their son cease and any reference to a marriage be forbidden to mention in their hearing. Another dream was about Keturah's parents trying to continue their ministry without her, perhaps finding someone new to fill her place. Normal plan or not, it was still painful both for me and for them.

My curiosity began to grow, and I wanted to see what Marco was doing; but Keturah grabbed my arm to prevent me. She seemed to know what was going on and knew it was better to let them finish. She tried to get my thoughts on other things like the great move of God that afternoon there in Tyre. It indeed was a marvelous time, and the way God was using us was something that would stay with me for the rest of my life; but I was going to be married to this wonderful young lady sitting beside me in just a few hours. As great as God had been that afternoon, it was hard not to be thankful for the greatness of Him bringing Keturah into my life.

Keturah and I continued to discuss just how to go about the ceremony and finally agreed that ten o'clock in the morning would be a better time. This would allow some extra time to make preparation in the daylight. It would also give our dear friends a little time to carry out their plans to help us celebrate.

What had come to life as a last-minute plan was now coming into reality. A precious and memorable event was starting to unfold right before the two of us.

Marco came up from the galley and scolded us for not already being turned in for the night with such a big day ahead of us. I was so tired that I normally I could have fallen asleep just sitting down on the bunk, but tonight, my thoughts would not allow me to find rest. I could hear Marco and Sirerah in the galley, and now Alexus and Cirro had joined them. Pots were once more clanging, but this time I could tell that they were actually using them to cook with. I finally went off to sleep to the aroma of fresh meat being roasted in Marco's oven. My sleep that night was broken with several short dreams, some which were brief visions of what the wedding might hold. Others were more disturbing ones, ones that portrayed angry parents demanding that the foolishness of their son cease and any reference to a marriage be forbidden to mention in their hearing. Another dream was about Keturah's parents trying to continue their ministry without her, causing guilt to rise up in my heart. After this last dream, I determined that it was of no use to attempt to find any more rest in my bunk. I sat up in the darkness, wanting to clear the flood of thoughts and feelings in my head, only to find that my being awake allowed more room for doubt to grow. It wasn't that there was doubt concerning my love for Keturah. That was sealed in my heart for eternity. It was that I doubted myself to know what was in God's heart for this wedding day.

"Nikos, come with me," I heard someone softly whisper and felt a gentle hand pull me from the bunk, leading me to the galley stairs. It was Captain Vitas. When we reached the ship's deck, he sat down and motioned for me to sit beside him. "I could tell you were having trouble sleeping. And somehow, I have been able to know your thoughts. I am convinced that you are under attack and your peace of mind is being threatened. This, my dear son, is the work of the devil trying to destroy your happiness and what God is shaping together for His chosen ones," he said softly out of respect for those still sleeping and also wanting to protect the private nature of our hearts.

"It's a very real thing. I have found over the years that the devil seeks to find your weakness and then works away at it like a plague. He'll take all you let him have."

"Well, he can't have Keturah! She's mine, and no one will dare do her harm while I have breath left in me," I broke in.

"You have to do just that. Stand firm against him and let him know that he has no power over you as long as you do so in the name of Jesus. I am not upset the least bit by this attack. It only goes to prove that you are moving in the right direction to fulfilling what God has for you. That is why the devil is working so hard to confuse the plans. That is why I had to get you up here and talk with you. I sensed there was a greater danger for you tonight than there was back in Jerusalem. I need to pray with you now if you don't mind."

"Please do. I am grateful for your help," I answered as I embraced him, placing my head on his shoulder.

"Dear Lord, we cry out to you this night for help in defending the heart of our precious brother and friend. Lord, you know all about what is going on. And only you can stop the devil in his tracks.

This young man is about to marry the fine woman you made especially for him. Help make this day one that he will cherish the rest of his life. Settle his heart and make firm the foundations of his mind so that the doubt and fears will not find footholds. Be jealous for this one who is like a son to me. Bless and protect him from this day forward. And, Lord, I thank you for helping me know how to pray about things I had no previous knowledge of. I can tell just this instant that I'm getting this right. Thank you for answering our prayers and for loving us so much. We pray all these things in the name of Jesus Christ. Amen."

I found such a flood of help pouring over me. The heaviness of my concerns left, and the doubts that were tormenting me began falling away like dead scales. Once more, that familiar ability to know God was with me again. I was getting so much help that I couldn't find the ability to speak to Captain Vitas to let him know what was happening, but from the look on his face, I didn't need to bother. He was being equally blessed, and we both sat there in silence, grateful for such a loving God.

"We'd better make our way back to the bunks. You'll need all the rest you can get! There is a lot ahead of you today," the captain softly spoke after we had relished in the anointing that was on us for nearly an hour.

"I wonder what time it is. Seems like I've been awake for over half the night."

"I'd say it must be close to three or maybe half past, going by the stars. You can find a couple of hours to sleep if you can get calmed down."

We both quietly made our way back to the bunk room below. As I reached my bunk, I felt an urgent need to reach out for Captain Vitas. As I put my hand on his shoulder to stop him and turn him toward me, everything in me wanted to let him know how much he meant to me and what he had done to help all of us on this voyage. I embraced him and held on with all my might, but the only words I could manage to get out were, "I love you so much!" I knew I had met a man like few people ever meet in life. It was so much easier to understand the things of God when there was an example right in front of me. As he went on to his bunk, I finally laid back in my old bunk, overwhelmed with more blessings that I ever deserved. My heart was flooded with memories of how God had touched me in so many different ways and led me to so many people. Even now, He was preparing to begin a new chapter as Keturah and I were to join our hearts as one for the rest of our lives. Sleep finally came as I lay there, completely exhausted but most adequately blessed.

"Wake up! How can you sleep on a day like this? Get up! We have things to get done," Marco spoke abruptly as he shook me nearly out of the bunk.

"Fine. Just let me gather-" I started to say but was cut off.

"No time for that! Come on! We have to go back to the city to get a couple of things. I need you to pick them out."

We passed through the galley where Alexus and Cirro were fixing something to eat for the crew. By the time we reached the streets that led back up to the shops of the city, I was almost awake. One of my first thoughts was that whatever Alexus was cooking didn't exactly smell like our usual breakfast.

My next thought was, What is Marco going after?

"I know what you're thinking! Where are we going, right? Well, you can't expect me to let my best friend marry such a fine girl without having a gift for her, can you? You are going to buy her something special."

Marco answered my question even before I voiced it.

"What might that be?"

"Oh, you'll know it when you see it."

Just about then, we stepped into a little shop that had jewelry and other trinkets for sale. I had never seen so many items gathered in one place before. Marco guided me to a small case that contained several rings.

"See anything in here you think she might like?"

"Well, I don't know. I don't even know what these things cost, and I'm not sure how much I have to spend. I guess that little ring there looks like what she would want to wear. It has such fine engraving on it. She would like that I'm sure."

"How much for this?" Marco abruptly asked the owner, grabbing the ring from me before I had a chance to finish my inspection of it.

"Eye for quality! One of my best pieces. Usually I get fifty denarius. But for you, what say forty?" the man spoke in broken language that we could understand.

"Twenty-five, and not a denari more!" Marco responded without hesitation. "Quickly now! We must be on our way if you don't wish to sell."

"Thirty is my best, but-" the man started to say, but then a broad smile came over his face and he took the ring from Marco, looked it over carefully, and then said, "Twenty-five will be fine!"

Marco reached into his pocket and pulled out a few coins, and soon we had purchased a beautiful ring. Now my concern was if it would fit her finger. After we left the shop and headed back to the ship, I tried to repay Marco for the ring, but he would not let me.

"Let your gift to Keturah be my gift to you. It has been purchased with friendship and loyalty.

Let it be given in the same."

We had returned to the old ship, and most of the crew was waiting on the dock for us. Levi came to me, wanting to know if I had any direction as to who was going to lead the wedding ceremony. I did, but I wanted to make sure Keturah didn't have something different in mind, so I sent Marco to ask her. He returned with a quick reply.

"She feels that you should take charge, being as you are going to be the head of the house. She's ready and waiting on you."

"Very well, then. Captain Vitas, Ben, Levi, and Artemis, please gather around. I want you all to have a part in our wedding ceremony. I feel a great honor to have all of you participate. Your friendship gives value to your words, but your integrity reflects the truth and honor of them. I would like you, Captain Vitas, to begin the ceremony and the rest of you to follow him. I appreciate the blessing of having four godly men presenting our union as man and wife to our holy God. I'm ready if everyone else is."

"Marco, escort the ladies out, if you would," Captain Vitas said.

When Marco returned, he held the hands of the two most beautiful women I had ever seen.

Keturah was adorned with a flowing gown that was nearly as lovely as she, and her mother also had on a beautiful dress. When I had directed my attention to Keturah, she nearly took my breath away. She was exceptionally beautiful. Her eyes sparkled like diamonds, her hair was pulled back and fell behind her like cascading falls, her face was radiant, and her skin had the softest tone. She was almost more than I could take. This lovely woman was going to be my wife in just minutes. I did not deserve such a beautiful partner in life, but I knew in my heart that her outward beauty was only a dim light in comparison to her inner beauty. Keturah stopped for a moment to look at those gathered for the ceremony and then looked at me. A brilliant smile spread across her face, and that inner beauty came beaming out.

Marco led the ladies to Levi and presented Keturah's hand to her father. Amid tears, he took her hand gently, leaned down to kiss her cheek one last time, and forced a smile to cover his aching heart as he led his daughter to present her before those who would be uniting us in marriage. As they stopped before me, he spoke.

"Nikos, love her more than I have loved her, and she will never be lacking. She has been a most precious gift from God, and now she is His gift to you. Love and honor her as long as you have breath. I love you, my son," he whispered to me.

My heart was being torn from my chest. Yes, I was gaining this lovely wife and wonderful partner, but he was turning loose one who had been such a part of him, one who was such a help, and one who held such a place in his heart. I could understand his suffering and felt caught between feeling selfish for taking this from him and being so overwhelmed with joy knowing Keturah was going to be my wife. I did not know how to deal with these feelings. I promised God that at every opportunity I would try to share our lives with them. I wanted to hold Keturah so close, hoping that her very being would bring peace to the moment.

"Let us begin," Captain Vitas said, capturing my attention. "Shall we pray?"

He led us in a prayer that was most certainly direct to the heart of God. I felt a great lifting of the feelings that had been weighing so heavily. Everything came into a clear focus. Those of us gathered on that dock knew what was in each other's hearts, and there was such a sense of unity that we had not experienced before. Although I could clearly hear Captain Vitas's words, I found myself going in and out of a sort of vision. One instant, we were standing on the dock, and the next, we were gathered in a magnificent courtyard with tall columns and crystal clear pools. Our wedding party would still be in the same positions but would change in appearance with the vision. We would be clothed in long, luminous white robes, except for Keturah. She was still in her wedding dress. This vision came and went a few times, alarming me at first and then becoming more intriguing as it repeated. The only conclusion that I could reach was that I was given the privilege of seeing our wedding as if it was actually seen in heaven. It was more than I could understand. I resigned myself to fully appreciating and participating in what was at hand and figuring out the rest later. The captain finished a wonderful prayer not only for the two of us but for our families and even our dear friends. He had such an eloquent way with words and could reach the heart of God so quickly. He was a person whom I wanted desperately to imitate.

"Nikos and Keturah, this is now your time to confirm and seal your love for each other before these gathered here and before God. If you agree without any reservations, come and pledge yourself to one another," Captain Vitas said.

I reached out to take Keturah's hand and stepped forward before Captain Vitas. We knelt together and bowed our heads, asking God's blessing on what we were about to do. I then arose, lifting Keturah with me, and we turned to face each other.

"Keturah, I promise to hold your heart in my hands each day, carefully considering what I can do to care for you, to show my love for you, to honor you, and to lift you to God each day. It is my desire to have you grow in your love for me as each day mine grows for you. I promise to do all that I possibly can to honor this vow and hold close the great honor of having you as my wife. I love you and offer myself to you with only God Himself coming before you," I vowed.

"Nikos, I have been blessed to have met you. I know your promises to me are from your heart and know they are true. I, likewise, promise my love to you and offer myself to you. It is my desire to follow you, to be of help to you, to listen to you, and to pray for you. I want to be the mother of our children in God's time and walk with you in each step you take. I pledge to be one with you in all ways, and may God be pleased with me each day. Our lives have grown together. And today, we commit to being one. Where you go, I will follow. When you have need, I will do my best to help. When you are hungry, I will feed you. When you speak, I will listen. When you hurt, I will help heal. But never will you be without my love. My place is now beside you as long as we trod this land together. I will gladly be your wife. I love you, Nikos." Keturah spoke softly but with conviction and assurance.

Levi stepped before us now and asked that we join hands with him. Marco must have sensed what he was about to do, as he stepped forward to hand me the ring we had purchased earlier. He smiled briefly and then returned to his place.

"My children. Yes, my children. Nik, you have become like a son to me. As you take my daughter for your wife, I ask that you would always honor me by loving her as I have loved her, honor God as He has loved her. As I let go of your hands, join yours together, never to be separated until death. Seal now this union with a kiss before those joined here as witness before God," Levi spoke with his face covered in tears.

As I took her hand from Levi, I took the ring and placed it on her finger. It fit perfectly and looked stunning on her. As we kissed, something worked in my heart. There was all the soft tenderness of it, of course, but there was also a definite sense of the official significance of it.

"Well, there's not much left to be done but present you as man and wife," Ben said. "Nik, you have become like to son to me as well. You have proven yourself many times over. Your heart is set right, you have set a good course, and now you have the best first mate any captain could ask for. It has been one of the greatest privileges of my life to have known you and Keturah. Friends and family, may I present to you Nik and Keturah, in whom we are well pleased. Artemis, my friend, will you ask the blessing on this fine couple?"

"Dear Lord, we come before you to ask a lifelong blessing on this man and his wife. Keep them well in body, clear in mind, not long in hunger, safe in danger, and humble in spirit much the same as you have been doing for them, Lord, these past many days. This world can be made better because of them, Lord. Help them each day to get to what you have for them, and provide for them along the way. Bless their children and their families. Thank you, Lord, for sharing them with us. They have helped change our lives. And for that, we are most grateful. Amen."

I hadn't thought our wedding would have made me feel any different than before about Keturah, but it did. Even though our love had not changed or grown that much during the service, there was a marked difference. Maybe it was the vows that made it feel that way or the words that were spoken, the anointing. I just felt married!

"If we're finished with the ceremony," Marco spoke up, "I would like to say something to my best friend. Nik, we have been friends a long time. I had feared losing our closeness and even felt a little betrayed when you met Keturah. I now realize those fears were not founded. We might not get to spend our days together as we once did, but part of you will always be with me. You have taught me so much and have helped me find the true purpose in life. We started out together to find more about a man called Jesus and ended up finding much more than a man. Your desire to know Him has led each and every one of us closer to Him. You have been the driving force that kept us going. I don't know where we will end up, but I consider myself blessed to have known you. I love you, my friend. And now that Keturah is a part of you, she is included in that love. God bless you both."

"Well now, let's not get all wet with the crying and all. We got a surprise for you. Carry that bride on board, and let the celebration begin. Come on, Cirro. Let's get the party started," Alexus called out.

The two of them dashed up the ramp to the ship and waited for me to bring my new wife aboard. I picked her up and hugged her close, and then we made our way up the planks. Cheers went up from all those around us, and even a few people had stopped along their way to watch our wedding. Marco invited some to come celebrate with us. As we reached the ship's deck, I let Keturah down, and we both ran to see what our friends had prepared. Before us lay a table full of food among decorations that were simply beautiful. I had never seen anything that came close to the attractiveness of it, even at the best of events back in Athens. As the lids were lifted, steam arose, carrying with it some of the most enticing aromas from the food they had fixed. My concerns about a proper celebration of our marriage were no longer valid. Our friends had outdone themselves.

It was nearing the noon hour when Captain Vitas announced that we would be setting out to sea in a few minutes. We had enjoyed a fantastic meal and even danced to some music that our new guest played for us. However, it was now time to leave this amazing country and begin our journey home. As our new friends left the party, they helped untie the ropes and set the old ship free to roam the seas. We drifted out from the docks, waving good-bye to Israel and her people. A breeze came up, and the command was given to hoist sail. Alas, good-bye, Israel.

# CHAPTER TWENTY ONE

# HEADED HOME

The captain had taken on a couple of deckhands, and with help from some of us, we made good progress for most of the day. About midafternoon, we changed out of our good clothes and cleaned up from the celebration. Quietness came over most of our group, not reaching the point of sadness but perhaps a loneliness. I decided not to be concerned, for I was definitely worn out.

As darkness came during the late evening hours, Captain Vitas announced we would be sailing through the night. He knew these waters well, and the breeze was carrying us along at a good speed. As bedtime neared, there was some conversation as to where Keturah would be sleeping. I knew it was meant in a lighthearted way, but I would not allow much to be made of it. I had determined that she would spend the nights with her parents as long as we were at sea. It seemed to be the most honorable solution and would be best for the both of us to wait to seal our marriage. There was no further mention of the subject for the rest of the voyage.

The next several days provided good sailing and gentle seas. We made great progress. The days were filled with the routine duties of cleaning the deck, repairing sails and rigging, cooking, and taking turns at the wheel. Our voyage home was considerably different than the one to Israel. Going there, we were filled with questions. Now we had many answers. On the way, we had a crew of seamen. Our crew now was made up of dear friends and a couple of men who were rapidly becoming dear friends. It seemed that many of the tasks that had been difficult on the way to Israel were now much easier. I knew for a fact that the fellowship among us contributed greatly.

We were so well-supplied that Captain Vitas chose to stay on course rather than stop for fresh food. Our cargo was to be delivered to Miletus for the most part, and we were to pick up some goods in Ephesus. As long as the weather and winds held, he wanted to continue on, and we gladly obliged him. On two separate occasions, we sighted ships we thought might have been pirate ships, but both of them sailed on without giving us much notice.

The voyage home was uneventful to the point of becoming almost boring. I had Keturah beside me much of the time. We talked about what we might do when we reached Athens and tried to get a vision of our ministry together. Although we were able to identify some general ideas, we couldn't settle on what our day-to-day work was to be. Levi heard us talking about it and told us he had a suggestion.

"Let's begin to gather for prayer, seeking God's direction for the two of you as you reach your country. I sense that the both of you will be heading up this work, regardless of who among us follows you. Nik, do you have any leading as to what you feel God wants you to do?"

"I am still in awe at the mighty work of God in those people back in Tyre. God used me to get a fire started in those people. He showed me which ones to call on to take up the teaching I had started. My purpose with them was to tell them of the love of Jesus and His salvation for them. My next job was to equip those who could lead others on to this knowledge. They would then be able to testify from personal experience of the work of the Holy Spirit to those living around them. I believe that He wants me to go into places in Greece and Italy to tell people all about this Jesus we have found. I know that the Holy Spirit came upon Keturah,

Marco, and me in great power as we spoke to people who normally could not understand our language but yet knew what we were telling them. This is the general understanding I have of my ministry. It is in which direction we should go and how I am to support my wife, where to stay as we travel. These things I do not know about. Not that they trouble me, yet I am concerned."

"My heart tells me you are speaking in agreement with the spirit. It is natural for a man to be concerned for the well-being of his wife and family. I can remember when Sirerah and I first started helping people we didn't even have a place to stay or food to eat. All we knew was that we were to help those we met along the way as we walked the roads. There were times we were so hungry and cold. It hurt me so deeply to see Sirerah shivering as we huddled by a tiny fire. I knew she hadn't eaten in at least two days. But in all that, she never once complained. And I vowed if she could endure without complaint, then I sure didn't have any reason to complain. If you were to ask her today about those times, she'd likely tell you she doesn't remember them. But if you ask her about the people we have met over the years, she could probably put a name to most everyone. We didn't know anything about money, food, or shelter. We did know that we were called to love people, love them as Jesus would. We have absolutely no regrets or complaints. Now let's commit to coming together in prayer for your direction every chance we get until we dock in Athens."

We made that commitment and gathered for a prayer time quite often. The prayer time continued for the rest of our voyage, and Levi often was able to get a vision for people in several different places. We took careful notes of those places and tried our best to write down all the details he could offer. It was on paper Ben had bought for me back in Joppa, knowing how valuable it would be to me. After having spent the night with sails lowered and anchor dropped, the morning light brought with it the outlines of a city off to our right.

"That'd be Miletus you are looking at. We'll dock there within the next couple of hours. I'd say we made extra good time on this part of our journey," Captain Vitas said.

We were soon securing the ship at the dockside, and cargo was being hoisted up from below.

Everyone was busy doing all they could to help unload the ship, and for the most part, we were doing a good job of staying out of one another's way as we worked. We were nearing the last of the barrels that had to be rolled into the nets to be lifted off the deck when I noticed Ben sitting down and holding his side. It was evident that he was having trouble, and I ran quickly to him.

"What is it, Ben? What's wrong?" I asked.

"I'm just wore out and getting too old for this," he replied with a little chuckle in his voice. As he tried to speak, he had to stop to gasp for breath. "I want to keep going, but I think my heart's giving out on me. Hold me steady for a bit, Nik, would you?"

"Sure I will, Ben. Someone bring me some fresh water! Marco, get a couple of those sacks of grain for him to rest on!"

My shouting had alerted most of those on deck to Ben's need for help. Captain Vitas and Artemis came running up. Soon, all of our group was gathered around Ben as he rested on the grain sacks. His color was returning, and he didn't have to struggle for his breath as much, but he was still not doing well. Even the crews on the docks stopped their work to see if Ben would be all right.

"Does anyone know a doctor in this town?" Marco yelled out.

We saw a couple of men leave and assumed they had left to get medical help. Artemis said he thought a poultice would work if he could find the right herbs to make it with. He asked Marco to go with him to help gather what would be needed. I felt helpless to do anything but try to make Ben comfortable. I wondered how long it would be before a doctor would arrive or how long it would take Artemis to find the herbs. Then it hit me, and I felt totally unworthy of being a minister of our Lord, Jesus. It was then that it had occurred to me to be in prayer for Ben. Not the first thought or even the second. No! It had taken me this much time into a critical situation like this before I thought about praying for his help. I was extremely aggravated at myself but made a mental note to deal with this later. Right now, I needed to pray for my friend Ben.

As I was kneeling to pray, I noticed that Levi and Keturah were already on their knees and must have been for a little while. I felt conviction rushing in, but I knew now was not the time to wrestle with it. I had to work hard to keep focused on praying for Ben and not get distracted by the guilt I felt for my inadequacies.

Marco came running up with Artemis not far behind. The two worked together to mix up a concoction of paste and powders and folded it in a piece of cloth. Artemis held it between his hands for a moment to warm it just a little and waited until he could feel warmth coming from the poultice. He then placed in on Ben's chest, over his heart. Ben lifted himself a little and said he was feeling a little better as Artemis worked to help him. Just then, the dock workers returned with a doctor.

"Looks like you got him about the best help we can give him. That poultice should let those parts in his heart relax and open back up. It's a little strange, though, for him to be able to speak and recover this soon. It usually takes days or weeks to get back what this man has after a heart has such a strong spasm. I don't know which god you were praying to, but he must have answered," the doctor said.

"It was God the Father, creator of the universe and the Father of Jesus Christ that they were praying to, Doc. He isn't just any god. He's the only God. And yes, He answers our prayers. You want to know more about Him, just ask one of these folks around you. They'll tell you about Him," Ben said.

"I might just listen to you. You seem to know Him pretty well yourself," the doctor replied.

He continued to examine Ben, checking his pulse and his breathing. He listened to his heartbeat through a horn he carried and tried to speak some encouragement to him as he finished his exam.

"You need to slow down and let these young men do the heavy work. You're not quite as young anymore. In fact, you are lucky to still be alive right now from the sound of your heart. You are going to have to take it easy."

"Take it easy! Never have found that to be a way but what leads to trouble. I've never considered going that way before, and don't plan to now. I do appreciate your advice, Doc. But that I just can't do. I will watch about picking up the heavy stuff if that will rest your mind," Ben replied with a genuine smile that told the doctor that his advice had been truly appreciated.

The doctor finished his examination and walked away a few steps to talk with some of us he knew would be helping Ben.

"He has suffered significant damage to his heart and needs to rest for several days. No more activity than very short walks, say from his bed to the table. Nothing more than that, or he will experience more damage. Try to keep him still and keep that poultice on him. Even with plenty of rest, I'm afraid he doesn't have much time left, weeks or a month or two most likely. I'm sorry to be the bearer of sad news, but you should know. He seems like such a fine man."

Captain Vitas and Artemis helped Ben to his bunk below deck, and they did all they could to make him comfortable. It didn't take the rest of us long to finish unloading the cargo and picking up our shipment. Most of the work was done with very little conversation, and the mood became somber.

Heaviness came over all those who knew Ben, and their hearts began to grieve as they realized his condition. Even those of us who were in prayer for him felt that his time was nearing its end. In all the effort to care for Ben, most of us didn't even give thought to the noon meal. By the time we were settled down from the cargo handling and making sure Ben was given the best care we could give, it was near midafternoon. It had only been a few hours since Ben's attack, and now most of us were filled with grief and sadness. Even though we tried not to let it show, Ben could sense what was happening among us. He called for Captain Vitas, and the two had a few words in private. Not long after, the captain announced that we would be hoisting anchor and setting out to sea, headed for Ephesus.

The crew obediently but silently went about their tasks and soon had the ship setting out with the sails filled with the wind. It was strange, but the sound of the waves splashing against the hull seemed much louder than normal; the old ship creaked a little more than usual. I don't know if it was just my imagination, but the timbers seemed to groan as if they sensed our sorrow. It was soon evident to all those on board just how much Ben had become such a close friend and what he meant to all of us.

"Nik, you know that Ben doesn't want us to be so downhearted about this. He would be the first to scold you if he knew how we were acting. He just might get up and do it because I think he's finding out how much we are moping around. We need to help cheer everyone back up, get their spirits lifted.

We're acting like we've been defeated and might as well surrender. I'm not ready to do that just yet, so let's get to work helping put an end to this moping around!" Keturah said.

As we sailed northward toward Ephesus, Keturah went about doing her best to raise the spirits of those on deck. She continued by going below and chatting with Ben while she prepared some food in the galley. By the time evening came and the sun was resting on the horizon, she was carrying food to all the deckhands and the rest of us. She never stopped long in one place, but she never gave up on offering words of encouragement. I don't know where she found the help, but nonetheless, she was dishing out encouraging words with every spoonful of food. Darkness had just set in when Captain Vitas called out to lower the sails and drop anchor. He didn't want to weave through the maze of tiny islands off the coast of Ephesus in the dark.

Since most of the chores were done early this night, I decided to spend some time with Ben.

Keturah joined me below deck, and we began talking with Ben. He had regained some more strength and could talk without much effort. It was a little difficult to keep him still in the bed, but we did the best we could. After some lighthearted conversation, Ben spoke to us.

"I appreciate all everyone has done for me today. It means so much, but I have a favor to ask of you. I know my days are but a few now. I can feel it inside. This is what I want you to promise me. Ever since I was old enough to set out to sea, I had always figured I'd be buried at sea if I should be killed or die. That's just the way of seamen. Never bothered me much. Fact is, I didn't dwell on it hardly any. But now, now it seems somehow important that I be buried on land, on land in Greece. Now that I know about Jesus and how he died for me, I want people to know my name. And when they see it on my grave marker, maybe they'll be reminded how much I want them to know Jesus too. I don't mind dying so much. It's just I enjoyed being with you all. I will miss you, dear friends. I don't know if I will last 'til we get to Athens. But if not, promise you will carry me off ship when we dock there. Find a place not far from the water to place my body, and come by once in a while to read my name, Ben Ides, on my marker. Stop there for a while so I can touch your heart."

"You'll always be in our hearts, Ben. And we will do what you have asked. I consider it a great privilege to have come to know you. You have been a tremendous part of our search to find Jesus. You have helped others find Him as well. Looks like you might be the first of us to actually meet Him, and I'm glad for that," I answered.

We sat quietly for a few moments, tears rolling down our faces. There were tears of sadness mixed with tears of joy. He had been so much help ever since we met him, and his years of experience on water and on land were of great benefit. He had taught us a great deal in his short time with us and was now teaching us more in his time of passing. Most of my tears were those of gratitude for the gift of knowing him.

We both hugged Ben and told him we loved him and then made our way to our beds for the night. I spoke briefly with Captain Vitas about Ben's request, and he wholeheartedly agreed to help us fulfill our promise to Ben. He figured we would be reaching Athens in five or six days and expressed hope Ben would make it that long at least.

The weather held fair, and we made good progress. There were several other ships that we passed, but none of them appeared to hold any danger for us. It seemed as though we reached Ephesus in record time, and the cargo was handled smoothly. In fact, things went so well that we gained a good bit of time. The rest of our voyage was uneventful, and the weather was nearly perfect for our last stretch to home. Marco and I had a little more time together, as our duties were easier to fulfill. I found the opportunity to ask him about his brother, Stephan.

"I'll be most glad to see him again, but I hope my parents have had enough time to calm down.

I'm not looking forward to the scolding I fear is coming. I trust Vito was able to get him back home safely."

"He sure had me on edge that night. I'm glad we didn't hurt him when we tackled him. Maybe we've been gone long enough that your folks will not even think about Stephan's little trip. They will likely be so glad to see you."

"I can almost guarantee that my mom will thump me on the head and then tell my father to give me a thump as well just as soon as she sees me. It's just her way. Then she will grab me and hug all over me for long enough that it gets embarrassing for a guy my age."

It was good to get a little lighthearted and spend some time with my old friend. I was reminded just how much a friend he had always been. We sat silently, enjoying each other's company for a while longer, and then turned our attention to the work at hand. It wasn't long afterward that we heard, "Land Ho"

# CHAPTER TWENTY TWO

# A GRAND PASSING

O ne of the crewmen shouted from up in the rigging, as he had sighted land ahead. The end of our trip. I ran to the galley to tell Ben that we were soon to tie up at Athens. As my eyes adjusted to the dim light in the galley, I could see that Ben didn't look well. His color had left him, and he was having a difficult time breathing. I knelt beside his bunk and put my arm around him to help lift him just a little.

"We're almost home, Ben! Hold on just a little longer and we'll find you the best place to stay any man has ever had, a good, soft bed in a room with a gentle sea breeze making the curtains dance and food fit for a king. It'll be the very best we can find," I told him, mostly speaking from an image that was forming in my mind as I spoke to him.

"That will be fine, Nik. But for now, help me make it up on deck. Hanging out in the galley isn't a place for a seaman to be when a ship's heading into port. No sir! My place is right up on deck, like all the other crew."

"All right, Ben. Let me get Marco to help, but you have to promise to stay still when we get you there. Promise?"

"Sure, Nik. Just hurry, if you will."

I could tell there was more going on with Ben than he was letting on. I quickly got Marco, and the two of us had Ben on deck with little effort. We sat him in a chair so he was facing the front of the ship and had a good view of the horizon as the shoreline rose up from the sea.

"Nik!" Ben called.

"Yes? What do you need, Ben?"

"Nothing. I just wanted to tell you that I think I saw into heaven last night. It was such a beautiful place, better than any place I ever saw down here. Seems I might be going there soon. I'm going to miss all you so much, but don't grieve over me. I got such a peace inside about dying, more than I can figure out. I don't think I'm gonna make shore, Nik, but tell all of them I love them and hold fast to their faith in Jesus Christ. I have found Him to be very real and worthy of our trust. Good-bye, my friend," Ben spoke in a voice that was trailing off

He was holding my hand as he spoke to me. When he finished speaking, his grip slowly eased until his hand was simply lying in mine. He seemed to go off into a sleep, his breathing slow and shallow. I knew his passing was now at hand. Even though we had been prepared for it, I found it most difficult to accept. Marco had slipped off to find Keturah and the others. I felt as though part of my inner being was being ripped apart. My heart was aching at the thought of losing my dear friend. It was when I felt the tender hand of my new wife touching my shoulders and back that I sensed healing starting to take over the place of the agony in my heart. She wasn't trying to stop the hurting, but she was letting me know that the healing would come.

The life of Ben Ides continued on, but his earthly body had served its purpose. His breathing became slower and more labored, followed by a brief coughing spell, and then he departed from this world. As we were gathered around him, a hint of a smile once more came over his face. Oh, what comfort there was in that.

"It is not easy to experience this time of sadness, but I can assure you it is not a time of loss. We have not suffered a loss but rather have been blessed with a great opportunity to have known Ben. Even though he will not be physically with us, he will be in memory and in spirit. He has gone on to be a blessing to others in the kingdom of heaven and has left us with a chest full of treasure. I trust each of us will come to appreciate the full value of these treasures as we continue on," I said with the confidence of the Spirit Himself

We fashioned a stretcher as best we could and gently placed Ben's body on it, covered him with a piece of canvas, and laid him beside the entrance to the galley. Sails were lowered, allowing us to gently come into port. As the old ship glided ever closer to the dock, I began to recognize some of the buildings and landmarks of my hometown. My heart was filled with a flurry of emotions and images. It began beating so strongly that I could hear the blood pumping in my ears. Keturah came up to stand beside me as we both took in the sights of the great city of Athens.

"So, this is home to you? It's such a beautiful place. I don't think I've ever seen such architectural marvels in all my life. Can you see your home from here?"

"No. My family lives beyond those hills over to the left. It is not too far inland. You're right. The city has a lot of beauty in its buildings. But unfortunately, there are a lot of skilled works that are dedicated to gods and objects that have no worth or value. But you asked if this was my home. I don't know if I can answer that question for you just now. It could well be that we won't have a home for a while. I know we have places to go and people to see. We'll have to trust God to provide a place to lay our head and for food, just as your father did. But for now, I am getting anxious for you to meet my family and for them to get to know my new wife."

# CHAPTER TWENTY THREE

# RETURN TO ATHENS

T he old ship slipped gently into the dock, and ropes were soon cast around mooring posts to hold her secure. We noticed several people making their way down to the docks. As they came nearer, we recognized many of them, old fishing friends and people from the shops where Marco and I had worked. Captain Vitas made his way to the boarding planks and stepped ashore to attempt to find someone who could help us make arrangements for Ben until he could be properly buried. As eager as we had been to reach Athens, none of us seemed in any hurry to leave the old ship. Artemis stepped up and took hold of my arm.

"Come on and introduce me to these friends of yours, Nik. I might need to get a job with one of them."

He led the way as Keturah and Marco followed me down the planks. Hearty handshakes and slaps on the back greeted us for a good distance down the docks. Finally, Marco and I found ourselves looking at the old fish market where we had birthed plans for our voyage. It was strange how it had not changed since we had left it many weeks ago, but so much of our lives had been changed forever.

"Marco! Marco!" someone was shouting. "Marco, you made it home!" a young boy shouted as he lunged upon Marco and wrapped his arms and legs around him.

It was Stephan, Marco's little brother, who had tried to stow away with us. The tears in Marco's eyes revealed how thankful he was that his little brother had made it back home safely.

"Is Momma still angry with me for letting you get away on the ship and then me sending you back home with Vito?"

"She was sure enough upset when Vito brought me back home. I got a good switching over that.

She even gave me a whack or two on account of you leaving home. But now she has gotten over the anger and has mostly been missing you. I'd say she'd probably smother you with hugs if she was to see you walking up to the house now."

"I hope you're right. I sure have missed all of you. You won't believe all that has happened on this voyage. I have so much to tell you that I don't know where to start. Anyway, let's get home to see Momma."

I turned to the others in our group and told them that Marco was going to his family and that I wanted to take Keturah to meet mine. Artemis and Captain Vitas were seeing after Ben's body, and the rest of the crew were helping carry off the cargo that was left on board. Keturah's parents said they would wait until I had introduced Keturah to my parents before they came by.

As we walked the streets leading to my house, I was overcome with the awesome experience we had just been through. I began to weep and felt overwhelmed at just how much we had been able to experience the work of the Holy Spirit. My thoughts were only turned aside when I began to realize how I was going to introduce my wife to my family. My wife! These were people who had been working to arrange my mate, and now here I was returning from a voyage that they had absolutely no knowledge of with a young lady I was about to tell them was my wife. And that would be the start of it. What would they think about all the miraculous experiences I had to tell them about? My heart was beating so strongly within my chest that I knew Keturah must hear it herself It wasn't that I had any embarrassment or shame of what I had to tell. It was that it was going to be so difficult for them to understand and comprehend. Keturah took hold of my hand, and almost at once I could feel the strength and confidence rising within me.

We walked down the cobblestone street hand in hand, looking up at the magnificent buildings on the hillsides above us. Growing up in a city like Athens might have kept me from appreciating the architectural beauty of the many structures that existed here. Keturah, on the other hand, was enthralled with their magnificence. After telling her what most of them were, I promised to take her on a tour throughout the city. Almost before we knew it, we turned the comer to the street that led to my family's house. Word of our arrival must have spread very quickly because my mother was headed down the street to meet us as quickly as she could walk without breaking into a run. She was determined to remain a lady of proper dignity no matter what. It was almost comical to see her trying to balance the role of a woman of stature with a mother longing to embrace her son. In the last ten yards, the mother tipped the balance as she broke into a run that ended with her arms embracing me and cries of joy and laughter spilling out all over the place.

"It's so good to see you again, Nikos! We've been so worried and missed you. Where have you been?" she asked without ever stopping to let me answer.

I knew it would be useless to try to stop her until she was finished, so I just let her go on. Being completely honest, I must say that I thoroughly enjoyed the comfort of my mother's hugs. I was now a man, a married man at that, but those hugs imparted such security and comfort. I hadn't realized how much I had missed them. She provided me with the feeling of being sheltered under her wings as a hen gathers her chicks underneath herself for protection. With Keturah, I felt as though I was providing that protective shelter to her.

Finally, she relinquished her hold on me and slipped back enough to place her hands on my face. "Look at you! You look tired and so thin. You not eating? Never mind! I'll fix you something to put the color back in you. You look so precious. I just can't find it in me to be angry with you," she said as she held her hands against my cheeks and distorted my face.

"Mother," I tried to begin to speak. "I am so glad to see you. I have so much to tell, but there is one thing you must hear. I want you to meet my wife, Keturah. Keturah, this is my mother. It is my desire that the two of you can find the love in your hearts that I have for the both of you," I said in an effort to work on any resentment that might be building.

A look of astonishment came over my mother's face and then was replaced with an awkward look of not knowing what to say. She nervously began to reach out her hand to Keturah and was rewarded with the warmest smile I had ever seen on my wife. Without delay, I stepped around behind them and placed my arms on their shoulders and suggested we made our way back to the house.

As we walked, I was able to tell my mother the high points of our journey. I wanted to be sure that I told her about Jesus and what He had done for me personally before my father came home. He was much more set in his ways than my mother was. I hoped to be able to at least tell her about Keturah and her family and of what Jesus had done in my heart without my father interrupting with the objections I expected of him. All too soon, we reached the front door to our house. I had not even begun to tell her some of the wonderful things that had occurred on the voyage. Once back on her ground, she regained control and did her best to make Keturah feel at home. When she was satisfied that she had accomplished that, she flew into the kitchen and began putting together food for us. My heart became flooded with emotions: guilt for the anguish I must have caused her, joy at being her son, thankful and relieved that she was so welcoming of Keturah, lost in what would be the next part of my life.

It was only a few moments before Mother returned with a platter of bread, meat, and other food. She scampered about the room, trying to make sure every need was met. She took Keturah by the hand and pulled her to the table as she frantically beckoned me to join her.

"Quickly now! Eat! Then I want to hear your stories. When and how did you meet Keturah? I'm so anxious to hear all about it," she said as she pulled out a chair to join us at the table.

Her eyes were filled with tears, and a few made their way down her cheeks. I wanted them to be tears of happiness for Keturah and me. I felt such a peace within that I didn't want to disturb it by continuing with stories from our journey. It would have been selfish of me to bask in the peacefulness of the moment when I knew my life's purpose was now to tell of Jesus and His desire for people to know Him.

Most of what seemed important had been retold when a noise from just outside the front door announced the arrival of my father. Nervousness again arose within me, but I nonetheless gathered strength to get up and met him at the door. Almost at the same instant, our hands grasped the doorknob, and I felt it turn within my hand. I helped pull the door open into the room and swung it back out of the way so I could have a full view of my father as we locked eyes. I could see he was shocked at first to see me. Then, as his eyes began to dart from side to side, I could tell he was recounting the last several weeks. I was hopeful of seeing a smile come upon his face. Finally, I saw his hand begin to raise and reach out toward me. As his hand raised, a smile also came upon him. He grasped me and pulled me to him with a powerful embrace. Even for a young man, I was in no hurry for this embrace to end. I felt the very heart of my father, a man of standing in the community, a man who had significant influence, one who had power over people and set the standards by which they lived or died. But now his heart was pouring out such genuine love and tenderness. This was part of my father that was rarely revealed. Oh, it wasn't a weakness that was being shown. Far from it! In fact, I realized as he was holding me that this tenderness of heart was the very bedrock that his integrity was built on. His position in the city didn't come from manipulating and taking advantage of people. It came because he could be trusted.

I was amazed that I had just now come to realize this. He hadn't changed, but I had. I was able to see people with a different heart and through eyes that had been enlightened by the light of God burning within me. Here I stood, a married man of nearly twenty years of age, weeping in the arms of my father. But I didn't care. I had no reason to be ashamed. I felt a new freedom. What others might consider to be signs of weakness and lacking manhood only served to reveal their lack of knowledge of what true strength and character is based upon. I was being abundantly blessed in the arms of a wonderful father. I was grateful.

A knock at the door ended our time of embracing. It was Marco.

"I'm sorry to interrupt your time with your family, Nik, but Captain Vitas has made arrangements for Ben. We will be gathering in about an hour down by the docks. They found a nice place up on the hillside on the other side of the harbor. I knew you would want to know."

"Marco, it is good to see you," my father said as he put his arm around him. "What is this you speak of about Ben and a place on the hillside?"

"Ben Ides was a man we met on the voyage. He became a very close friend who taught us much. He passed away just as we were coming into port, and we are going to have his funeral this afternoon. I wish you could have known him," I answered. "Keturah and I will go with you now, Marco."

"Do you care if your mother and I join you? We'd like to meet your friends and say farewell to this man who meant so much to you," my father said.

"That will be wonderful! You can not only meet our friends, but you can meet Keturah's parents as well. Ben became very dear to all of us. We will surely miss him."

"I'll go back and tell the others you will be coming. Captain Vitas has asked you and Artemis to speak as we lay him to rest," Marco said softly to me.

My mother gathered the food from the table and cleaned up after us, constantly asking questions to do with Keturah and her family. My father was listening intently to all that was being said. My parents did not mean to be hurtful with their questions, and I respected their right to ask; but it was getting to be a bit more than I was willing to subject my new wife to.

"Please listen to me for just a moment. Keturah and I met and fell in love almost immediately. I wasn't searching for a mate, but God put us together. She is a wonderful person, and her parents are the most loving people I have ever met. They have spent their lives helping other people. They have rooted their lives in something much richer, giving what they have to those in need, forming integrity and compassion every day of their lives. I want you to get to know my wife and to come to love her as I do, but please trust us now to know each other. Meet her family for yourselves, and then search your hearts to see if we have not found greater wealth than is in all of Athens. But for now, it's time we need to be heading down to meet the others."

The four of us walked back down to the docks and soon found the rest of our group gathered around Ben as he lay covered with the old canvas from the ship. Captain Vitas greeted my parents, and others were introduced. Keturah gladly introduced her patents to mine, and after a few seconds of eyeing one another, they seemed to be getting along well. Although they had little in common, they began to find much to talk about. Barriers that I had thought might stand between them just didn't materialize. In fact, each of them seemed to be eager to know more about one another. Their conversation only ended when Captain Vitas announced it was time to carry Ben to his burial place. Marco and I took hold of the head end of the stretcher, and Levi and Artemis took the foot. Captain Vitas led the way, holding his hat over his heart. Several others followed. Some were seamen who knew Ben. Others were those who only knew those of us who knew him. It was quite a large group for a man who had no family we knew of

We made our way from the dock up a hillside that overlooked the harbor. There were several other graves there, and the spot was well kept. We stopped beside the pile of freshly dug earth and gently lowered our friend to his resting place. Captain Vitas motioned for Artemis and me to begin. I encouraged Artemis to speak first, and he recounted the day he met Ben and how close the two had become. It was difficult for Artemis to get the words out that were in his heart, not that he couldn't find them but that they were so heartfelt that the emotion overpowered him. After I had spoken briefly about how much Ben had meant to each of us, I concluded the service by promising Ben that we would do our very best to carry on the work he had so greatly helped us start.

We stood silently around the grave for a good while, each of us reflecting on the precious memories we held. It was quite a testimony to Ben to have touched these people standing around him now. His touch was always soft and gentle, even when he attempted to disguise his true nature with gruff and growling ways. I began looking at those standing beside me, reading their faces to find what was in their hearts. I saw heartache, loneliness, sorrow, but not grief Somehow, we all knew there was no reason for grief Ben was now far ahead of us on our journey to find Jesus. Now that was something to rejoice about. I wanted to sing or shout but restrained myself for fear of being misunderstood, not sure if it would be appropriate.

I also noticed my parents. They were intently watching us as we said our good-byes to Ben. I could see in their faces that they were amazed at how our group had become so closely knit. They seemed to be searching to find out how a man that we had met only months ago had became closer than family. The concept of loving and caring for strangers was not built into their culture. They did not seem to be against the concept. I believe they were getting more and more curious. I made a mental note to help nourish their curiosity. That could be a solid entry point into understanding our whole purpose: learning to be like Jesus.

# CHAPTER TWENTY FOUR

# A PLAN UNVEILED

The next few days were spent with our group getting to know the families we had in Athens. The crew had family members in or around Athens. We were asked a lot of questions, ones coming from hearts that wanted to know more of what we had experienced that was now so evident in our lives.

There was a healthy curiosity growing that was greater than I had even hoped for. Overall, it was a most pleasant time of resting and recounting. My mother was eager to show love to Keturah and Sirerah.

Whatever fears and doubts I might have had about their acceptance were now far removed. I was deeply grateful for the relationship that was growing stronger each day.

We made a couple of sightseeing tours of the city. Those who saw the beautiful buildings and sculptures for the first time were left spellbound.

Even the people on the streets displayed a warm hospitality toward our group. The overall reception we were receiving in Athens was so much more than I thought it would be. For now, I took part in basking in the warmth of the welcome we were given.

Nearly a week after we had docked that I began to feel the urgent need to be about ministry, a testifying, preaching ministry. I spoke with Keturah, and we made plans to set up a small area near the downtown Athens. We didn't have any food or other items to offer that the people didn't already have. We simply wanted to offer what we had to give them and not confuse the message with material things.

For the most part, the people in that area did not have much need for worldly things, most being more prosperous than much of the world we knew. It was the spiritual needs that were causing Keturah and me to feel burdened for this town. We knew it would not be an easy task ahead of us to convince those who were living a comfortable life to realize that it would mean nothing in the end if they were not willing to give up the worship of manmade gods and come to know the life-giving God who was driving us to tell His story. When the morning sun was rising, Keturah woke me to tell me something that had come to her in the night. She wanted us to sing songs that told of Jesus as a way of introducing us to the people who would walk past. She knew several songs that would help open their ears to what I wanted to tell them.

"Mother even has a harp to play to help us. She always has a song in her heart and enjoys playing when she can. What do you think?"

"Sounds like someone helped us with a plan," she answered.

Realizing the need to have some money to buy food and things we would need to live on, I decided to see if I could get a job at the old fish market. I needed something to help provide for my wife. It wasn't right to expect to live off my parents now. They had offered to let us stay as long as we wanted. For now, though, the fish market would be a place to start.

I spent over three hours working the fish market most mornings. I found the work not overly difficult and enjoyed meeting the customers. Some of them were ones I knew from earlier days, and some were new. The one thing that was new this time was that I had an inner desire to know the spiritual condition of the people. Over the last months, I had learned to read people and could tell with a degree of accuracy about how important spiritual matters were to them. It became a matter of balance to be curious and yet not be intrusive, especially while I was being paid to work at the market.

After the fourth day at the market, I concluded that, generally speaking, most people in Athens and the surrounding area had needs spiritually, but most of them lacked a solid foundation to build a spiritual life around. It rested mainly on tradition and social custom. These observations only served to convince me of the need to be about the ministry of teaching the message of Jesus, the Christ. I resolved to finish out my two weeks at the fish market, out of the respect to the owner, and then committed myself to not being restricted in ministry by the constraints of regular employment. I could not let a job stand in the way of the urgency of reaching people with the truths we had discovered. I knew that such a commitment might sound like foolishness to most people, especially when I had a wife to support, but I felt such an undeniable calling to obedience to this. And when I made that commitment, a rush of confirmation flooded my inner being.

Later that afternoon, I shared my decision with Keturah. She outwardly agreed with me, but I could see some hesitation in her eyes.

"You are wondering how we will live from day to day and what we will use to supply our work, aren't you?" I asked.

"Well, yes. You are reminding me so much of my parents and how they simply trusted each day for provision. I don't remember ever going without what we needed to survive, but there sure were times when it took a good bit of trust and faith. Now that we are married and on our own, it is a little scary. It's that we are in a different land with people who are not accustomed to following the God we know. We have a lot to overcome, and there are a lot of people who aren't ready to accept the teachings."

"It is a much more challenging task we are about, but I am convinced that these people need to hear our message. What hope do they have unless they can find the eternal hope that Jesus offers? These people have hunger in them just as those did in other places we taught. I have seen it in them, even in the last few days. I know it will be tough going for a good while, maybe even dangerous. That is why I want to speak with your parents. I want them to be in agreement that you travel with me. If they feel it is too risky for you to go, I want you to stay here while I go ahead, at least until I get a feel for how people receive the message we have."

"No! I am your wife now. My place is beside you, wherever that may be. My heart belongs to you, along with my allegiance. We have set out to do what God has called us to do, and I must put that before the concerns of my parents. If there is danger, we will face it together. I feel that same need to share that hope with these people. We are a team."

There wasn't much discussion for the rest of the evening. I found a rough map of southern Greece and plotted out a route that would cover several cities and towns. I figured it would take about two months to travel the route if we were to limit our stops to a day or two. I had a strong feeling that there would be times when our visits would last longer in some areas. But for the immediate plan, I wanted to get Keturah, Sirerah, and my mother to start singing on the streets of Athens. After all, that was the last plan God had given to us, and I had learned that prompt obedience was crucial to accomplishing what God had for us to do. As soon as I had finished at the fish market tomorrow, I would join Keturah and those who wished to help down in the main part of the city.

# CHAPTER TWENTY FIVE

# THIS WE HAVE FOUND, AND IT IS TRUE

T he ministry on the streets was very successful. At first, only Levi and Sirerah joined us. But later on, several of our group came to help. It was not unusual for five or six of us to be talking one on one to people while they sang. Some would walk away, waving our teachings away; yet others listened intently and would often let us pray with them to accept Jesus into their hearts.

Part of Athens was beginning to change. It was evident enough that some of the city fathers took notice and felt threatened. We were asked to leave and stop teaching. The request was given with a firmness and authority that indicated they were serious. We knew it would no longer be productive to continue as we were, but we also knew that there were people who needed to hear the teachings. It was decided that we were to find some of the people who had accepted the teachings and understood them, equip them to continue on in our place. They were not to be as visible as we had been, but they could carry on what we had started. We would also return from time to time to help encourage and further equip them. We had planted a few seed, and now it was time to move on and let those seeds sprout to produce fruit of their own.

The ministry continued in much the same way as we traveled throughout Greece. There were many new friends, and our group grew in number. We were even able to split off into smaller groups and cover more area. We met opposition at nearly every place we stopped; however, we also had great success in nearly every place. By the end of our first year of traveling Greece, our group had grown in size so that it was a period of several weeks before we would see some of the original crew. We were always thrilled to see each other when opportunity brought us together. There would be a time of recounting all the amazing events and miracles we shared in Israel. We would have fond memories of those we had met along the way. Marco explained how he tried to step back to let Keturah have her rightful place in my life. His relationship with me had never diminished, and he felt that my feelings for him had remained as strong as ever. It was just that it was now necessary to share time with someone else.

That is the way it is with God. His love for us remains just as strong and steadfast as ever, even though He has others He loves just as much. He is God, and He is able to love the whole world. He didn't wait for us to love Him before He demonstrated that love to us.

Life for our group will continue on. There will be happiness and hardship, victory and defeat, new life and death, joy and sadness. That is life here on earth. It is our part to enjoy what we can and find the strength to persevere in the struggles. If we were to rely on our strength, we would not succeed.

It is only by God's grace, strength, and mercy that we can make it. The things of life here are only for a brief time in light of eternity. The few things that will last into eternity will be known to us as we are obedient to our true Father.

God let Keturah and me know that we were blazing a trail that others would follow. They would be bringing the same teachings but with more detail and clarity. Our mission was to prepare the way and cry out to those we met that there was one true way. We were most thankful to be given a part in kingdom work.

Marco and I had started this journey as we sought to find answers to questions that formed in our minds as we heard of a new teaching of a man named Jesus. Our journey consisted of many steps, each one bringing us closer to finding what our hearts were driven to. Our journey now continues. It is not over. There is no place for it to end as long as we still have breath. This journey shall continue on, reaching all parts of the earth where there are people who have not heard of the teachings of Jesus.

Many powerful and anointed men will have followed our path.

*We are first called to know Him and then to tell the world what we know of Him. He has not asked us to wait until we have earned degrees and positions of authority before we undertake our calling to tell others. Marco and I began with a simple urging. Our hearts were driven to find out what was truth. Our hearts were driven to find people who could help us find truth. Our hearts were driven to appreciate people and genuinely care for them. Our hearts found the truth. He changed each one of us. Our hearts were then driven to tell of the truth. What was it that caused our hearts to be driven? If I have failed to provide the answer to that question in this book, then I apologize with deep sincerity and I beg you to seek someone who can help you find that answer. He is very real, and He can be found. It is my desire that you will be encouraged by this writing and that your faith will be strengthened. I have not put into words anything that is impossible for God to accomplish. May God bless you and help you on the next step of the journey.*